THE SOUL OF SHAMANISM

THE SOUL

of

SHAMANISM

WESTERN FANTASIES,
IMAGINAL REALITIES

Daniel C. Noel

CONTINUUM • NEW YORK

1999

The Continuum Publishing Company
370 Lexington Avenue
New York, NY 10017

Printed in the United States of America

Library of Congress Cataloging-in-Publication Data

Noel, Daniel C.
    The soul of shamanism : western fantasies, imaginal realities / by
Daniel C. Noel.
        p. cm.
    Includes bibliographical references and index
    ISBN 0-8264-1081-2 (pbk.)
    1. Shamanism. 2. Spirituality. 3. Jung, C. G. (Carl Gustav),
1875–1961. I. Title.
BF1611.N64 1997
291.1′4—dc20   96-32504
                                                      CIP

Grateful acknowledgment is made for permission to quote from the following
material:

The Forbidden Forest by Mircea Eliade, translated by Mac L. Ricketts and Mary P.
Stevenson. © 1978 by the University of Notre Dame Press. Used by permission.

Healing Fiction by James Hillman. © 1983 by James Hillman. Used by permission
of James Hillman.

Re-Visioning Psychology by James Hillman. Copyright © 1975 by James Hillman.
Used by permission of HarperCollins.

The Dream and the Underworld by James Hillman. Copyright © 1979 by James
Hillman. Used by permission of HarperCollins.

For My Magnificent Children

And in Loving Memory of
T.A.M.M.

CONTENTS

Preface • 9

Introduction: Merlin Returns • 13

PART ONE • 24

WESTERN FANTASIES:
LITERARY SOURCES OF THE NEW SHAMANISM

1. Booking a Magical Flight • 26

2. Telling Tales of Fictive Power • 42

3. Lying with Shamanovelists • 63

4. Studying with Shamanthropologists • 83

METAXY, THE MIDDLE • 106

ENTERING JUNG'S HOUSE:
WHERE A MODERN MAN REDISCOVERED THE SOUL

PART TWO • 118

IMAGINAL REALITIES:
POST-JUNGIAN RESOURCES FOR SHAMANIC IMAGINING

5. Realizing the Radical Legacy of Jung • 120

6. Dreaming the Underworld Journey • 139

7. Imagining with Animal Powers • 162

8. Suffering the Recovery of Soul • 181

Conclusion: Comprehending Merlin's Cry • 204

Notes • 225

PREFACE

This is a book about shamanism as Western scholars, storytellers, and seekers have imagined it—and as we in the West today might reimagine it into the future.

Scholars have defined it variously, sometimes becoming secret storytellers (or would-be shamans) in the process. Openly avowed storytellers and other imaginative artists have not only portrayed the figure of the indigenous shaman but have also kept alive ancient memories of the West's own native shamans. However, they make these contributions without being able to claim the scholarly adherence to objective factuality of the historian of religions or the anthropologist. Scholars, on the other hand, are seldom able, like storytellers, to refine our skills at reimagining more consciously and creatively any personal relationship we might wish to have to this exotically fascinating subject.

Seekers of today, meanwhile, have been left with this entanglement of scholarship and story in our picture of the shaman. In this book I envision such seekers as people in search of a spirituality alternative to the mainstream of Western institutional religion, in particular a shamanic spirituality of indigenous healing wisdom. This is a spirituality these seekers hope will be directly applicable to their difficult lives at the end of this modern age.

As a scholar, I nevertheless consider myself one of these seekers. If all learning is personal, as my adult students have helped to teach me, then the roles of scholar and seeker overlap. In the end, the former must serve the latter. Scholars are certainly in search of understanding, which seekers scarcely can do without as well. So I am both of these, and my book of passionate assessment and advocacy is addressed to them both.

I am not a secret storyteller, though I would wish to be an openly avowed one. I cannot quite claim that role in this book. But there is the suggestion of a story showing through, I hope, an intermittent narrative about a scholar in search of the soul of shamanism for very personal as well as seriously academic reasons.

I am definitely not a shaman, let alone a would-be one. I do rely, however, upon a radical legacy in psychology and psychotherapy that has been handed down from a man, C. G. Jung, who I believe to have been the closest thing to a Western shaman the modern age has seen. I rely very heavily indeed on certain aspects of his life and thought as these have been extended by his successors in post-Jungian "imaginal psychology."

Although I write as a scholar of religion and culture specializing in the psychology of religion among other areas, I am, finally, not a psychotherapist, either. But I count myself a colleague of these radical post-Jungians and I here advocate their perspective, deeply aesthetic as well as psychological and therefore supportive of the skills the storyteller can teach us. I find it the most appropriate perspective from which to assess the tangled picture of shamanism in the Western imagination, focusing on the most recent decades. Of equal or greater importance, I advocate their viewpoint as one that can allow us, seekers and scholars together, to reimagine into the future a more authentic Western shamanism than we have had thus far.

What I have produced, then, is a text in which assessment predominates in the first half and advocacy, having arisen there, takes over for the rest, overtly driving assessments in the second half.

After an opening chapter which introduces the figure of Merlin as an "archetypal" Western shaman whose legend frames my text, underscoring my conviction that only a Western version of shamanism will work for us now, a first main section of four chapters evaluates the "New Shamanism" of Mircea Eliade, Carlos Castaneda, Michael Harner, and others. Their efforts, as "shamanovelists" and "shamanthropologists," in fostering this popular psychospiritual movement are seen to be largely literary. This work of imaginative construction—never admitted as such—has promoted unconscious Western fantasies of immediate access to indigenous healing wisdom. In contrast, the writing of the experimental novelist Ronald Sukenick is seen to model a more mindful interaction with the genuine "fictive power" of imagination behind such fantasies. Sukenick stands for an honest literary lying that can help us all to "become sorcerers," as he once wrote of Castaneda's potential.

A middle chapter next probes aspects of the life and work of Jung, showing how he was in a real sense a Western shaman and, thereby, a kind of modern Merlin. His own initiatory descent to what he called the objective psyche, leading to the insight that inner images are the soul's substance, provides the radical psychological legacy realized in the work of the post-Jungian imaginal psychologists. These are the theorists and therapists—James Hillman, Thomas Moore, and Mary Watkins, among others—whose ideas I have put together with my own in assessing neoshamanism and which I adapt and advocate in the second half of the book. Their work offers the indispensable resources for arriving at another New Shamanism: an imaginal shamanism specifically for Western seekers.

As the four chapters of Part Two indicate, this version of neoshamanism parallels what we know of indigenous shamanisms by consciously engaging with imaginal realities in the dream underworld and in waking dreams with their animal powers of imagining, especially as these involve the woundings by which the soul most often heals. I intend to demonstrate that if Jung rediscovered the soul, it is his successors, the imaginal psychologists, who assist us in our personal and cultural attempts to remedy its evident loss: to recover it in ourselves and our world—truly a Western shamanic journey worth making.

In presenting this Western shamanism of soulful spirituality, I also advocate that we cannot and need not continue to take indigenous healing treasures with nothing to give in return but our "good intentions." A neoshamanism that moves from Western fantasies to imaginal realities might have something more appropriate to submit in exchange instead of misappropriating these people's spirituality as we have stolen their lives and land.

A concluding chapter returns to the Merlin legend to recapitulate the book's findings and to suggest further paths for discovery and reflection. As we ponder Merlin's final withdrawal from his outer shamanic practice as part of a patriarchal society and his entrance into the British and Breton landscape of Western story, and thus into Western psychology, we find the modern emergence of shamanism evoked in our soulfully seeking imagination.

MY DEBTS IN WRITING this book are many. I would like to acknowledge them all. Since the imagining that is involved in the fantasies and realities of a Western shamanism is provoked above all by the direct experience of reading, I owe a particularly large intellectual debt to the writers I quote and discuss, especially James Hillman, Thomas Moore, Mary Watkins, Ronald Sukenick, and Count Nikolai Tolstoy. Other writers to whom I am indebted will be obvious from my frequent citations of their work.

Those who have also explicitly and personally assisted this project, some from the earliest days of its gestation, even when they may not have known it, include Brian Bates, Mary Baures, Diane Bell, Alan Bleakley,

David Carrasco, Jerry Cullum, Vine Deloria, Jr., Richard de Mille, William G. Doty, Ailo Gaup, Renata Gelineau, Sam Gill, Chellis Glendinning, Susan Grimaldi, Ronald Grimes, James Hollis, Noelle Imparato, Lily Jung, David L. Miller, Christopher Noel, Richard Noll, Mac Linscott Ricketts, Lawrence Sullivan, Bradley Te Paske, and Michael Whan.

Still others deserve thanks for their support during my own experience of what felt like shamanic dismemberment during the time the book was trying finally to get written: Tom Absher and Erika Butler, Rebecca Armstrong, Lynn Brady, William Doty (again) and Joan Mallonee, Christine Downing, Ethne Gray, Patrick Green and Jane Slaughter, Richard O. Hathaway, Thomas Idinopulos, Paul Knapp and Tamarra Kaida, Lynda Latta, Roy Levin and Gabrielle Dietzel, Howard and Evelyn McConeghey, David McKay, Thomas McKenna, Joanna Meyer, David L. Miller (again), Nancy Morrison, Christopher, Rebecca, Jennifer, and Susannah Noel (also see the dedication), Michael Perlman, Paul Phillips, Robert Segal, Lynda Sexson, John R. Turner (for help above and beyond), and Michael Whan (again), along with my colleagues and students in the Adult Degree Program of Vermont College over twenty-four years, recently the Pacifica Graduate Institute, and briefly the Religious Studies Department of the University of Colorado, Boulder. To my editor, Frank Oveis, I express gratitude for his practicality and patience.

None of these helpful people is in the slightest way responsible for my errors (let alone any misuses of their work). I apologize to anyone I have inadvertantly failed to acknowledge. To the hospitality of St. Deiniol's Library in May of 1996 I owe the joys of being able to focus uninterruptedly on final revisions and this Preface. They emphatically bear no responsibility for my un-Christian endeavor in their corner of Myrddin's Precinct.

ST. DEINIOL'S RESIDENTIAL LIBRARY
HAWARDEN, CLWYD, NORTH WALES

INTRODUCTION

MERLIN RETURNS

We are drawn to the shamanic spirituality of other cultures, indigenous cultures in particular, because we seem, many of us, to receive little ecstasy or healing power from our Western heritage. Cut off from our own primal life-ways by distance and disaffection, the example of Native American, Asian, Australian, or African shamanisms is tempting medicine, and we experiment with workshops and tours—or at least visit the local bookstore for the latest fascinating account of someone else's supposed apprenticeship.

In my case it was certainly reading Carlos Castaneda which first drew me, at the close of the 1960s, toward the exotic treasures of what I took to be shamanism.[1] Admittedly what I found was held at arm's length experientially by my attempts to process his brand of "nonordinary reality" through some rather abstract academic analysis. Still, there was plenty of experiential intensity for me in working for several years on a 258-page study of the "don Juan" volumes for Warner Books in 1974, only to have someone—Castaneda? his agent? his editor?—keep my contribution to Warner's "Writers for the Seventies" series from ever being published. It surely "stopped my world" abruptly enough to give me the flavor of what Carlos was described as having to cope with down there in the Sonora Desert, three thousand miles from my Vermont study. I continued to ponder the possible message for my life in this strange publishing sorcery as I tracked the Castaneda books well into the 1980s.

But none of this quite prepared me for the experience of a Hopi Bean Dance on Second Mesa in northeastern Arizona one cold February night in 1987.

My Norman ancestors probably had crossed the Channel from France to England before crossing the Atlantic to Virginia and later migrating to Georgia and Mississippi (where I was born, not without some Celtic blood as well: my middle name, Calhoun, probably derives from the Scottish Colquhoun). This was my way of being implicated in the Western heritage, though millions of others of assorted ethnicities have been enlisted into it just as deeply through migration—sometimes brutally forced, as we know— and assimilation. I had made several trips back to the British Isles as a tourist and even as a tour leader. But until I spent a sabbatical in Santa Fe that year, I never fully understood that I was and am an "Anglo."

In the American Southwest, anyone of non-Hispanic European ances- try is referred to by that term, a subcategory of the "Euro-American" or, even more broadly, the Western heritage. I was made to rethink my own cultural identity there by the powerful presence of living Hispanic and Native American traditions which are, at best, very much less obvious in Vermont. All around me in New Mexico was "contrapuntal" evidence— food, architecture, accents, festivals—that would not let me ignore my her- itage and its apparent spiritual shortcomings, for I was able to get a comparative glimpse of religious resources that assuredly did not seem avail- able in *my* native culture.

I suspect that this context of cultural self-revelation and alienation is one that shapes the experience of most of the Anglos and other Westerners who have come inquiringly to the New Shamanism that Castaneda inspired over twenty-five years ago. It definitely shaped mine, as I sat in the kiva—an impossible privilege born of being at the right place at the right time, with my mouth shut—on that February night and observed Hopi dances and songs through the long hours of the full moon. I had no preparation to understand the experience beyond the sketch of the Powamu ceremonial in Frank Waters' *Book of the Hopi*, and I had no way of knowing how much he knew that truly pertained to what I was watching.[2] The power was undeni- able. But the experience, overall, was bittersweet for me.

It was bittersweet because it brought home to me that I could never be more than a spectator at the occurrences of any non-Western ritual resembling shamanism, however much they filled me with respect, empa- thy, and envious yearning. If I was to fully explore shamanism on a person- al as well as an academic level, I would have to find a version appropriate to my own heritage.

In 1987 I had not tried the various neoshamanist options offered to Westerners by writers and workshop leaders like Michael Harner and Joan

Halifax, though I did not rule them out. For me, however, since I was fresh-ly aware of cultural roots I had too long taken for granted, research on the possibilities of a New Shamanism in the West began in earnest with another trip to the British Isles.

MAKING CONTACT WITH MERLIN–SHAMANIC MODEL FOR WESTERN SEEKERS

IN JUNE OF 1987 I made my sixth visit to England in fourteen years. I had been moved on previous trips, even genuinely enchanted, by the sacred spaces in the West Country of southwestern England. My tours there went to sites associated with the legends of those landscapes, and pursued topics like King Arthur and the Grail quest lore, including the role of Merlin.

But I had not connected these explorations with my interest in shamanism. I did not really know until 1987, for instance, that before Mer-lin became Arthur's advisor and court magician in the late-medieval texts, he had been seer, bard, Druid, Wild Man, and, at bottom, shaman. Beyond this, he could provide a model for my own native shamanism, or any West-erner's. I began to learn these lessons that June at Michael Whan's house in Harpenden, outside of London.

I had met Michael, then a social worker training to be a Jungian psy-choanalyst, because of Castaneda. In 1978 Michael had published an article on Castaneda in the Jungian journal *Spring*, quoting one of my own articles.[3] That got my attention, but, snakebitten by my experience trying to publish the study for Warner Books, I actually wondered whether his last name might be a hoax: don Whan.

The journal answered my inquiry by giving me Michael's address in England. He responded to a letter by saying his name was Scottish, had once been spelled with a "Qu" (Quhan, I think—not so far from my middle name), and had been changed to Whan so that non-Celts could pronounce it. In short, he was real, he was not Castaneda's don Juan, and we began a correspondence that has become a friendship. And he is the one who, assist-ed considerably by an heir of Leo Tolstoy, introduced me in a deeper way to Merlin as a master shaman for the modern West.

It was my first visit to Michael's house, and I was browsing his book-shelves. I ran into something that immediately intrigued me, something which Michael and I discussed. When I returned to the United States and could not find a copy, he kindly sent me one. The book was *The Quest for Merlin* by Nikolai Tolstoy, a descendant of the great Russian novelist.[4] Pub-lished only two years before my trip, his extensive study turned out to be only one of several recent manifestations of a Merlin resurgence. It has remained the most important one to me, however, because of the strong case it makes for Merlin's shamanism. I first read it in earnest after moving back from my Santa Fe sabbatical to New England. There I was, poised, as it were, midway between the New Mexico "Land of Enchantment" where I had learned I was an Anglo and the enchanted Anglo landscape of my ancestry and Western heritage.

Above all Count Nikolai taught me to take Merlin *seriously* as a shaman. In Disneyfied versions of Arthurian legend, he had seemed a slightly buffoonish old wizard, crankily charming but nowhere near psychologically captivating or grandly mythic. Tolstoy's quest, on the other hand, had revealed a composite figure with genuine evocative power for us today. As the Irish Suibhne, the Scottish Lailoken, and the Welsh Myrddin, Merlin had an identity with profound Celtic layers beneath the references to him in the medieval texts of Geoffrey of Monmouth and his successors, from Thomas Malory to J. R. R. Tolkien and T. H. White. Tolstoy even points to the possibility that in *pre*-Celtic times Merlin descended from a divine figure of prophetic inspiration especially worshipped in southwestern Wales (where the bluestones for Stonehenge were quarried) but identified with all of Britain—which one ancient manuscript calls "Myrddin's Precinct."[5]

And with these oldest mythological layers showing through and blending with more historically based ones of recent centuries, we have a role model for Western shamanism who seems to be resurfacing in popular culture today.

IN THE POPULAR media alone, the last fifteen or twenty years have seen many manifestations of Merlin. There was the Scottish folksinger Robin Williamson's bardic chant "Five Denials on Merlin's Grave" (followed later in the 1980s by performances in Wales of legends relating to Merlin from the mythic collection called *The Mabinogion*), Doug Henning's hit Broadway magic show *Merlin*, a short-lived TV series with Barnard Hughes called "Mr. Merlin," and Nicol Williamson's memorable portrayal in John Boorman's film *Excalibur*. The writers who have retold Merlin tales in these years include Mary Stewart, whose four-novel *Crystal Cave* series gives prominent place to the arch-mage; Marion Zimmer Bradley in her stunning feminist revisioning of Malory, *The Mists of Avalon*; and Jane Yolen with her highly inventive stories in *Merlin's Booke*.[6]

Scottish writer and musician R. J. Stewart has put out several nonfiction books dealing with the implications for spiritual practice of particular aspects of the medieval versions of Merlin's life and exploits. *The Prophetic Vision of Merlin, The Mystic Life of Merlin*, and *The Way of Merlin* do not focus on Merlin's shamanism *per se*, but valuably stress his relevance to our current experience. In addition, Stewart has produced *The Merlin Tarot* and edited a series of anthologies stemming from annual Merlin conferences held in London in the late 1980s, when authors knowledgeable in ancient British lore and its symbolism such as Geoffrey Ashe, John and Caitlin Matthews, and Gareth Knight participated. An American researcher, Norma Lorre Goodrich, also published her study, *Merlin*, which concentrated on a contemporary Christian saint as the possible historical basis for the medieval Arthurian Merlin. At the end of the 1980s Count Tolstoy added his new novel of Merlin, *The Coming of the King*.[7]

Any rundown of these recent reappearances of Merlin would have to mention related books like Ward Rutherford's *The Druids* and the Australian writer Nevill Drury's *The Shaman and the Magician*, correlating shamanic states of consciousness with Druidic practices and with European traditions of esoteric magic or occultism, respectively. More recently than these books from the late '70s and early '80s there have been similar works: John Matthews' *Taliesin: Shamanism and the Bardic Mysteries in Britain and Ireland* in 1991 and Tom Cowan's *Fire in the Head: Shamanism and the Celtic Spirit* in 1993. Or there is Brian Bates's *The Way of Wyrd*, in which this English psychologist fictionally recreates the world of an Anglo–Saxon sorcerer–healer in Dark-Age Britain.[8]

Bates's shaman figure, Wulf, would have lived not too long after the time when the historical Arthur, a British (Celtic) or Romano-British warlord, staved off the fifth-century advances of the Germanic Saxons from across the Channel. Merlin's roots were themselves Celtic, I had learned, if not pre-Celtic, but by the time his story was set forth by Geoffrey in the twelfth century, the Romans had come and gone, the Angles and Saxons had overrun all but the westernmost Celts, and the Danes (Vikings) and Norman French had succeeded the Saxons in the historical palimpsest.

That was five centuries ago, and since then we have had Spenser and Tennyson, Arnold and Swinburne, down to the twentieth century, so Merlin has had his earlier revivals. Nevertheless, as this most recent one at century's end proceeds—Jean Markale's *Merlin: Priest of Nature* was translated from the French in 1995, the same year that a novel, *The Return of Merlin*, appeared by Deepak Chopra, an American physician born in India, who has a wide following—it is clear that something unforeseen is happening.[9] Who would have thought such a figure, so remote from our hurried and unromantic technological world, could still move us, still enchant us—indeed, still advise and heal us?

And yet, quite improbably, Merlin returns, incorporating and appealing to the many strands of the Western heritage. Granted, he may speak to an escapist mood in many of us who are not convinced that modern progress and a cybernetic future will solve all our ongoing human ills. Beyond this, however, he offers himself as a positive resource the West would not have expected to need: an archetypal model for renewed shamanic seeking, for the rediscovery of the soul we have lost.

MANIFESTATIONS OF MERLIN IN JUNGIAN PSYCHOLOGY

AS THE TERM "ARCHETYPAL" implies, I see a strong Jungian connection in the Merlin resurgence. Indeed, for me it has become an indispensable connection. Even before my visit to Michael Whan's house in 1987, I knew that Jung's wife and fellow analyst Emma, together with Marie-Louise von Franz, had written about Merlin.[10] I also knew that another of Jung's associates, Heinrich Zimmer—best remenbered for his work on the myths and symbols of India and for his mentoring of the young Joseph Campbell—had done so as well.[11] But until I made contact with the shamanic Merlin through Michael's good Jungian offices, I failed to see the deep significance of these writings for my interest in the making of a modern Western shamanism.

Entirely aside from any conscious involvement with Merlin's shamanic guidance, I had been preoccupied for some time with Jung's travels in England and had learned many details. Among his trips, one in 1939, just as Tolkien's *Lord of the Rings* and White's *Once and Future King* were coming to birth, was especially evocative.

It was on a 1979 visit to England that I was able to interview Mrs. Anne Baynes at Reed House, her home in Surrey. She was the widow of H. G. Baynes, a founder of Jungian psychology in England and one of Jung's most valued assistants. Forty years earlier the Bayneses had accompanied the Jungs on a journey from Surrey out to Glastonbury, in Somerset, because of Emma's research on the psychology of the Arthurian Grail quest, with its many reverberations in that town's folklore.

Up to her death in 1955, Emma Jung worked on her book about this material, a book which von Franz, herself a distinguished Jungian analyst and author, later finished. As I sat in the garden of Reed House at sunset, Anne Baynes described a dinner party there on the evening before the two couples were to make their 1939 pilgrimage to Glastonbury. A third couple had joined them: Heinrich and Christiane Zimmer. Since that was the year when Heinrich Zimmer's essay, "Merlin," was published in a Swiss journal that the Jungs would have known well, and given the imminent Glastonbury sojourn, I see it as inevitable that Merlin was a subject of dinner conversation. However, I did not know enough in 1979 to confirm that with Mrs. Baynes, and by the time I did she had, sadly, passed away.

In any case, a quick perusal of Emma Jung and Marie-Louise von Franz's book, *The Grail Legend*, indicates that Zimmer's perspective is alive and well in that volume's final five chapters: they are all on Merlin. Likewise, von Franz refers to the Zimmer essay in her own biographical study, *C. G. Jung: His Myth in Our Time*, which closes with a chapter entitled "Le Cri de Merlin."[12]

Once Michael Whan had put me onto Nikolai Tolstoy's *Quest for Merlin*, I began to reconsider these Jungian texts. It became clear to me that not only was Jung himself fascinated by Merlin, but that he actively *identified* his psychology, if not his own personality, with Merlin's powers.

THE VON FRANZ BIOGRAPHY of Jung underscores the Jung–Merlin connection by retelling the tale of the aging Merlin's disappearance. This was probably a late Anglo–Norman or Breton addition, but no less "telling" for us than earlier layers, and certainly well-suited to my own particular ancestry. The theme of withdrawal has him imprisoned under a spell by his heart's love, young Viviane or Niniane (or Nimue: there are numerous spellings), to whom he had relinquished his magic. Merlin's cry can still be heard in the forest, it is said: this element of the legend definitely captivated Jung.

We know from Jung's autobiography that during the process of constructing his retreat tower at Bollingen on Lake Zurich, starting in 1923, he chiseled images and sayings on a large granite cube mistakenly brought by the builders. He later recalled that he had had the idea to inscribe the phrase "Le Cri de Merlin" on the back face of his Bollingen stone because

> what the stone expressed reminded me of Merlin's life in the forest, after he had vanished from the world. Men still hear his cries, so the legend runs, but they cannot understand or interpret them. . . . His story is not yet finished, and he still walks abroad. It might be said that the secret of Merlin was carried on by alchemy, primarily in the figure of Mercurius. Then Merlin was taken up again in my psychology of the unconscious and—remains uncomprehended to this day![13]

Uncomprehended, that is, by those who remain insensitive to the imaginal language of the unconscious psyche. In his own life and work, Jung *listened* to the imagination, both the inner images of night dreams or waking dreams and the imagery of the *anima mundi*, the soul in the interiority of the world's things. And he did so at some personal cost. He did not, after all, carve "Le Cri de Merlin" on his stone. But he chiseled the face of Mercurius as Trickster—surely an aspect of Merlin's shamanism, as Tolstoy empha-sizes—on a nearby wall when it seemed to be laughing out at him in the shapes of masonry, sunlight, and shadow.

Jung, as an old man dictating his autobiography in the six years left to him after Emma's death, knew that both her researches and Zimmer's 1939 essay had stressed Merlin's disappearance and subsequent forest cries. For me, these two interlinked events of legend, heeded with a Jungian sensitivity to the imaginal, reveal the mode of Merlin's *re*appearance today, giving us a central clue to how he becomes accessible again to our Western experience, especially the experience that draws us to the New Shamanism.

Certainly Merlin remains invisible, and thus *not* accessible to our liter-al and direct appropriations and manipulations: no straightforward formula will give us his imagined powers. But he *does* return, to judge from this large clue, with our renewed attentiveness to the cries of the unconscious in the languages of the imagination, the murmurs of the imaginal or soul realm connecting mind to body, spirit to nature. These are the intonations of a self-effacing magic that abandons ego-dominance for dialogue in depth.

Such is the attentiveness we Westerners lost as we went about the busi-ness of "modernizing" the planet through science, technology, commerce, and colonialism (with not a little help from Christianity). Now, however, at the culmination of the modern age, we hear Merlin's call once more, I sense, in our Western attraction to the "irrational" shamanisms of indigenous cultures with their healing wisdom. But I also see the recent popular appeal of non-Western shamanisms as capable of awakening our imagination to our *own* native shamanic resources. These are no longer available to us from tradition-al practitioners in our culture—we have discarded their wisdom as thought-lessly as we have been destroying the indigenous cultures we now envy. But such resources are powerfully represented by the variegated figure of Merlin, shaman of our cultural memories—and by his successors, starting with Jung, in the school of imaginal psychology. With their recent insights realized in our seeking, we not only can hear Merlin's cry coming through the contem-porary fascinations of neoshamanism. We can begin to comprehend it as well.

This book makes that effort at attentiveness and comprehension. It attempts to show that it is a conscious relationship with the imagination that Merlin calls us to—a "way" of imagination, if you will, that can contribute to recovering the lost soul of the West and Westerners in a truly shamanic maneuver. Only with this effort, I am convinced, can we gain something that we may offer to indigenous cultures besides our dangerously acquisitive yearning to have *their* spiritual gifts.

And to find our Western way of imagination, as Merlin returns to tell us, the imaginal realities that can deepen and heal us, we must start by reimagining our major dealings with the concepts—or, as we shall find, the fantasies—surrounding shamanism itself.

REIMAGINING "SHAMANISM"

THE OLDEST KNOWN RELIGIOUS practice on the planet has returned to Western culture to fascinate us afresh in a most unlikely age. It has returned in recent centuries called "modern" and recent decades sometimes called "postmodern." Western modernity and postmodernity, however, have seemed nothing if not hostile to traditional religious beliefs and behavior. So how did this seeming archaic revival come about? What is its current state in such an apparently inhospitable cultural environment? And what are its implications for the future of our spirituality in the West?

I speak, of course, of "shamanism," a term I have already used but now want to highlight with quotation marks. Very tentatively it can be said that the traditional practice involves undertaking an ecstatic or trance "flight" or "journey"—more an ordeal than a pleasure trip—in order to encounter "spirits" from whom the practitioner obtains healing insight for the benefit of his or her community. The additional words in quotation marks will concern us at one point or another in the following chapters as we explore in detail the past, present, and future of "shamanism" in the West.

These explorations will be undertaken with a particular Jungian point of view that will become more explicit as we proceed. As a preliminary rationale I can say that the Jungian school in psychology, beginning with certain key perspectives of Jung which are then creatively extended in the "post-Jungian" work of James Hillman and colleagues with their "imaginal psychology," seems to me best equipped to *understand* the making of a modern Western "shamanism." At the same time, this imaginal approach *converges upon* the latter enterprise, I believe, with its own significantly shamanic characteristics which will need to be set forth with some care. It all revolves, as I hope to make very evident, around *the centrality of imagining*. And this is a centrality that the post-Jungian viewpoint I will be employing reveals both within human personality and in the outer worlds of culture and nature.

It is the imagination, we shall find, radically taken as beyond mere make-believe, that emerges as the driving force and validating authority of the reappearance of "shamanism" in our midst. If such a reappearance can also be called a reconstruction, a making, then modes of imagining—fantasy, fiction, fairy tale, and the like—have been its building blocks at every stage, especially as mediated through the writing and reading of books.

Moreover, these imaginal modes require, I will insist, our conscious acknowledgement and interaction for any authentic version of "shamanism" to be a possibility in the West's future or ours as individuals caught up in its heritage. Again, it is imaginal psychology, perhaps uniquely, that can provide this authenticating acknowledgement and interaction, helping us to heed Merlin's cry.

To be sure, these claims need spelling out and supporting as only the entire book can do. It will attempt this by discussing the magical books and powerful ideas of others—sometimes deceptive, often difficult. Along with this discussion, I will recount my own personal experiences as a participant–observer in both neoshamanism and imaginal psychology during the years since the former first began with Castaneda's initial and initiating volume in 1968. On the other hand, before there was a New Shamanism there had to be "shamanism" itself, which did indeed start a long time before Castaneda.

WESTERN WRITERS AND TRAVELERS have known about the figure denoted by the Tungusic term *saman* for at least three hundred years. It was in 1692 that two Dutch diplomats accompanied a Russian embassy sent by Peter the Great to China that passed through the Siberian homeland of the Tungus people. One of the Dutchmen later published a description of a "family shaman" from these people.[14] Thereafter the Western scholarly imagination has not ceased to invest with debatable and often conflicting characteristics the "ism" it added to the Tungusic term. It has been said that "shamanism" has a South Asian Buddhist *origin* or else has a South Asian Buddhist *overlay.* "Shamanism" is *distinct from* trance-possession or else is *defined by* trance-possession. "Shamanism" *is a religion* or else *is not a religion* but a set of behaviors or else a social role or else a "psychomental complex"—as the Russian ethnographer Shirokogoroff put it in the title of his study of the Tungus, published in English in 1935.[15]

And so on. Scholarship has imagined the shaman as witch doctor, sorcerer, schizophrenic—as the first artist, the first actor, the first psychoanalyst.[16] Gloria Flaherty, in writing of the shaman as the dark shadow of our eighteenth-century rationalist Enlightenment, throws up her hands at all the theoretical disarray and calls for a "shamanology" that could address these conflicting claims.[17]

Meanwhile, there was one scholar who seemed authoritatively to settle such confusions for many fellow scholars. He also seems to have done so for most of the fervent seekers who felt they had begun to find personal spiritual meaning by reading Castaneda and his successors. They were finding meaning for their lives in what seemed to be a newly accessible Western version of the shamanism that the scholar had been writing about long before Castaneda.

This master scholar, the most significant precursor to the New Shamanism, really its forefather, was Mircea Eliade. To visit where he is in this story, we need to book a magical flight.

PART ONE

WESTERN FANTASIES

LITERARY

SOURCES OF

THE NEW

SHAMANISM

This is an invitation to imagine again.

To reimagine what we have already imagined—but mostly imagined unconsciously, passively. What we shall find is a fantasy, or set of fantasies, called the New Shamanism, created by the imagining of scholars, storytellers, and seekers. We shall need to look long and hard at how this has happened, for the future possibility of a shamanic spirituality in Western consciousness and culture depends upon such a careful reimagining of the true sources of neoshamanism. Those sources, we shall discover, are above all literary, not literal. In other words, instead of direct access to the objective facts or actual experience of indigenous shamanic wisdom—neoshamanism's Western fantasy of the exotic Other—we have the unacknowledged imaginings of the authors and readers of a series of key books.

When we do acknowledge our participation in the production of this fantasy and its bookish initiations, we encounter a surprising possibility: we can consciously, actively follow our imaginings into imaginal realities, shamanic otherworlds for Westerners. By radically shifting the ground under the neoshamanism of Mircea Eliade, Carlos Castaneda, and Michael Harner, among others, from factual accounts—which they can never entirely be—to "literary lying," we gain access to an authentically shamanic imagining in the process of rereading their writings or attending the workshops derived from those writings. In other words, once we learn to stop taking literally the shamanovels and shamanthropology that have given birth to their new spiritual movement, we can all "become sorcerers" in another sort of New Shamanism. The chapters of Part One strive for that learning.

1

BOOKING A MAGICAL FLIGHT

e are at thirty-five thousand feet. Below us is Iowa, or perhaps it is Illinois, hidden beneath clouds. In the cabin every third person is lost in a fat novel: Clancy or Grisham, Danielle Steel or Belva Plain. I am on the aisle. Next to me is a man in his forties. Next to him, in the window seat, is a petite woman of about the same age. She has taken out a book called *Shakkai*, by Lynn Andrews.

Andrews, I know, is the author of a series of popular works on shamanism, starting with *Medicine Woman* in 1981.[1] There she recounted her paranormal experiences, as a Beverly Hills art dealer, with a Cree mentor, Agnes Whistling Elk, in western Canada. After *Medicine Woman* was followed by successor volumes referring to the same Native teacher appearing in places as improbable as the Yucatan and the Australian outback, it became clear to reviewers that these were almost certainly works of fiction. They may even have been ghost-written, and Native American representatives have often picketed Andrews' expensive workshops.[2]

Aware of all this, I ask the woman next to the window what she thinks of *Shakkai*, set in Japan. She says she finds it fascinating. I gently suggest that there have been criticisms of Andrews' factual reliability, indicating that I am studying shamanism, and that even now Mircea Eliade's big tome on the topic is in the carry-on bag at my feet.[3] The woman admits she'd heard that not everyone believes Andrews' books, but she feels *Shakkai* tells a good story. That's what counts for her, she goes on, adding significantly that her work as a physical therapist does not fulfill her spiritual needs.

About this time the man in the middle seat weighs in with the rather surprising information that he's been to one of the Andrews workshops and found it worthwhile. Despite his appearing to be a staid business type—he turns out to be a consultant to doctor-managed clinics—he'd once lived in an ashram and knows his way around the world of alternative spirituality. He agrees with the window-seat woman that the factual veracity of works like Andrews' is less important than their being a good read with a few meaningful principles to impart. He is unaware of any reason Native people would have to protest such books, since they promote the spiritual wisdom of Native teachers.

I attempt to argue that perhaps Native wisdom is being misrepresented in Andrews' pseudofactual works, and that their claims of credibility might be a feature worth pondering. The dust jacket of *Medicine Woman*, I can't help recalling, proclaims that although it "reads like an adventure story . . . readers will experience it as a factual account on the order and importance of The Teachings of Don Juan." This reference to Carlos Castaneda's bestseller had placed her book in the recent movement of neoshamanism which his writings inaugurated starting in the late 1960s. And it had thereby claimed, in effect, that that movement, through Castaneda, is based on fact. I am not so sure, though I am sure that it matters.

But I am clearly outnumbered by my affable row-mates, bright health-care professionals with an appetite for archaic and unconventional healing, flying high above the clouds of my academic doubts, suspending disbelief willy-nilly if not willingly while cruising the friendly skies of something like a New-Age faith. Up here most passengers, only partly for distraction from confinement and fear, seem up for any writer's narcotic page-turner. Among the latter are the suspect scriptures of a Western neoshamanism that promises direct contact with ecstatic transformation to trusting consumers on the path of personal growth. Who can blame them for being fascinated?

I bury my nose in a less engaging text: Eliade's dry but supposedly factual descriptions of Asian and Arctic shamans on their magical flights, together with his interpretation of these journeys from the standpoint of the history of religions. As I read I continue to wonder about the neoshamanic lift-off and uplift provided by his popularizing successors. They are able to purvey the fiction of physical experience through the disembodied experience of reading books. They provide a flight that is not without its own powerful magic.

Throughout the burgeoning subculture of New Age neoshamanism (it is at least in some respects allied with the New Age), at workshops I've attended, in conversations with some of its leaders, and in issues of its main periodical, *Shaman's Drum: A Journal of Experiential Shamanism*, the constant cry is to move beyond analysis to practical experience, not to study shamanism but to study with shamans. But the movement, launched by the reading of Castaneda's works and then those of others like Lynn Andrews and Joan Halifax and Michael Harner, is—largely unbeknownst to itself, it seems—overwhelmingly bookish.[4]

Aside from Andrews, these founders all have Ph.D.s in anthropology, hardly a credential unreliant upon critical reading. If they have subsequently overturned scholarship for shamanship, "experiential shamanism" in the New-Age West still depends on the books they keep publishing and people keep reading, notwithstanding any debunking I might know about. And we all like a good story.

My knowledge of the bookishness of these simulated shamanic flights will take me, I see, to the shamanism surrounding our flighty behavior with books. But first I want to establish how fantasies of flight came into Western readings of shamanism to begin with. Before Castaneda it starts with Eliade, and not just in his shamanism book. I place my seatback in its full upright and locked position for the descent into Chicago.

Professor Eliade Imagines an Ism

A WICKED WIND off the lake slices through my optimistic jacket as I sprint for the shuttle to the downtown conference. It was in wintry Chicago, at the University, that I'd missed the chance to study with the great Romanian historian of religions in 1959 when I was studying, instead, the relation of religion to literature. Now, thirty-five years later, I am to give a paper on his interpretation of shamanism at a hotel in the city where his long career as an emigre scholar had culminated.

Over the intervening decades I'd passed through most of my own career in academe, teaching mainly in "nontraditional" programs where my interdisciplinary interests were indulged. My students in the late '60s, experimenting notoriously with hallucinogens, were the ones who pointed me toward the topic of shamanism. Initially this was by way of the exotic offerings of Castaneda, about whose immensely popular renditions of Mexican Indian sorcery I wrote my own commentaries during the early 1970s.[5] In the course of this work, and in later tracking the neoshamanist spirituality Castaneda inspired, I had occasion to consult Eliade's sprawling overview volume compiled in the late 1940s, *Shamanism: Archaic Techniques of Ecstasy*.

I used this book as the definitive encyclopedia of all things shamanic, and was unaware of its judgements ever being criticized. Certainly none of the neoshamanist writers I was assessing ever questioned Eliade's views. Andrews' writings might be fiction, but those of Eliade remained authoritative as scholarship, even as a kind of science.

I did note that in 1987, the year after his death, one of Eliade's younger colleagues at the University of Chicago, Jonathan Z. Smith, produced a strong critique in a book called *To Take Place*,[6] calling into question Eliade's dealings with the idea of the "Center" in religious traditions, a concept that turns out to be important to the latter's interpretation of shamanism. Smith also criticized Eliade's misreading of an Australian aborigine myth of a "sacred pole" which the divine ancestor figure supposedly climbed up and disappeared into the sky. Quite to the contrary, Smith observes that "the usual Australian pattern is not one of celestial withdrawal," as Eliade had implied, "but of terrestrial transformation and continued presence."[7] This bias, too, I eventually learned, meant much for Eliade's scholarly shaping of the "ism" that had produced our Western category of shamanism.

BUT IT WAS NOT until the 1990s that I caught up with other objections offered by anthropologists who rejected Eliade's insistence that certain "patterns" of religious belief and behavior were worldwide, or who contradicted his armchair analyses of particular cultures' shamanisms.[8] By then, however, I had also encountered another work of Eliade's that revealed a secret about his book on shamanism—and about that entire category as scholars had constructed it and readers had consumed it.

I had known that Eliade wrote fiction—"on the side," I assumed—and had even read his *Two Tales of the Occult*, set in India.[9] Still, I saw little specific connection between this activity and his scholarly achievements. Then, in 1991, as a visiting faculty member at the University of Colorado in Boulder, where I was teaching a seminar on "Shamanism: Traditional and New," I was given a gift. It was a copy of a collection entitled *Waiting for the Dawn: Mircea Eliade in Perspective*, donated generously by its coeditor David Carrasco, another of Eliade's former students and my temporary colleague there.[10]

Among its several virtues, *Waiting for the Dawn* reprints an essay from 1978 in which Eliade discusses the relationship, deeply important to him, between the two apparently very different aspects of his work. He refers especially to a creatively indispensable "oscillation between research of a scientific nature and literary imagination."[11] If I had been too preoccupied by my religion-and-literature studies in 1959 to take Professor Eliade's University of Chicago courses, it seemed he was meeting my interests more than halfway that spring in Boulder. Eliade's essay then gives examples of his dual vocation. Most significantly, he describes his work on the novel *The Forbidden Forest* as an interruption, starting in 1949, of his writing of the big book on shamanism.

STARTING WITH A SHAMANOVEL

The Forbidden Forest, translated into English in the late '70s, is long, over six hundred pages long.[12] It tells the story of a group of Romanian intellectuals living through the war years of 1936 to 1948. Sometimes tedious to read, its occult incidents are nevertheless intriguing and its imagery is revealing. A major group of these images can be called celestial or ascensional, indicating a novelistic imagination preoccupied with upward flights and elevated vistas. Intersecting with this imagery is the occultist theme of otherworldly spaces hidden in this world—as in secret rooms.

The main character, Stefan, is already, at the start of the novel, obsessed with spending his days in a hotel room he maintains in secret so as to eavesdrop on the couple next door. He also paints there, over and over on the same canvas, his paranormal perceptions. He hopes in this way to find clues to the camouflaged miracles he believes are happening, unrecognized, in ordinary reality all around us. When he recounts a dramatic childhood experience of this sort we see that his secret room fixation has to do with a paradise above: a theme with which, I now suspected, Eliade's scholarship was similarly preoccupied.

Stefan is in the process of showing his lover Ileana and his friend Biris his hotel room for the first time. In so doing he is prompted to tell them the story of "the room *Sambo*":

> "I was about five or six years old," he began, his voice hushed, "and I found myself with my family at Movila. We were living in a kind of villa-hotel that had two floors and about fifteen or twenty rooms. In the dining room we sat next to a group of very mysterious young people. They seemed mysterious to me because although they spoke Romanian, I couldn't understand very well what they were saying. . . . And one day I turned my head suddenly toward their table at a moment when the discussion had become exceptionally animated. I heard one of them—the one who seemed oldest because he had a mustache—say something, and I saw him raise his arm toward the ceiling apparently to indicate a direction. I heard him utter in a solemn voice the word 'Sambo.' Suddenly they all fell silent. They bent their heads and looked down at their plates. Then one after another they

repeated: '*Sambo!*' '*Sambo!*' . . . At that instant I felt a thrill I had never known before. I felt that I had penetrated a great and terrible secret. . . . Through a providential circumstance I had turned my head at the exact moment when the man with the mustache pointed out the place where their secret, *Sambo*, was found. It was above us, there overhead on the second floor."

Furtively and with a pounding heart the boy does discover, that very afternoon, an upstairs room, filled, it seems to him, with a mysterious green light:

"And just then, at that moment I understood what Sambo was. I understood that here on earth, near at hand and yet invisible, inaccessible to the uninitiated, a privileged space exists, a place like a paradise, one you could never forget in your whole life if once you had the good fortune to know it. Because in *Sambo* I felt I was no longer living as I had lived before. I lived differently in a continuous inexpressible happiness. . . . I wasn't hungry, I wasn't thirsty, I wasn't sleepy. I lived, purely and simply, in paradise."[13]

What does this passage of "fantastic" fiction have to do with shamanism? And with our Western attempts not only to understand but to emulate it, to join its trance-journeys, even from our armchairs, book in hand? Everything, I was beginning to learn.

MAC LINSCOTT RICKETTS, one of the translators of *The Forbidden Forest*, had also written an essay on the creation of the latter in which he informs us that Eliade interrupted his work on the shamanism book to start his novel on June 21 and the week following in 1949. This is precisely the time of the astronomical and Christian calendar to which the novel's Romanian title, *Noaptea de Sanziene*, "The Night of St. John," refers. The summer solstice affected both the author and his chief protagonist Stefan very strangely, and the events of the novel begin and end twelve years apart on that same mysterious night of the year.[14]

The idea for the novel came to Eliade, Ricketts tells us, "en route home from an excursion to the Abbey of Royaumont outside Paris,"[15] which is also where one of the last scenes in the narrative takes place. Meeting his long-lost mistress Ileana there, Stefan proceeds to "escape from history" (a favorite theme of Eliade the scholar) with her as the two are involved in a fatal car crash at the end of the novel. Remarkably, this fictional event revealed to Eliade only in writing about it the meaning of the car that had obsessed Stefan throughout the novel, from his first meeting with Ileana in a Romanian forest on St. John's Night, 1936, to that same day of the year in 1948, when they die.[16]

As already should be evident even from this brief account of the events that bracket the plot, the significance of time and history is crucial to the novel—the reminiscence about the secret room also hints at this. But the imagery of space is important as well to the preoccupations of Eliade and his characters in the story. The forest of its English title, where Stefan first meets Ileana, is where he thinks an escape from history may be possible on solstice night. This is the Forest of Baneasa near Bucharest, but the forest surrounding the Abbey de Royaumont near Paris is just as much—or more—a place of such escape, an escape made more desirable by the sufferings of the Second World War.

Additionally, the mysterious space *Sambo* of Stefan's childhood is only the most memorable of the secret rooms he cultivates as he eavesdrops on neighbors in a succession of hotels. There he listens for clues to the camouflaged, or occult, miracles happening but hidden in the ordinariness of "profane" space and time all around us. This suggests a parallel realm with similarities to shamanic otherworlds. Indeed, as becomes evident when the novel's influence on the shamanism book is fully traced, *The Forbidden Forest* can be called a "shamanovel." And this is a term which further intimates the shamanic powers at play in the reading of any work of fiction (including works masquerading as nonfiction). We will be defining it further as we proceed.

THE SECRET ROOM WHERE SHAMANISM WAS BORN

THE INSISTENT IMAGERY of ascent in particular—to the paradisal upper room of childhood, of course, but also to the royal mountain setting of the final forest—is a major feature of Eliade's spatial and temporal preoccupations in this novel. The escape from history sought by Stefan is an escape *upward*, reversing the "fall" *into* history.

Several other scenes support this inference. There is a figure, Anisie, who functions for Stefan very much as a kind of shaman. He lives in the mountains and, like other peasants in the region, seems to embody them. Based on his memory of a theological conversation he had had with Anisie, whom he calls "Emperor," Stefan tells his little son a fantastic story of the latter's accompanying God, who has appeared on earth, to a strange summit sheepfold—a structure which God proceeds to fling "into the heights of heaven":

> "'Behold, Emperor!' God says once again. The Emperor Anisie raised his eyes to the sky. 'I don't see it anymore, Lord,' says he. 'I don't see the fold anymore. . . .' God patted him on the shoulder and said to him, 'Tomorrow you will find the fold still here on the top of the mountain. It will only stay in the sky overnight. I put it there to protect it from men. . . .'"[17]

Another especially powerful episode of this imagery of ascension comes from the scene of Stefan and Ileana's parting several years before their climactic meeting at the Abbey de Royaumont. They are on an outing to the Palace Hotel in Bussaco, Portugal: "here in this ancient royal castle," as Stefan describes it, "built on a hill, hidden in the forest. . . ."[18] Earlier that day they had climbed a nearby mountain, where

> sometimes the wind shook the topmost branches of the trees momentarily and then all was still. The cedars were left behind, lifting their limbs high above the forest, dominating it. But the trees became more dense as the two approached the top of the mountain. Then at a bend in the path they caught sight of the cross—*Cruz alta.*[19]

This sign of a *celestial* Christianity with its high cross is noteworthy. But so are the trees, which figure throughout the novel as the images that help make its forests—starting with the one in the Bucharest area "where once there were marshes," as Stefan often repeats—into heaven-aspiring affairs. Stefan's dream of an airplane flight over the ocean that brings to his mind the Forest of Baneasa also adds to the *aerial* connotations of this place, a place which gives its name to the title of the English translation of the novel.

Temporal imagery is not neglected in the parting of Stefan and Ileana: their Portuguese outing occurs on New Year's Eve. Yet the recurrent vision of the philosopher Biris, near death under torture toward the close of the novel, strongly reiterates the spatial metaphors of spiritual yearning heavenward:

> . . . he thought that it was the eve of Easter and he was standing on the deck of a ship, holding a lighted candle in his hand. It seemed to him that the flame lengthened and mounted ever higher, a slender filament of light. He followed it with his eyes as it touched the arch of the sky and pierced it. He tipped his head back in order to see it better, and there high above where the light penetrated the heavens a radiant face appeared. Undoubtedly it's God or Jesus Christ, he said to himself, and he awoke overcome with emotion, his spirit flooded with a happiness that was beyond belief.[20]

Along with this quite astonishing vision there are still other examples of sacred space as well as sacred time—the former promising access to the latter—in this huge and finally despairing narrative. It is despairing because only in death, for the characters in *The Forbidden Forest*, is any escape from the profoundly profane time of the mid-twentieth century possible. The shamanism *of* the novel does not entail giving the characters a shamanism adequate to their healing *in* the novel—and, Biris's vision aside, neither do their loosely held Christian beliefs appear to help their spiritual state.

The main point remains clear nonetheless: it is only the elevated spaces of the novel's world that offer any hope of a way out of the history that so tormented Stefan, Ileana, Biris, Anisie, and the other characters—as it tormented their creator and his fellow Romanians in the period between 1936 and 1948.

And just as escape is always sought above in the novel, so "ecstasy," as the shaman's defining experience, seems most often to take these figures higher, I recalled, not lower, in the scholarly survey Eliade wrote in tandem with his novel at the end of those same years. Were ascensional emphases that Jonathan Smith had found elsewhere in his work, with their connection to the symbolism of the "Center," unduly prevalent in Eliade's scholarship on shamanism?

Pondering this as a probability I began to be convinced that, as a representative metaphor, *Sambo* was indeed the secret birthplace of the "ism" that this great scholar has bequeathed to us. In other words, I suspected that even his authoritative "objective" account is tilted, beyond the thousand sources he drew on in the late '40s and the ethnographic evidence since, in the direction of that hidden room in his novel: upward. My rereading of *Shamanism: Archaic Techniques of Ecstasy* confirmed that it is in fact shaped to exaggerate the shaman's upperworld journeys and to ignore—or demonize—the equally defining underworld travels.

DESPITE OCCASIONAL even-handed statements suggesting their equal importance, a careful inspection does reveal a preponderance of celestial over infernal examples in Eliade's text. I went through roughly half the book—258 of its 511 pages—comprising seven of the fourteen chapters (I spared myself further tedium by assuming the other half would not wildly diverge). Counting reported shamanic testimonies together with the author's explanations accompanying them, I came up with 338 heavenly destinations to 131 lowerworld references, a ratio of 2.58 to 1.00. More important than this arithmetic, however, is Eliade's treatment of each type of imagery.

First there is his use of the term "infernal" itself, which he employs almost interchangeably with "underworld." This terminology inevitably casts an aura of evil around the downward journey, and it is true that what we find in Eliade's shamanic infernos are usually "demons" rather than the much more benign "spirits" encountered on skyward flights. Also, among the descents that are described, many are treated only as preludes to celestial journeys, not as worthwhile ends in themselves.

The claim, made early in the shamanism book, that Arctic, Siberian, and Central Asian cultures mostly have sky gods as their "Supreme Beings"[21] is at least open to question. As is the underlying notion that all such shaman-istic cultures have supreme beings in the first place. Often in Eliade's view these supposed High Gods have "withdrawn" in the course of cultural evolu-tion, so that if recent data do not support their existence or importance to a culture's current beliefs, this does not count for him as disconfirming evi-dence. Similarly suspect is his idea of "decadence" in the history of religions, which he uses here to prop up his claims that widespread priority is given by shamans to celestial gods or goals.

How this works is that a presumed "Old Shaman," a primordial ancestor shaman of mythic times, who may be involved in narratives of easy communication with the highest heavens, is taken as the defining model for all later practitioners. These latter shamans and their practices, often less celestial in orientation, are then seen as decadent examples, and are thus undervalued as data in establishing what a shaman is and does.[22]

Another crucial set of comments comes in Chapter 8 on "Shaman-ism and Cosmology," the twenty-eight pages immediately succeeding those in which I tediously tallied ascents and descents. While this chapter does not mention the tainted tale of the Australian aborigines' sacred pole, it does start out by declaring something that Smith would find just as dubious, given his review of the source data: ". . . the symbolism of the 'Center,'" writes Eliade, ". . . appears to be of considerable antiquity, for it is found in the *most* 'primitive' cultures."[23] As Smith had shown, however, Eliade's abo-rigine pole is the only example he gives from such cultures, and it is a clear misreading—or ignoring—of the evidence.

Beyond that initial offense, the chapter, which proposes to deal with the "three cosmic zones" of heaven, earth, and underworld, again over-whelmingly favors the ascensional.

It does this in its cataloguing of pillars, trees, mountains, and ladders that represent the "Center" in various cultures where movement between the three zones is available to shamans and similar practitioners. There are only eight or ten references to the lower world—two of these, aptly enough, rele-gated to footnotes—in the twenty-eight pages with their scores and scores of heavenly examples. Furthermore, Eliade makes generalizing statements at sev-eral places in the chapter that contradict—or ignore altogether—his own three-part cosmological schema of upward and downward connection.

For instance, he claims that ". . . the cosmological concept of the three communicating zones . . . is a universally disseminated idea connected with the belief in the possibility of direct communication *with the sky*."[24] And he continues by saying that ". . . every altar, tent, or house," as a micro-cosm of the interconnecting vertical World Axis, "makes possible a break-through in plane and hence an *ascent to the sky*."[25] Then again he goes on to assert that in archaic cultures only the shamans "know how to make an *ascent* through the 'central opening.'. . ."[26] Later still he writes that "it is at the 'Center' that the break-through in plane, that is, communication with the *sky*, becomes possible."[27] Conversely, "*ascending* a mountain always sig-nifies a journey to the 'Center of the World.'"[28] This means that shamans—whose major experience, according to Eliade, is one of ecstasy, where ecstasy is equivalent to flight and flight is almost never other than upward—must be traveling toward the "Center" on *every* ecstatic journey.

Or so must Eliade have been *imagining* the matter. And this was my main finding in the paper I gave at the Chicago conference, marshalling the evidence discussed above.

I was not so much concerned to discover, as Smith does, an undue reliance upon ancient Near Eastern cosmological models which fail, finally, to support Eliade's overgeneralizing of the imagery of interlocking centers and ascents. Rather, I was interested in assessing his psychological *attraction* to such imagery. I was interested as well in how it determines his monumen-tal contribution to the definition—and the experience, as we read his schol-arly study or books that presuppose it—of shamanism by the modern West.

THE BOOK AS A SHAMAN'S DRUM

MY CLOSE INVESTIGATION of Eliade's scholarly text had established that *the secret of shamanism as a Western construct is indeed in that secret room of the novel where his imaginative preoccupation is revealed.* But the secret is not sim-ply that shamanism is less focused on magical flights to the heavenly "Cen-ter" than Eliade was.

A few blocks away from where I was studying literature and religion during that Chicago fall of 1959, Eliade was writing in his journal. He noted that his essay "Le Vol magique" ("Magical Flight"), reprinted the same year, "illustrate[s] the importance of the symbolism of flight and of ascension to explain the deepest and most secret longings of man: his desire to break away from the earth, to transcend the human condition, to be free."[29] Later that winter he signalled his own need for such liberation in another journal entry:

> The meaning of my "learning": . . . I would compare my immersion in the documents to a fusion with the material—to the limit of my physical resistance: when I feel that I'm suffocating, that I am being asphyxiated, I

come back up to the surface. A descent to the center of dead matter, comparable to a *descensus ad inferos*.[30]

Here he also may be revealing the impetus he felt toward fiction writing as a celestial journey up and out from the "descent into hell" of his scholarly research. Perhaps this is exactly why he had to interrupt the writing of his shamanism book to work on *The Forbidden Forest* with its high-flying imagery, imagery that then doubled back to dictate the emphases of his interpretation of shamanism.

As these inferences of mine imply, even as long ago as 1959 I was priming myself to consider another of "the deepest and most secret longings" of humans. It is one that is certainly not unrelated to the need for ascensional liberation that Eliade identified as an historian of religions, though it does not require his degree of scholarly immersion. As I was busy reading about religion and literature, the theological ramifications of Camus and Sartre, Melville and Faulkner, I was stoking a fascination with the longing to imagine, the need to dream up and tell stories, and the imagination as the soul of Western spirituality in an age of science. It is certainly the soul of any authentic renewal of shamanism in the West.

WHAT WAS HIDDEN in the room called *Sambo*, and in *The Forbidden Forest's* other locations that echo it, was the imaginal core of shamanism as the latter has been constructed in the West above all by Eliade's definitive scholarly book, written at the same time. The hidden secret was not his particular preferred symbols—for who can deny that his favored symbolisms of ascent do play a significant part in shamanism as in other cultural expressions?—but the primacy of the symbolization process itself, which the power of those symbols over Eliade's scholarship reveals to us. There may also have been other factors contributing to that symbolization process: his years in India and study of yoga may have helped shape the imagining underlying his scholarship, as, more diffusely, may a male bias toward being in control from above and beyond. In any case the hidden meaning of Eliade's originating contribution remains the one represented by that secret room.

The core or soul of the West's idea of shamanism is not factual at all, but fantastic, fictive, a work of imagination.

This may sound like a negative reduction of a powerful spiritual practice to mere make-believe. But it is not. Quite to the contrary, it presumes nothing against the reality of what may be experienced in indigenous shamanisms. It simply suggests that Westerners might find a positive shamanic power for themselves in their own practice of mindful imagining, including the imagining that goes on while books are being written or read.

For modern seekers a book, perhaps one of Eliade's, could be the best "shaman's drum" to induce a flight to the friendly skies—or the unfriendly underworld—even if reading cannot replicate every archaic technique ascribed to shamanism. The few Westerners who have participated in tribal shamanisms have testified to experiences that seem to overthrow our comfortable categories. Such experiences definitely appear to transcend our ordinary reality of resting in a comfortable armchair or airplane window seat with a fascinating book. Nevertheless, reading is a generally unrecognized example of the sort of imagining that can be shamanic for any of us once the power of that imagining is understood and honored.

Eliade, a master of his academic field, may never have been fully aware of the force exerted on his shamanism studies by his imagined memory of that small boy penetrating a great and terrible secret—despite his own autobiography containing a childhood room with green drapes, secretly enjoyed, and influential years growing up in an attic apartment.[31] It was the imaginative fiction, though, not the hard facts, that shaped our shamanism through his sensibility, as he worked on his two books in tandem back in 1949. The point is not to fault his flawed scholarship on traditional shamanism; the point is rather to learn from it the secret that can serve a Western recovery of shamanic powers.

FROM BLIND READING TO MINDFUL IMAGINING

SO FAR, THE OPEN SECRET that the neoshamanism movement was founded on fiction has hardly been seen by most of those readers who are, like my fellow airplane travelers, drawn to the movement. My impression from students and others over the years is that such seekers have been led to assume the solidity of "shamanism" itself, sanctioned by Eliade's scholarship which apparently authorizes as fact the story his studies have been telling. These same Western seekers, according to my informal inquiries, are also inclined to avert their eyes from any controversies over factual reliability of the kind Andrews' books have occasioned. Or, if they are aware of this issue, they often declare that "it doesn't matter" whether the writings are fact or fiction—just as the woman next to the window valued Andrews' *Shakkai* as a good story, whatever its factual credibility. My suspicion, however, is that as an avowed spiritual seeker herself she was reading it for more than entertainment value. It was a literal guidebook for her seeking, it seemed, and probably gained thereby a quasifactual status.

What this suggested was that maybe in the actual Yucatan or Australian outback with a factual Agnes Whistling Elk it wouldn't matter whether Andrews' writings, marketed as fact, are fictional. But in the armchairs (or airplanes) where the author's fiction engages her readers' fantasies, it does matter. To deny this seems like a kind of willed blindness over this one exotic spiritual option that may reflect a more general cultural condition. Today we all desire to find a faith that will suffice, a desire made desperate by a social environment in which organized religion no longer feels binding to many of us and yet where science, defining truth, devalues the imaginings upon which spirituality depends. (For nonscientists like me, even science may be a fantasy, but it is one that dominates all the others in the name of "scientific fact.") Given this situation it is understandable that, as yet, when seekers are shown something like Eliade's secret room *Sambo* by their reading, something that shows forth the centrality of imagination, they cannot or will not see it.

But it is books that are also responsible for this blindness, I reflected as I left Chicago on another literal flight, retreating to the relative balminess of a visit to Albuquerque. An open secret not seen, an open book not consciously read, seems a case of what used to be called "blind faith," now invested in an unconscious worship of facts. Readers like my traveling companions act as if blind to the fictionality of a text like *Shakkai*, even when they are shown it is fictional, since they seem to find its "principles" factually persuasive. The book in their hand is indeed a shaman's drum to take them on a magical flight above the book, and yet they do not recognize that that is what it is doing. They thereby relinquish the chance to interact with the process on a conscious level.

Paralleling the "sonic driving" of the shaman's drum, the book transports us with a kind of "semantic driving." It induces an imagination we cannot necessarily "access" in the sense of easily finding a fixed body of "information." It can cost us more than computer skills to take this mindfully shamanic flight with books, which may be why page-turners and pot-boilers sell best: their evocations follow conventional narrative formulas and are therefore less demanding that writer and reader alike be conscious of their experience.

MICHAEL TAUSSIG, one of Eliade's sternest anthropological critics, raises another possibility in this regard which we need to take preliminary note of, as it will point us forward to an important discussion later on.

In a long 1989 essay, he has a section entitled "Shamanic Flight: The Magic of Narrative" where he denounces these two ideas we have been finding linked together. In other words, he, too, sees the shaman's journeying and the storyteller's telling as interlinked. But he feels that the beginning/middle/end flow of conventional stories can be a pernicious magic because it helps to pass off unfairly the idea of a successfully completed shamanic process (a rare exception, in his view) as a "fictitious rule."[32] The indigenous visionary experiences we have called "shamanism"—a label he dismisses as "a made-up, modern, Western category"[33]—do not, Taussig claims, proceed in an orderly fashion like a traditional narrative pattern, as Eliade's model implies. Such experiences are more likely to entail an open-ended uncertainty which lacks the cathartic resolution of an Eliadean magical flight, where the practitioner is assured by the pattern of heroically returning with the healing balm.

Shamanic ordeals, asserts Taussig, thus in actuality resemble modernist (or postmodernist) experimental fiction

> in which parts are only loosely connected one to another, there is no centralizing cathartic force, and an array exists of distancing techniques involving and disinvolving the reader or spectator and thus, potentially at least, dismantling all fixed and fixing notions of identity.[34]

We shall return to Taussig's large and rather unsettling proposal in Chapter 3. Suffice it to say here that as we become mindful of both Eliade's secret room of celestial imagining and the Eliadean flight on which traditional narratives can take us, our perception of the actual processes at work in each allows us to experience a shamanovel—a literary flight—of another sort, perhaps one closer to what Taussig is talking about.

Meanwhile, without such mindfulness, Eliade's novelistic reveries about his upper room, imagined almost half a century ago, together with the more recent literary constructions of neoshamanists like Andrews, continue to shape the expectations we carry into the weekend workshop with our drum and rattle or the eco-tour to meet a medicine man in Ecuador. But it is now time for the secret to be out and acknowledged as the basis for any authentic Western shamanism in the future. The true power is in an imagining with books that may be, or may as well be, shamanic. At any rate it can scarcely be improved upon by us educated Westerners, equipped as we are with a critical consciousness we can never entirely quiet.

Every persuasive book by the latest shaman's apprentice only provides us with another occasion to imagine. It all depends on whether we reimagine our practice of reading. Whether we become aware of the shamanic flight that the book in our hands has already begun, making it a mindfully interactive experience. Or whether we miss that conscious possibility through passive immersion in our reading, as we are mesmerized by narrative's traditional magic to ignore the book we are holding and instead hold with a Western delusion of direct access to some non-Western shamanism. And even that literalized fantasy can always be reimagined, deliteralized, as we have started to do to our mindless involvement—certainly *my* mindless involvement—in Eliade's massive narrative of shamanic flight.

There is no escape from our literacy. But if we resist literalism, there can be an ecstasy with it that need not be blind, and that can be the beginning of a truly shamanic imagining. For Western seekers that is the first lesson to learn about the magical flight books like Eliade's point to and provide: the source of their magic, the real origin of the ecstasy. Other lessons will follow, examples besides that of Eliade—or Andrews—will be brought in, other ways to mindfully imagine will be explored.

Meanwhile we must not forget that consciously shamanic imagining can start where we are right now, with me writing a book and you reading it, encouraged to reimagine others, perhaps some less analytical and more novelistic than this one needs to be, that first kindled your fascination to find out more.

2

TELLING TALES OF FICTIVE POWER

It was Mircea Eliade's *Shamanism: Archaic Techniques of Ecstasy*, translated into English in 1964, that was the great prototype and scholarly authority for the neoshamanism movement to follow. However, it was in actuality, as we have seen, an authoritative *imagining* more than a factual account of what traditional indigenous shamanisms had been or might still be outside of Western culture. Those who rely on it as a reference benchmark in trying to bring shamanic practices to Western seekers—in effect, to replicate or simulate such practices—are thus in truth dependent on his ascensional emphases. And these were mainly heartfelt fantasies, perhaps spiritual fantasies, imposed upon data that only partially supported them.

We have also seen that these emphases are more straightforwardly presented in their nonfactuality in his novel *The Forbidden Forest*, not translated until 1978. By then, neoshamanism was well underway. Anthropology, often critical about the lack of social-scientific rigor in Eliade's history of religions approach, had done something curiously un-rigorous for a social-scientific field. This was something that Eliade, for all his personal spiritual leanings, would not have dreamed of doing as a scholarly interpreter. Anthropology had started a new religious movement.

In our attempt to move beyond Western fantasies to imaginal realities, it is worth exploring how this unlikely achievement came about. To do so we must begin with another neoshamanist book and its important literary reverberations, an investigation of which will then take us, by Chapter 4, into the strange story of shamanthropology.

ONCE UPON A TIME WITH DON JUAN AND CARLOS

ONCE UPON A TIME in a dusty Arizona town on the Mexican border, a short, stocky Latin-American man approached an old Indian at the bus depot and inquired about the latter's knowledge of medicinal plants.

The first man's name was Carlos. He was a graduate student in anthropology at UCLA, the University of California at Los Angeles, looking for data which he might use in a thesis on how the Yaqui Indians of the southwestern United States and northwestern Mexico employed various plant substances for healing and the stimulation of religious visions. A friend had told Carlos that the old Indian, whose name was Juan Matus, or don Juan, was reputed to be a *brujo*, a sorcerer, who had extensive information on the so-called power plants.

What then transpired as the tale continues is that Carlos, already an apprentice to the concepts and categories of his anthropology professors at UCLA, entered a very different, and in many ways *conflicting*, apprenticeship to don Juan's "way of knowledge." As Carlos later depicts one of his first lessons, "There was a strange cleavage between my pragmatic experience . . . and my rational deliberations. . . ."[1]

Following Carlos, we learn how difficult and frightening it can be—but how fascinating—for an educated Westerner to be initiated into what is apparently a Yaqui form of the oldest path of healing power on the planet.

For some readers, what I have synopsized thus far is an unfamiliar narrative. For others, I imagine it is a vivid part of their not-too-distant past. For *all* readers inspired or intrigued by the return of shamanism to the West, in any case, it is absolutely essential to review Carlos's story with care.

This is because the future possibilities of what has come to be called the New Shamanism, or neoshamanism, are rooted in its origins as a movement. And those origins lie not only with Eliade but even more so with don Juan and Carlos several decades ago—or rather with our reception of their relationship.

The "strange cleavage" Carlos experienced was the conflict between the "ordinary reality" of UCLA Graduate School, or of Western culture in general, and the "nonordinary reality" out of which don Juan seemed to be operating much of the time. Worse, the conflict eventually deepened and widened to the point of a fearsome schizophrenia on Carlos's part.

Here is how he says it happened:

Over the four years between 1961 and 1965, Carlos tells us, don Juan introduced him to the bizarre world of the power plants: peyote cactus, a mixture of mushrooms, and the Datura plant or Jimson Weed (which don Juan called "devil's weed"). These are the three hallucinogens which Carlos was taught to harvest, prepare, and ingest. Under their influence, instead of merely gathering information on the plants as he had intended, Carlos underwent experiences which challenged his every assumption, including his overconfident assumptions about the importance of data-gathering and, indeed, the nature of true knowledge.

The most significant of these experiences came after Carlos was instructed to apply a paste made from the devil's weed directly to his body. He describes vividly how he *flew* through the night gliding on his back, tilting his head up to make vertical circles or changing directions by turning it to the side. "I enjoyed such freedom and swiftness as I had never known before," he recounts.[2] Carlos's stupendous flight was clearly a version of the shaman's ecstatic journey—something few modern Western persons had ever experienced in this dramatic fashion outside of dreams or drugs. And, as Carlos discovered, the devil's weed paste did not necessarily account for his amazing waking dream.

When he discussed it with don Juan the next day, he pursued tenaciously the question which most of us, if truth be told, would also ask after such an experience. In one form or another it is a question which would dominate Carlos's consciousness for years to come. For reasons we will get to, it deserves to dominate ours still today as seekers after shamanic spirituality: "*Did I really fly, don Juan?*" While answering in the affirmative, the old sorcerer was not about to confirm Carlos's conventional view of the "reality" of the episode:

> "You flew. That is what the second portion of the devil's weed is for. As you take more of it, you will learn how to fly perfectly. It is not a simple matter. A man *flies* with the help of the second portion of the devil's weed. That's all I can tell you. What you want to know makes no sense. Birds fly like birds and a man who has taken the devil's weed flies as such. . . ."[3]

But Carlos persisted, anxious to pin don Juan down and make him admit that the flight was, as he said, "in my imagination, in my mind alone"[4]—and therefore not truly real:

> "Let's put it another way, don Juan. What I meant to say is that if I had tied myself to a rock with a heavy chain I would have flown just the same, because my body had nothing to do with my flying."

Don Juan looked at me incredulously. "If you tie yourself to a rock," he said, "I'm afraid you will have to fly holding this rock with its heavy chain."[5]

THE "CARLOS" WHOSE EXPERIENCES with don Juan I have been retelling is, as most readers will have recognized, Carlos Castaneda, the author of *The Teachings of Don Juan*. This is the book which, more than any other, reintroduced shamanism to the West as a possible spiritual practice.

The passage I have just quoted is probably the most frequently cited one in the entire book, for it is the philosophical as well as experiential high point of Castaneda's rich narrative. And don Juan's reply to Carlos's dogged questioning is remarkable, still not fully appreciated, I suspect, even decades later. It "takes off" as surely as Carlos did, flying in the face of ordinary logic and levitating the chain, the rock, Carlos—and the reader.

From our vantage point as readers of this extraordinary tale, we are sometimes tempted to feel superior to poor Carlos. Surely *we* would not always be such slow learners! Or would we? Like him (and for understandable reasons, as we shall see), we, too, I am afraid, cling to one way of understanding, grabbing always for conventional certainties. Until something—it could even be don Juan's words on the page in this passage, or Carlos's desperate questions—something suggests in a most bewildering manner that there *are* other ways of understanding things, other "realities."

If we are truly receptive to their story, don Juan and Carlos can disrupt our routines as readers of factual anthropology. The shaman's trance-journey, no longer a distant ethnographic curiosity, begins to *feel* disturbingly real. Our conceptual schemes may be scrambled by this reading. Our imagination may be made capable of actually *experiencing* Carlos's flight.

But if it *is* properly received, don Juan's alternative understanding cannot come easily to the Western mind. At first Carlos gave up his apprenticeship. Again, if we are honest we will admit we probably would as well. Given our culture's norms of sanity, especially before the late '60s, this radical a shift in basic perspective would threaten us with madness, the ominous outcome to Carlos's "strange cleavage." Certainly shamanism has never been far from schizophrenia, at least in the eyes of Western observers. Carlos sums up his experience by saying he succumbed to what don Juan called "the first enemy of a man of knowledge": fear.[6]

In September of 1965 he withdrew, he tells us, from don Juan's tutelage—although the old Yaqui believed their relationship would be resumed—and went back to UCLA.

READING CASTANEDA

THERE, WE KNOW, he wrote his book. The hardcover edition of *The Teachings of Don Juan: A Yaqui Way of Knowledge* came out with the University of California Press in 1968. It attracted enough attention for a paperback edition to be brought out by Ballantine Books the following year. And that edition sold hundreds of thousands of copies, making Castaneda a famous anthropologist, and presumably quite a wealthy one. More important to our purposes, in a way that Eliade never did, Castaneda had seemingly brought back the living experience of indigenous shamanism to a Western culture that had suppressed such a spiritual form in its own history, silencing its practitioners and consigning it to the irrelevant exotica of museums and musty scholarship. Or treating it as merely escapist romanticism, primitivist nostalgia.

What this also means is that neoshamanism was born for Western seekers with the reading of Castaneda's writing, a magical flight based on his book, an apprenticeship to his words. Needless to say, this was not the usual reaction to a work of social science, and most readers ignored the seventy-five pages of dry "Structural Analysis" and scholarly appendices that followed his main narrative.

But just as the New Shamanism had much growing to do before reaching its current status as a widespread psychospiritual movement, so Carlos was far from finished with don Juan. A second book, entitled *A Separate Reality: Further Conversations with Don Juan*, came out in 1971.[7] Here we could read about Carlos's resumed apprenticeship between 1968 and 1970, which emphasized the hallucinogenically assisted achievement of what don Juan called "seeing": the ability to perceive the world in a concretely different way, the actual perceptual experience of a nonordinary reality.

Along with a fellow sorcerer named don Genaro—a master trickster, practical joker, and something of an acrobat—don Juan pushed Carlos toward this nonordinary perception. As when he told his puzzled apprentice that Genaro, pulling himself precariously from boulder to boulder at the top of a high waterfall above them, was doing so by means of tentacle-like fibers coming out of his abdomen!

Don Genaro "felt that the waterfall was like the edge on which [you were] standing," don Juan explained, "and was confident [you] could also make it across."[8] Carlos did not, however, "make it across" into nonordinary "seeing" quite yet. Still, as with the first book, in this second cycle of apprenticeship the reader was challenged along with Carlos to fit these strange experiences into comfortable categories of understanding.

Suffice it to say that *A Separate Reality* followed *The Teachings of Don Juan* onto the bestseller lists in 1971, and in 1972 a third book emerged called *Journey to Ixtlan: The Lessons of Don Juan*.[9]

Journey to Ixtlan, it turned out, was a recycling of previously ignored notes from the first stage of the apprenticeship in the early '60s. Carlos now realized, he says, that everything don Juan was trying to do to him in those first years comprised an elaborate array of techniques for what was termed, a decade later, "stopping the world": the true prerequisite for "seeing" in don Juan's sense. Stopping the world is accomplished by interrupting the flow of interpretations which puts our ordinary world together for us, stopping this flow with a set of circumstances that are alien to it, such as the circumstances don Juan arranged for Carlos in his initial apprenticeship. These, we can recall if we have read *The Teachings of Don Juan*, included Carlos having to "find his spot" on don Juan's porch, meet "Mescalito," the peyote spirit, become a crow, and battle a woman sorcerer—as well as undergo the paramount shamanic experience of nonordinary flight with the impetus of the Datura paste.

But among those world-stopping circumstances of a shamanism reborn for the West, we also learned in *Journey to Ixtlan* that the use of hallucinogenic plants was not nearly as central as it had seemed. "My insistence on holding on to my standard version of reality," Carlos reflects back in the later account, "rendered me almost deaf and blind to don Juan's aims. Therefore, it was simply my lack of sensitivity which had fostered [the use of the power plants]."[10] This sensitivity can be accomplished in another way, as we will be trying to do in this book.

IF DON JUAN'S TRUE AIMS were to get the Carlos of 1961–65 to change his personality, stop the world, and "see"—ideally through nonhallucinogenic techniques—it is the events of May 1971, we now read, which gave Carlos the hindsight to understand his teacher's earlier goals. Part two of *Journey to Ixtlan* described these crucial events.

Among them were the apparent disappearance of Carlos's locked Buick under the influence of don Juan and don Genaro's sorcery, and a solitary encounter in the mountains with a talking coyote. Since none of these startling occurrences took place while Carlos was influenced by any of the three power plants, explaining what "really" happened was even more difficult for Carlos—and the reader—than in the earlier two books. Without a "drug-induced altered state" to fall back on we were forced, with Carlos, to rely totally on *don Juan's* explanations. As in the conversation following Carlos's magical flight, however, these were not only rather puzzling but more than a little disturbing. For instance:

> "Genaro never moved your car from the world of ordinary men the other day. He simply forced you to look at the world like sorcerers do, and your car was not in that world. Genaro wanted to soften your certainty."[11]

As for the talking coyote, don Juan pointed out that although Carlos's "body understood for the first time," what he encountered was not a coyote and did not actually talk! Carlos was incredulous at don Juan's seemingly *skeptical* attitude:

> "But the coyote really talked, don Juan!"

> "Now look who is acting like an idiot. After all these years of learning you should know better. . . . you *stopped the world* and you might even have *seen*. . . ."

> "Yesterday the world became as sorcerers tell you it is," he went on. "In that world coyotes talk. . . . But what I want you to learn is *seeing*. . . . [which] happens only when one sneaks between the worlds, the world of ordinary people and the world of sorcerers."[12]

Elaborating his earlier lesson about nonordinary flight, don Juan here totally canceled the literalism of Carlos's either/or perception, shocking us all toward imaginative flexibility.

Not surprisingly, with such provocative revelations *Journey to Ixtlan* was another bestseller, and by March 5, 1973, Carlos Castaneda had made it onto the cover of *Time* magazine. In an issue which also contained a review of the mysterious novelist Thomas Pynchon's new masterpiece, *Gravity's Rainbow*, *Time* correspondent Sandra Burton found Castaneda's personal life equally elusive.

Yet the cover story was generally very admiring of his magical field reports, quoting another anthropologist, Michael Harner, "a friend of Castaneda's and an authority on shamanism," who observed that "most anthropologists only give the result. Instead of synthesizing the interviews, Castaneda takes us through the process."[13] It was likely there would be a *fourth* volume.

That is, of course, exactly what happened. Indeed, with *Tales of Power* in 1974 we have not even come halfway in a review of Castaneda's output.[14] Like an old rerun of Peter Falk as Detective Columbo, he has never quite been able to leave his readers, despite having told *Time* in 1973 that "this [*Tales of Power*] is the last thing I will ever write about Don Juan. Now I am going to be a sorcerer for sure. Only my death could stop that."[15]

Today there are nine of his books, with more undoubtedly on the way. But I believe I have recalled for you enough of the main teachings and the flavor of the Castaneda texts to let us feel our way back into the reading experience at the source of neoshamanism, especially if we take a brief look at *Tales of Power* with our 1990s hindsight. Only by so doing can we build an adequate basis from which to move forward into further possibilities for this fascinating new movement—and for any personal participation in it.

That is, except for one all-important detail, generally unknown through the appearance of the first four books but by now even more of an open secret than Eliade's upper room of imagining. An exploration of this factor needs to be a part of our journey back to the origins and essence of neoshamanism—so improbably launched by an anthropologist like Castaneda—in order to then move ahead. The detail is that, as it happened, in following Carlos's story it seems we were really reading *fiction*, a kind of once-upon-a-time fairy tale, set in the Sonora Desert but most likely devised in the UCLA library.

Let me recount how this secret was revealed to me—I have already touched on it in the introduction—and start to show why it is so important for us to explore its ramifications.

"HELLO. THIS IS CARLOS CASTANEDA."

IT IS A COLD December day in 1974 when the phone rings in my Vermont kitchen and a voice that could have been that of Ricardo Montalban on the old *Fantasy Island* television show says "Hello. This is Carlos Castaneda."

By then I do not know what to believe. For the past year and a half I have been working on a study of Castaneda's first three books for Warner Paperback Library's "Writers for the Seventies" series. I had finished an acceptable 258-page typescript and was looking forward to publication when I was notified that Castaneda had refused Warner permission to use quoted material from his works. This is something that almost never happens when one publisher pays the other a permissions fee, as Warner had offered to do.

Since my book relied heavily on the extensive quotes in question (I was often discussing Castaneda's specific writing style and imagery), my entire project was jeopardized. In desperation I obtained Castaneda's California address from Sam Keen, who had interviewed him for *Psychology Today*. That interview was in 1972 (reprinted in Keen's book *Voices and Visions*), when Castaneda told Keen that "the idea that I concocted a person like don Juan is inconceivable. . . . I am only a reporter."[16]

By 1974, in the wake of the *Time* cover story with its references to Castaneda's mysterious personal behavior, I am aware that you cannot contact Castaneda by phone: if you write to him he might call you. So I have sent him a heartfelt request to reconsider his decision about the permissions fee and hope the phone will ring.

But the actual voice of the enigmatic anthropologist himself in my most un-mysterious Vermont habitat is, if not absolutely beyond belief, surely bizarre in the extreme. I am reminded that the origin of the word "phony" was the introduction of the telephone to a public unaccustomed to technological voice transmission. What the voice says is that he has no objection to my using the quoted material, and he will do what he can to help me. The matter is probably out of his hands, however, because when he signed with his publisher he had had nothing, "and now they've got me dangling." His agent, too, says the voice, had emphasized his state of dependence: "This year you are hot, baby," quotes the voice, "but next year you could be cold as Kelsey's bar"—or sounds to that effect. (Castaneda's agent, I learned, also brokered the best-selling novels of Jacqueline Susann.)

In short, the voice concludes, "in the *field* I am impeccable, but in *this* realm I have no power." Publishing sorcery had overpowered him, he pleads, though he certainly sympathizes with my plight and supports my wish to publish the book I had completed. And mine is a book, I assure the voice, which is an interpretation but in no way an attack. It should even whet readers' appetites for future don Juan volumes.

I quickly convey the support of the Castaneda-voice to the publishing powers in question at Simon and Schuster. Instead of solving my problem, though, their reply only thickens the plot. "Dr. Castaneda's decision," their letter intones, "is irrevocable." When I report this pronouncement to Castaneda in my next communique I get another call from the voice, which speaks to me conspiratorially about the behavior of the shadowy figures who are making him rich and costing me eighteen months of effort: "Those bastards," hisses the voice. "They want you to hate me for free."

ALL IN ALL, there were four phone calls that winter, but no remedy for my moribund book was forthcoming. Today evidence for its existence occurs only in its announcement as a future series volume on the back cover of Joseph Slade's study of—appropriately enough—Thomas Pynchon as a "Writer for the Seventies."[17] No doubt that worthy little commentary is out of print by now, just as the type has pretty much faded on my own doomed pile of manuscript pages.

Despite this considerable professional setback—a version of stopping the world I would have preferred not to experience firsthand, as I put it in the introduction—I could not hate Castaneda, "for free" or otherwise. His work had become too important to me, personally evocative as well as intellectually stimulating, to dismiss it or him because of this strange episode. It was admittedly hard to believe he did not have the financial and legal leverage, as a best-selling author, to grant my book its needed permission to quote from his works. To that extent he came to seem the culprit in my dilemma—and, if so, also a liar, or perhaps a trickster. If you took his tales factually, he had flagrantly misrepresented Yaqui culture. Still, at the time I was inadequately attuned to this cross-cultural issue and I could personally accept his trickery as a valuable teaching.

But when one of those shadowy figures at Simon and Schuster came out into the light as the author of a book called *Power! How to Get It, How to Use It,* I was more confused than ever.[18] Michael Korda was, in fact, Carlos Castaneda's editor, and the kind of corporate sorcery he recommended in his dubious little manual might well be extended to include using a relatively defenseless Vermont professor for batting practice.

I never did definitively learn who was wielding power over my poor project—nor did I learn why with any certainty. This brand of *brujeria* definitely got my attention, in any case. It felt like amoral witchcraft was being directed right at me, distressing yet potentially instructive. In its weird way, it brought don Juan's equally weird teachings home to my securely snowbound life, softening my certainty far from the shamanic exploits Castaneda had written about. It also made me begin to speculate about the *reliability* of the reporting he claimed to be doing in his books, now increased to four in number.

Once the voice of the phone calls had finished with me in early 1975, I took a long look at the sources of Castaneda's success and any clues to it that might lie in his new text, *Tales of Power.*

Still very much an admirer of the don Juan writings, I wondered with heightened and painfully acquired sensitivity why other people were. Perhaps by exploring why readers were so receptive to him I could also perceive what Castaneda was really up to as an anthropologist who had apparently gone beyond "going native" to preaching a shamanic gospel to the West. At that time I could not see what later became clear: I was attending to the birth process of the neoshamanism movement.

THE RECEPTIVITY OF THE COUNTER-CULTURE

IT IS DIFFICULT to dispute that the high sales of the first few Castaneda books resulted from the apparent endorsement of hallucinogenic drugs by don

Juan himself. The psychedelic cover of the Ballantine Books paperback of *The Teachings of Don Juan* clearly sought to hook the young (and not-so-young) adults of the late '60s and early '70s who were experimenting with various chemicals.

This focus on the power plants in Carlos's early years of training under his shamanic teacher was exactly in line with a craving for direct religious experience which had already taken many readers to one or another kind of illegal drug. It also made for delicious reading, in those rebellious years, to see such a straight character as Carlos constantly befuddled by his contacts with a disreputable old Mexican whose superstitious beliefs and behavior scarcely merited the attention of establishment authority figures. (It did not hurt, however, that don Juan's teachings all seemed to be anthropological fact.)

As a junior faculty member teaching in the academic field of religious studies at a small Pennsylvania college during those tumultuous years—just before withdrawing to the wilds of Vermont—I was situated very much within this social environment. Not at Columbia or Berkeley, I was nevertheless in the pipeline of the culturally and politically radical student enthusiasms produced by the 1960s. Indeed, it was several of my more rebellious students who brought Castaneda's first volume to me, suggesting I use it in a somewhat arcane course I was teaching in the spring of 1971. And it was my more rebellious side, I suppose, that agreed to do so. As a usually unadventurous academic with a spouse and family and a job to protect, I was nonetheless attracted, with other younger faculty, to the social critique and creative disregard for convention displayed by our liveliest students. Maybe there was some envy that we had missed out by being a generation too early.

In any event, like several of my junior colleagues I had already been purged for mildly dissenting activities at that conservative little institution, having received notice that I would not be granted tenure and would have to leave. This unhappy circumstance alone probably qualified me for admission to what the cultural historian Theodore Roszak had called the "counter-culture" in his widely quoted 1969 book *The Making of a Counter-Culture*.[19] But I was already drawn to several of the thinkers whom Roszak claimed were the theoreticians inspiring opposition to the establishment. Besides, I was instantly taken with *The Teachings of Don Juan*, about which Roszak had interviewed Castaneda as early as 1968 on an FM radio show.[20]

Accordingly, with little to lose and much-needed excitement to gain for my "Modern Interpretations of Religion" course, I made Castaneda with his recycled shamanism an honored guest in my teaching repertoire starting in 1971, when I also began to assemble my ill-fated book and look for another teaching job. After doing some adjunct teaching at Goddard College in 1972 I was able to secure a full-time position there in the fall of 1973, and quickly learned I had plunged even more deeply into the counter-culture. Poet Allen Ginsberg, the Goddard folklore assured me, had designated the experimental Vermont school "the drug capitol of America" during the '60s.

Although I continued to avoid the more exotic hallucinogenic options myself, I met people in the Goddard community who seemed to exemplify the "drug-induced" popularity of the early don Juan volumes. As Goddard students showed me, this was a popularity underscored by an issue of the "Fabulous Furry Freak Brothers" head comics devoted to the Yaqui sorcerer, and by a similarly loving reference in a Fleetwood Mac song, "Hypnotized."

And yet none of this counter-cultural psychedelica came labeled, at that time, as "neoshamanism." Nor did Castaneda, after a few public appearances and interviews such as Roszak's in the early years, make himself available for weekend workshops or tours to the Sonora Desert to meet don Juan. Moreover, all the media attention turned out to be merely the tip of a very large philosophical iceberg.

For one thing, as has already been noted, *Journey to Ixtlan*—the third book—made it evident that don Juan's use of hallucinogens was never an end in itself. What the narratives about him seem to have been after all along was closer to what another spiritual text, the New Testament, calls *metanoia*: conversion. Carlos and the reader of his story were being taught to change their lives, a challenge which went much deeper than drugs as recreational devices or a cheap ticket to salvation.

Don Juan's caustic remark, at one point, that Carlos had not really *disrupted* his accustomed routines but had only developed *unusual* ones could also be applied, ironically enough, to many of those readers who felt that by turning on chemically they were fully assimilating some sacred "Yaqui way of knowledge." Thereby, such readers presumed, they were automatically transcending the stuffy and unspiritual ways of conventional American culture. As we have also seen, beyond their short-term shock value Carlos's hallucinogenic experiences—especially when unaccompanied by don Juan's conversational cues—actually constituted one of the *least* disruptive techniques he underwent. Knowing in his old linear and literalistic fashion that he had been, or would be, under the sway of the power plants allowed the apprentice to *discount* their lasting importance, and so continue his life largely unchanged.

OVERALL, WHATEVER SPIRITUAL or psychotherapeutic validity there may have been in the "drug connection" to the early Castaneda books, it is now mainly aside from this source of their popularity that their teachings still have much to say to us. That is, while the psychedelic wing of the counter-culture was importantly receptive to Castaneda's reintroduction of shamanic experience, the *meaning* of the latter was not adequately captured by philosophies of drug advocacy like that of Timothy Leary. Additional factors, other sorts of significance, had to have been part of our reading of the don Juan writings (and still have to be) for them to harbor the secret riches upon which the New Shamanism of the West and its adherents may build for the future.

Only by a true transformation of perspective, adopted in soberest belief as well as during ecstatic episodes, we read in *Tales of Power*, the fourth volume, can Carlos or we ourselves learn the sort of knowing which is open to the mysterious "power" underlying our various versions of reality. Only through such a conversion can Carlos, as the representative of our unavoidably literate twentieth-century Western skepticism, be given an actual experience of something like indigenous shamanism.

But what is this power? This is what I wondered in the wake of my own personal encounter with the powerful publishing sorcery of Castaneda and/or Korda. Whatever it was, it had clearly come to occupy the central place in don Juan's teachings by the time we got to the fourth book, just as it was featured in the titles of the fifth, *The Second Ring of Power*, and the eighth, *The Power of Silence*.[21] My closer look at Castaneda's work in the light of his unaccountable behavior towards me had to discover what his writing meant by "power." Moreover, doing so would serve my larger goal, then and now, of finding the core or soul of Western neoshamanism. This movement, we have seen, had relied on Eliade's scholarly imagining but had been ignited by reading Castaneda's books, ostensibly anthropology but actually something else again.

While I studied *Tales of Power* in 1975, I gradually realized that a major aspect of don Juan's "power"—probably the major aspect—is what he had already referred to in *Journey to Ixtlan* as "nothing and yet it makes marvels appear before your very eyes."[22] This is the power that blows life into what we see when we see it, as Carlos experienced when he "mistook" a wind-blown bush at twilight for an impossible beaked mammal and was berated by don Juan for not *sustaining* the perception.

Depth psychology might speak of this power as "projection," or, more aptly, as the image-creating faculty of the psyche. Novelists and poets, literary theorists and philosophers have written similarly of the imagination. C. G. Jung and his successors, as we shall find, encompass and move beyond these translations of power to present us with deeply applicable ideas and methods of interactive imagining.

In the context of my probing of Castaneda I preferred a term which I borrowed from the experimental fiction writer and critic Ronald Sukenick: "fictive power." This would be the particular power of the imagination to make the fictions or stories, the half-conscious narrative collections of images, in which we actually live. It is the power, in other words, to spin out the web of story-shaped description which comprises our world, our reality. We could even, I thought, arguably expand the title of Castaneda's fourth book to *Tales of Fictive Power* and use it to define his entire series of nine.

Interpreting Castaneda's "power" as "fictive power" certainly seems justified by don Juan's discussion in *Tales of Power* of what is perhaps the most enigmatic concept in all the books: the *nagual*. The words "nagual" and "nagualism" have reasonably accessible denotations among anthropologists studying Mesoamerican religion. They pertain most often to the Aztec-derived belief in an animal double who could roam at night and cause sickness.

In *Tales of Power*, however, the *nagual* (which in the later books becomes an honorary title for don Juan and his fellow shamans who teach apprentices) is more generally used to refer to the transcendent or the ineffable, which is described as a medieval theologian might approach the Godhead, only negatively or through its effects. Don Juan explains that the *nagual* is not mind, soul, thoughts, state of grace, heaven, pure intellect, psyche, energy, vital force, immortality, life principle, God, or even nothingness. Nor is it the philosopher Kant's "transcendental ego," nor experience, nor intuition, nor even consciousness. But he does allow that it can best be understood in terms of "power" and it gives rise to *creativity*.[23] Hence, again, my recourse to Sukenick's term "fictive power," the power which is nothing and yet creates out of thin air, the power manifested for instance, in magic tricks and tricksters' tales.

But there is another reason why I consider this term so definitive as a designation for the meaning of the don Juan books at the heart of neoshamanism: not only is fictive power operating *in* these narratives; it is "echoed" by the power *of* the books.

THE MAKING OF A COUNTER-CULTURAL FAIRY TALE

SAM KEEN'S 1972 interview with Castaneda was not the first publication to raise questions about the factuality of the don Juan texts. A month earlier the

National Book Award-winning novelist Joyce Carol Oates had done the same in a letter to the *New York Times*. When I wrote to her with my opinion that we simply could not know yet if Castaneda might be giving us fiction in the guise of anthropology, she answered me cryptically. She said that she had enjoyed the first two volumes, "but now that it's a 'hoax' I doubt that I'll read the third. . . ."[24]

Since she had offered no firm proof in either of her letters that the books were indeed a hoax, I, being a fan as well as an interpreter of Castaneda, remained unconvinced. *Time* magazine, as I have indicated, looked askance at Castaneda's shifting autobiographical information but did no outright debunking of his books in its cover story of March 1973. And meanwhile Sukenick had written about the books that same winter in the *Village Voice*. He softly rebutted his fellow novelist Oates and supported Castaneda's credibility by deciding that "these are works of art . . . but works of art don't have to be novels."[25]

Between the winter of 1972–73 and late 1974, when my own book ran afoul of Castaneda or his publisher, I was frankly up in the air as to whether his work was fact (however artfully arranged, as Sukenick suggested) or fiction (however faithful to *someone's* shamanism, as Oates implied). I even felt back then that the very ambiguity of the issue could itself be powerfully informative: not having a final verdict might force us to ponder the terrain *between* the usual options. As don Juan had prodded Carlos to do on more than one dramatic occasion of nonordinary flights, disappearing Buicks, or loquacious coyotes.

This was my noncommittal middle-ground position even after my Warner book was bewitched and I became more personally involved in Castaneda's possible trickery. *Tales of Power* in 1974 did not appear to me to settle matters, either, although Oates once more disagreed.

She felt that this fourth volume confirmed her earlier judgment that don Juan and the books about him were novelistic fictions. Her review for *Psychology Today* of Castaneda's latest installment was entitled "Don Juan's Last Laugh," and I found it appealing that she did not actually denounce the author she had accused of hoaxing a huge reading public. One of her major statements in that piece almost sounded like praise. "Perhaps it takes a writer of fiction," she declared, "to intuit the work of a fellow artist: at any rate it seems to me beyond a doubt that this series of books is art, not mere reportorial observation."[26]

Oates's viewpoint, it turned out, was not so different from Sukenick's, which held fiction and story to be subtle ingredients even of factual objectivity. And my attitude was close to his, since his *Village Voice* review-essay contained the term "fictive power" which had struck me as so central to understanding don Juan's teachings—and their reception by the reading public.

THE CLOSE SCRUTINY I was giving these complex matters continued to occupy me throughout 1975 as I put together an anthology of reactions to the don Juan writings in order to recoup some of the lost effort of my earlier book project for Warner. While there were many important contributions to *Seeing Castaneda*, as I called my collection, the letters and review-essays by Oates and Sukenick—which I was quick to include along with the *Time* story, the Keen interview, an excerpt by Roszak, and much else—were closest to my own evolving estimate of Castaneda's absolutely crucial role. He was conveying a form of shamanism to the West, and doing so through what might be a hoax.

For me fictive power, the world-creating artistry of the imagination, still applied mainly to meanings *within* the four books. But I was beginning to feel an "echo effect": that same power might also be applicable *outside* them—applicable, that is, to their larger role within the Western counterculture of spiritual seeking. And, as part of that culture, to the relationship between the books and their readers. This could be the case, it seemed to me by 1976, even if there were just an unconfirmed possibility that Castaneda's writing *might* be fiction. It would be especially true, however, if Richard de Mille were to be trusted.

Just as my *Seeing Castaneda* anthology was being published in the fall of 1976 a new book by de Mille, a Santa Barbara psychologist, also appeared. *Castaneda's Journey: The Power and the Allegory* claimed to establish conclusively what others up to then had only suspected or insinuated: that Castaneda's books—shelved in the anthropology section of libraries by the Library of Congress cataloguers and labelled "nonfiction" by their publisher—were not factual reports at all, but creative writing, "made-up" stories, and therefore fraudulent.[27] Fraudulent but also, to judge from the style of *Castaneda's Journey*, mostly in good fun. De Mille's book was a wisecracking detective story in which the author, with great gusto, tracks down every bit of evidence showing that Castaneda had hoaxed us all. Carlos, not don Juan, it seemed, was the real sorcerer: a lovable trickster with some valuable philosophy to teach who had, in the bargain, dangerously blurred the boundary between fact and fiction, reality and imagination. How this is supposed to be dangerous, according to de Mille, is a topic for a later chapter.

Of course, with a little checking, defenders of Castaneda like me could determine that he was in fact awarded a doctorate in anthropology by UCLA. The abstract of his dissertation was available, and the dissertation itself, virtually identical to *Journey to Ixtlan* but with the title "Sorcery: A Description of the World," sat on a nonfiction shelf of the UCLA library.

And yet that, argued de Mille, is exactly where Castaneda's "field work" took place to begin with: in the library, not the desert.

De Mille's book goes to impressive lengths to show the many unacknowledged borrowings in the don Juan narratives, ideas and incidents taken from truly factual accounts by other anthropologists. None of them, by the way, has anything to do with *Yaqui* culture—a point that Native American critics have noted with understandable indignation.[28] There were also revealing discrepancies of sequence in the books and a highly unlikely use of English colloquialisms in Carlos's supposed translation of don Juan's Spanish.

Although UCLA never admitted to being either tricked or a co-trickster, and Castaneda continued to put out his books as literal ethnography, *Castaneda's Journey* had piled improbability upon improbability about them until it finally did seem just that to me: at least *improbable* that the first four volumes I had found so fascinating were factually reliable reports.

But what did this eventual verdict mean for my assessment of the importance of Castaneda's work? And what does it mean for us today as a clue to uncovering the essence of neoshamanism as a basis for understanding or personal involvement?

FICTIVE POWER BRINGS A NEW SHAMANISM TO WESTERN SEEKERS

NEOSHAMANISM WAS BORN because of fictive power, the fictive power not only *in* Castaneda's *Tales of Power* but more importantly *of* the entire four-volume fairy tale he had produced by 1976. This is the fictive power that led those of us on the counter-cultural Left, in search of literalistic validation for our psychospiritual (and psychedelic) visions, to misread the fairy tale as fact. This is also the fictive power we can reclaim as a treasured resource of the imagination for a future shamanic practice in the West—once we realize and reflect upon our misreading.

As I look back on neoshamanism's beginnings from the vantage point of the 1990s this was what the strong weight of Richard de Mille's evidence pointed to, even without final proof—which de Mille sought to supply in a later 1980 critique he edited, *The Don Juan Papers*.[29] And aside from de Mille's debunking there were the intuitions and speculations of the fiction writers Oates and Sukenick. These, I felt, could go with any growing doubts we might have about Castaneda's reliability to nudge us toward a less literalistic notion of what his writing was up to.

Books we were led to believe were factual anthropological field reports of actual shamanic experiences, and which, after several years of attentive reading, we could begin to see as teaching the puzzled apprentice something akin to fictive power, turned out by the mid-1970s to have been the most surprising demonstration of how that power actually worked—namely, on us, on our process of credulous reading.

It is significant, of course, that we did not see this outcome clearly (if at all) until several years had passed. That is, by 1976 it was really too late for aesthetic suspicions or a de Millean guilty verdict against Castaneda to prevent the trickery of his fairy tale telling from working its fictively powerful spell upon most of the many readers of his first four books. (Some readers even went to Mexico to find a don Juan who only existed in the pages of the books.) The fictive power operated unconsciously, under the cover of factuality, as it had to for maximum effect in a culture which has worshipped facts for several centuries and lowered the status of the imagination to a frivolous and marginal nonreality. Best-selling novels, understood as "mere" fiction, would not have given birth to neoshamanism as a social movement.

In this regard it is also crucial to understand that the forces leading us to equate fiction with falsehood and factuality with an exclusive access to truth were the same forces that destroyed our native Western shamanisms of continental Europe and the British Isles. They are the same forces of hyper-rational literalism that don Juan had to undermine for Carlos through his teaching of shamanic experience as described *within* our literalistic misreading of the tales. They are also the forces which Castaneda, as the unmasked *creator* of "don Juan and Carlos," can help us to counterbalance in ourselves if we *consciously* receive the lessons of his hoax.

IN OTHER WORDS, once we attain such a mindful sense of how the fictive power of Castaneda's hocus-pocus hooked us, then the trickery with which don Juan sought to soften Carlos's literalistic certainty can truly soften ours as well, opening for us—and opening us for—imagination's flexible reality. This is the way to deliteralize our reading, joining Castaneda's created characters in their genuinely shamanic flight of fictive power.

This is the way, as well, to renew or reempower shamanism in Western culture more generally. A conscious interaction with fictive power as a counterforce of imagination, hidden but available as a Castanedan birthright of the New Shamanism and as a legacy of Eliade's authoritative imagining before his, provides the most promising avenue ahead for Western seekers after shamanic spirituality. Attunement to imagination's fictive power can lead the way forward from modern Western culture's deeply anti-shamanic attitudes to the nonordinary reality, the imaginal reality, that shamanism needs to draw upon.

Admittedly the modern distrust of imagination is itself an immense impediment, within ourselves as well as the culture. It seems we need a kind of shamanic healing, or soul-recovery, just to reconnect to the possibility of renewing any version of Western shamanism. But beyond the indispensable remedy of pondering the Castaneda phenomenon—which we will continue to do in the next chapters—there are resources available now in the West, especially in the Jungian school of depth psychology to be probed in the second half of this book, for validating imaginal experience in full view of our skepticism toward the nonliteral. The tools are at hand for empowering *imagination* so that it can healingly empower *us* to envision an authentically Western neoshamanism.

Besides, any other Western option for renewing shamanism, even one that may seem to offer a more direct path to indigenous wisdom from non-Western cultures, runs a risk we cannot afford: literalistic delusion as well as neocolonialist presumption. This issue will require further thought later. For now it is enough to say that we cannot, as Carlos did when interpreting his magical flight in the first book, presume to bypass what he took to be "in my imagination, in my mind alone," as though flying in that realm is unreal, an indirect approximation of actual experience. Don Juan, as I read him, did not devalue the imaginal in that way, and neither would Castaneda when he told *Time* something his fictive persona had trouble seeing: "using science to validate sorcery . . . robs the world of its magic and makes milestones of us all."[30]

As modern Western seekers, we long for "direct experience" beyond rigid dogma and bureaucratic institutions, even beyond "book-learning." It is most of what we mean by preferring "spirituality" to "religion" as the designation of our quest for deeper meaning in our lives. But we must realize that, setting aside narcotic excursions, which are variously problematic in our culture, the only direct experience of nonordinary reality we can claim as Westerners to be truly ours—and recognizably shamanic—is the experience of imagination's power in fictions and fantasies, dreams and reveries, or the arts of literature and the like.

Moreover, the fictive power that perplexed Carlos in the books and that Castaneda employed in writing them may be, as we shall see, ours to become conscious of but not, most basically, a product of our will. This means that the imaginal reality produced by fictive power is no more something the human ego simply "makes up" than is the underworld or upperworld of the tribal shaman. As our Jungian explorations will make clear, imagination is a larger affair by far than "make-believe," and much closer than Western science has supposed to something shamanic that is happening *to* us.

Meanwhile, for many writers on shamanism, and for most of the people I have personally asked about it, Castaneda's having presented a counter-cultural fairy tale as factual anthropology is nevertheless shrugged aside as irrelevant to the truth or value of his writings. Except for readers who turn away in anger at being hoaxed, it seems that to Castaneda's many fans it simply does not matter that the books have turned out almost certainly to be fiction, just as my airplane companion was unfazed by the probability that Andrews' *Shakkai* was in actuality a New-Age fable. This common reaction is another matter in need of further examination in the next chapter and later. For reasons already hinted at, it fails to discover the fictive power at the core of the New Shamanism—which only confronting Castaneda's trickery in depth can do. Now is the time, over twenty-five years after *The Teachings of Don Juan*, when a maturing Western movement for reconnection to shamanic healing needs to find this rich legacy in its Castanedan origins. Assuredly we also need to do so as individuals attracted to such a resurgent spirituality, either as fascinated students, earnest practitioners, or both.

Today we have the chance to challenge a statement Oates made in her review of *Tales of Power* back in 1974 and to confirm a very different one from Sukenick's discussion of fictive power the previous year. Lamenting the situation she saw, Oates claimed that "the mysterious 'power' that once belonged to the West, in psychological terms, will never be experienced again in our lifetimes."[31] But quite to the contrary, as we shall see in detail, it is *precisely* "in psychological terms" that we can follow through on some evocative advice that Sukenick had already offered:

> Once philosophy was stories, religion was stories, wisdom books were stories, but now that fiction is held to be a form of lying . . . we are without persuasive wisdom, religion, or philosophy. Don Juan shows us that we live in fictions, and that we live best when we know how to master the art. . . . The sorcerer, the artist, sees beyond any particular form fiction may take to the fictive power itself, and in the absence of powerful fictions in our lives, maybe it's time for all of us to become sorcerers.[32]

Or, as "don Juan" himself said when "Carlos" asked him what "once upon a time" means: "It means once upon a time, or maybe it means now, today."[33]

Indeed, today is the perfect time to make this counter-cultural fairy tale come true. We can do this by finally seeing that the fictive power of imagining is what made its telling shamanic for us as readers. And it is what can make us "become sorcerers" ourselves if we will interact mindfully with such imagining. In learning this lesson of seeing through to and engaging with fictive power, other shamanovelists, professed writers of fictions, can be our master teachers.

3

LYING WITH SHAMANOVELISTS

The audience in the large lecture hall is listening to the visiting speaker with interest and respect. He is a handsome man, middle-aged and well-dressed, with a foreign accent that adds to his charm. I am attending his lecture on "The Power of Lies" more because of his topic than his fame as a novelist. Mario Vargas Llosa, fresh from a failed presidential candidacy in Peru, is talking about the political ramifications of writing fictions—or the differences between lying in politics and literature. Everyone in this auditorium at the University of Colorado, considering Vargas Llosa's remarks in the aftermath of the recent Persian Gulf War, seems receptive. Except for one anthropologist.

It is the question-and-answer period now. After several friendly questions and comments, including one by me about Carlos Castaneda, a man rises, identifying himself as a member of the Anthropology Department. He asks for Vargas Llosa's response to an anecdote. It seems the anthropologist has just returned from the jungles of Peru, where he has had interactions with people from the Machiguenga tribe.

Vargas Llosa had written about the Machiguenga in his novel of 1989, *The Storyteller*.[1] It tells the story of a young man from Lima, an eccentric red-headed Jew with a disfiguring birthmark, who had gone to live with the tribe and had become, most mysteriously, one of their itinerant ritual storytellers, moving from settlement to settlement in the Amazonian jungle. The novel, a bestseller in the United States, is dedicated to a relative and to the Machiguenga.

The anthropologist is unhappy with Vargas Llosa because, he says, he has read portions of *The Storyteller* to Machiguenga acquaintances, portions that recount Machiguenga stories and customs. He reports their reaction to what he has read to them: "They say you have misrepresented their culture. They call you 'El Mentiroso,' the liar. What do you have to say to that?"

The previously affable audience, humming with private conversations following the formal lecture, is suddenly silent, waiting for Vargas Llosa to reply. After a hushed pause, he does so. "Thank you," he says quietly.

I am stunned, at first, like everyone else, by this unexpected response to the anthropologist's unfriendly inquiry. Then I think: of course.

I cannot remember exactly what else Mario Vargas Llosa said that night. I cannot even recall many details of my own question about Castaneda or of his answer. It had to do with how much less pernicious the "lying" of the fiction writer is than are the lies of politicians or government regimes. And perhaps he acknowledged that Castaneda was somewhere in between with his imposture, falsifying Native Mesoamerican culture and much else if his lying were believed as nonfiction.

Here is part of why it very much matters that Castaneda fabricated a hoax—and why it very much matters that we confront our awareness of that fact. If the hoax does not matter to us we are not only led into colonialist misconceptions harmful to other cultures but we also cannot learn its lesson about *openly* lying in order to "become sorcerers."

Don Juan may show us that we live in fictions, as Ronald Sukenick pointed out, and yet his creator had hidden the fact that we were also living in fictions as we read his books. Instead of saying "Thank you" when Richard de Mille debunked him as a liar, Castaneda stuck to his story of not telling stories.

Not so Vargas Llosa, who accepted with gratitude his role of being a "liar." Which is to say, he gladly acknowledged that his was not a factual account of Machiguenga life and beliefs. It was clear, however, that he believed his sort of mindful lying in *The Storyteller* served truth in another way, the way of imagination's fictive power: a way just as valid as a literal ethnographic report but not meant to achieve the latter's traditional aim of factual accuracy. His novel, in other words, was not misrepresenting the cultural Other, as had Castaneda until unmasked, but representing otherwise, by way of conscious imagining.

In the modern West, beholden to science's standards, stories of nonliteral realities, imaginal otherworlds, had to be categorized as fiction, as lying—thus robbing them of their reality and their ability to offer us

much-needed meaning and healing. But a way back exists for Western seekers after a shamanic spirituality (and for the scholars who follow their travels). It is not a backward movement, really, but a way to *get* back a version of
our own lost shamanisms in the form of a soulful spirituality reliant upon a
new relationship to imagining.

Saul Zaratas, Vargas Llosa's Jewish protagonist, may have been able to
blend his life with the Machiguenga's in the story because he, too, was an
Other in Hispanic Catholic Peru as well as being an outcast by reason of his
physical disfigurement. Similarly, while supporting the cultural Others
among us in the increasingly multicultural West, gratefully receiving their
gifts, we whose heritage is European may need to find the Otherness in our
own history. This would be the pre-Christian wisdom left behind in myths
handed down or lingering still in the landscapes across the Atlantic, the legacy of Merlin's cry.

But with shamanism a fading memory from Europe's indigenous past,
and attempts at outer revivals riddled with unacknowledged fantasy, another
step is needed. There is another Otherness we need to honor, an inner Otherness which psychology has emerged, from the midst of modern science, to
indicate as a current resource for shamanic reconnection: the imagining psyche as our inner Other, and science's Other as well.

Here Merlin's cry is louder, and this will be our focus for the second
half of the book. First we must explore further the truthful lying of the fiction writer, the novelist who knows how we can become sorcerers in
Sukenick's sense, starting with Sukenick's own shamanovels.

THE SORCERY OF SHAMANOVELS

WE HAVE ALREADY seen how Mircea Eliade's widely influential discussion of
cross-cultural shamanisms was strongly shaped by *imaginal* preoccupations
more directly expressed in his novel *The Forbidden Forest*. We have therefore
called the latter a shamanovel, a text in which imagination is revealed as the
true wellspring of Western ideas and experiences of shamanism. Neither Eliade's shamanovel (seen in conjunction with his scholarly study of shamanism) nor Castaneda's series of nine—nor, for that matter, the works of
dissimulating successors such as Lynn Andrews—was presented by their
authors or received by their readers in full consciousness of this lesson, however. It took some deconstruction for us to find that these narratives were
built out of imaginal elements and fictive power, not primarily out of ethnographic facts, and to glimpse initially the positive basis there for a Western
shamanism, reconstructed through conscious imagining.

But writers like Sukenick—and he can stand in for a whole modernist/postmodernist tradition of experimentalists—provide us with another sort of shamanovels. These are self-conscious fictions that can both engage us in magical flights of reading and instruct us in holding their processes of imagination in our awareness like a lucid dream. Added to these features of Sukenick's fiction are his writings in literary theory, probing how the magic gives us flight, how we might be better readers, less passive passengers, even artful climbers and divers ourselves. Also, his involvement as a reviewer of Castaneda makes Sukenick an especially pertinent guide to the secrets of imaginal sorcery. Finally, his contribution may help us to understand Michael Taussig's difficult point about shamanism reflecting more a text of open-ended ordeal than an orderly narrative of completed flight.

Sukenick recalls that when he first read an excerpt from Castaneda's second book, *A Separate Reality*, he was finishing the last sections of his novel *Out*.[2] He says that he

> was astonished to find a number of similarities in incident and idea between *Out* and Castaneda's story. The more so in that the things in *Out* most parallel to Castaneda's book came out of my dreams, on which I have come to draw heavily in my writing. How could such a thing have happened, I wondered, unless I were a sorcerer or Castaneda a novelist. . . .[3]

From earlier statements we have examined we know that Sukenick believed the former to more likely be the case than the latter, but having confronted de Mille's revelations we can say that both are true. And not only both true, but equivalent, even identical. The novelist's sorcery and the anthropologist's novelizing come to the same thing—a tantalizing clue to how we can all "become sorcerers" that we will probe in the next chapter.

SUKENICK'S OWN EXPERIMENTAL NOVELS and stories both reflect and reflect upon that process. The substance of his novel *Out*, for instance, is on one level political, often comically so, but that is not its only level. The political melodrama, complete with phallic dynamite sticks and conspiratorial get-togethers called "meets," means that the word "plot" refers both to the designs of the conspirators and the structure of the narrative.

Heading out from the East Coast—the site of Sukenick's earlier fictions—the hero of *Out* encounters various characters who give him ambiguous clues to the meaning of the plot (in either sense of the word). Reaching the Great Plains he runs into Dr. Frank Stein, who tortures him into telling his life story. Reduced to nonsensical babble, he makes up the name

"Ronald" for himself and escapes, writing down a clue: "Evidence is ubiquitous suspicion is pervasive fantasy hardens reality seeps away."[4] This is certainly something more than politics in any narrow sense.

Sukenick is not only pursuing large issues of how we know (as is "Ronald"), but he also frequently places the inventiveness—the sorcery—of the acts of writing and reading, with the imagination that connects them, right in the foreground of his narrative. Toward the end of Chapter 6, Ronald announces: "Here we are in the middle of our book speeding along on the breaking crest of the present toward god knows what destination after the first word everything follows anything follows nothing follows the world is pure invention from one minute to the next. . . ."[5] Chapter 5, in the novel's reverse-numbered ten chapters, then begins the second half of the story, the journey out west, and the countdown speeds up for the reader as the white space on the pages grows.

Having arrived at the South Dakota Badlands, the hero meets Empty Fox, Sukenick's single most Castanedan character. Ronald and Empty Fox cross paths when they both hitch rides on the back of the same pickup truck, and coming into Rapid City there occurs what seems to be one of those coincidences the author has cited between his work (or dream work) and that of Castaneda. What is narrated in Chapter 5 is strongly reminiscent of a scene from *A Separate Reality*, discussed earlier, in which don Juan's friend don Genaro, a Mazatec sorcerer, climbs a steep ledge by a waterfall and performs acrobatic feats, leaping from boulder to boulder at the top of the falls and eventually disappearing with a phenomenal backflip. We need to consider at some length the actual language—nonstop, perhaps dreamlike—of the similar scene in *Out* in order to get the full effect of Sukenick's literary lying and flying. Perhaps it will also show us a shamanism less like Eliade's and more like Taussig's:

> Coming into Rapid City says Empty Fox we stop for a hitchhiker he climbs into the truck very stiff we pull him up a short fellow with crew cut pasty pudgy face not young he has a small valise the truck stops the three of us on the outskirts of Rapid City the little fellow opens his valise
>
> starts working with some struts and colored paper very quickly he has this box kite set up red and blue with small wings he gets in and takes off rises to the top of a tall cottonwood tree and gets off on a branch on one side starts climbing disappears on a branch opposite he's going to fall disappears his head pokes out around a distant branch he falls reappears at the very top of the tree disappears around to the other side a foot comes out from behind a branch a leg an arm waving then he reappears next to us on the ground I hug him he seems rather grumpy pulls away

closes up his bag walks down the road he's a clown he's going to the circus a van pulls up looks like an old bakery truck full of silly teenage girls we throw them off drive into town we get off at a corner in front of a bar the van moves on we can see through the rear window that the driver's seat is empty on the back of the van it says *the spirit moves us* this is a dream Empty Fox's dream or maybe my dream the truck drops us off on the out-skirts of Rapid City let's have a serious discussion says Empty Fox. What's your ambition.

I want to write a book like a cloud that changes as it goes.[6]

CLOUDS, WIND, AND WORLD-CREATING

THERE IS NO EVIDENCE in the text of *Out* indicating whether the novelistic dream quoted above was one Sukenick in fact had while writing *Out* in California or was one he experienced, awake or asleep, with the actual Sioux medicine man he has mentioned meeting in South Dakota.[7] Or was one he just "made up." In any of these cases it constitutes another tale of fictive power. In being a story it is not claiming to give a factual account of a Sioux visionary. But it does demonstrate as well as describe how the sorcery we need to learn encompasses both the "controlled dreaming" of creative writing (or reading) and a mindful relationship to the dream process itself (which we will explore in Chapter 6).

The language of this experimental novelist, in other words, conveys the truly shamanic quality that imagination can offer, dreaming or waking, to Western seekers who no longer have available a native cultural shamanism of their own. Taussig's type of unresolved shamanism here meets its kind of Western storyteller, a postmodern shamanovelist who shows us a wild imagining at work.

For example, the verbal image of the cloud—in this instance the novel as a cloud—is central in Sukenick's fiction and can, indeed, be called an *image* of fictive power, a concrete symbol for the sorcery of imagining. Already in his early story "The Birds" this imagery comes through the stream-of-consciousness language: "Nuthatch slick arctic acrobat seal bullets through blank air silence of the page the stream carries mainly on its glassy surface rippled clouds inventing themselves from minute to minute. . . ."[8]

It is worth noting that at this point Sukenick's cloud imagery connects up not only with the ongoing world-creation of the inventive acts of writing and reading but also with the specific influence of a poem by Wallace Stevens, a poet about whom Sukenick had written a book-length study.[9] The poem in question is "Sea Surface Full of Clouds," which concludes with its own vision of primal procreation: "Then the sea / And heaven rolled as one and from the two / Came fresh transfigurings of freshest blue."[10]

But perhaps the most important point to make here, easily overlooked, is that even reading these excerpts from writers like Sukenick and Stevens can actually start us imagining for ourselves; certainly their self-conscious use of imagery models for us a relationship to the imagination that can be shamanic in ways we shall be exploring in depth later on. And minute-by-minute invention seems a different sort of narrative process than Eliade's rather programmed sequence of the shaman rising and converging toward centered ecstasy.

As for Sukenick's particular model of the shamanovel, *Out* continues by offering another image for fictive power, a time-honored one: the wind. Empty Fox brings this image in with a little chant he sings when the two men leave Rapid City:

> Without the wind
> The kite is dead
> With it everything
> Is possible.[11]

This is reminiscent of don Juan telling Carlos that he had blown life into the tumbleweed at twilight when he had seen it as a beaked mammal. Also reminiscent of Castaneda's first shamanovel is Empty Fox's behavior when he and Ronald reach a campground in the Black Hills: he "finds a spot" on which to pitch their tent. He then takes off up a trail, as he says, "to make friends with the wind,"[12] later returning to tell Ronald that he has been "on the wing":

> What.
> Dreaming that's what I call on the wing I go very fast. I had a great dream very strong.
> What about.
> I make up a song. Goes like this
> It doesn't matter
> Where you start
> It all comes together
> It all falls apart.[13]

The phrase "on the wing," which we could connect to the magical flight of the shaman, nevertheless leads, we notice, to a concluding point about disintegration that Taussig might applaud. This aerial phrase further recalls Sukenick's story "The Death of the Novel," where the character named Sukenick admires crows—notoriously shamanic birds which figure in the Castaneda books—because "they know how to think so that their thinking is part of their world, like a wing beat, like the wind."[14] In this sorcerer's logic, then, dreaming of some kind is our closest thing to thinking like a crow, although, as in shamanism, ingesting hallucinogens may also do the job. Smoking hash is referred to as "on the wing" when Empty Fox and Ronald share a pipeful in front of the tent. As with Carlos, however, such aids are not compulsory; without a supporting cultural context their use can be a danger and a distraction from the necessary development of the imagination needed to "become sorcerers." Besides, this is a novel, not a factual guidebook.

The novel winds down with further adventures for Ronald, successively named Roland Sycamore and R. Chapter 1, which is almost all blank space, begins with a declaration reminding us of how acutely aware Sukenick is of his reader's experience of reading, including their reading (like his writing) as a kind of dreaming: "Wake up stop this is it drop everything stop all this is a message you've been reading now throw it away stop the wind is blowing the tide is flowing stop finish up and get out. . . ."[15]

Here is a self-consciousness about the actual process of reading that undermines it as an unconscious activity—the sort of reading which supports the magic of traditional narrative (or its misuse by a hoaxing writer)—and installs an even more impressive magic of mindful imagining instead.

ONE OF SUKENICK'S fellow fiction writers has said that *Out* releases "a true hallucinatory energy."[16] In other words, as we have glimpsed ourselves, it displays or even radiates fictive power as well as describing it: practicing the sorcery of a literary lying that shows us further shamanic possibilities of the imagination. Although *Out* is an especially effective example of this owing to its parallels with the contemporary writing of Castaneda, the same is the case, to a greater or lesser degree, with all his fictional works to date—a good reason for calling them shamanovels.

The images of fictive power, the world-creating capability of imagination, often persist from novel to novel. For instance, in his 1975 novel *98.6* the character named Ron (who is, not surprisingly, writing a novel), after his commune recites a myth about a god called "Flows-with-the-streaming-clouds," chooses the new name Cloud.[17] This underscores the divine prerogative of the writer as creator, and toward the end of this novel an idealized Israel is praised as a Holy Land where "artists are recognized as the creators not only of esthetic works but of reality itself. . . ."[18]

The artist, the writer, however much he or she can model how to become a sorcerer, is not the only creative practitioner of fictive power. All along in his career Sukenick has supported the slogan of the French writer Robbe-Grillet: "the main didactic job of the contemporary novelist is to teach the reader how to invent his [or her] world."[19] The focus on the inventive potential of the reader in the act of reading is striking. The statement sounds radical, revolutionary—certainly innovative. But two literary critics make an intriguing suggestion: that it would only qualify as innovative "in any society other than those primitive ones that are constantly in the act of creating their world day by day."[20] It is also necessary to recognize, recalling Taussig's critique, that such cosmic creativity is not without its own peculiar birth agonies, which must be as constant as the daily (or momentary) delivery of new worlds.

Whether anthropologists—or the "primitives" themselves, who deserve a different name—would entirely agree with the two critics' statement is not clear. The point to see, however, is the possible closeness between cultures where some form of shamanism may be practiced within a supportive context of belief and ritual, and modern Western readers, imagining with a book in their hands in a culture which has only fantasies to offer the seeker after some new access to shamanism.

To turn toward the power and process of imagining underlying our fantasies rather than their delusory content may actually bring us closer to the realities encountered and invented by the indigenous healers we have called shamans.

These connections between image-rich language in tales that take us on daredevil flights of invention, teaching us as readers to take off on our own ordeals, on the one hand, and the worlds of shamanism, on the other, are why the issue of Castaneda's presenting fiction as fact matters, and matters crucially for whoever seeks a way to reconnect to such worlds. By probing and pondering the Castaneda hoax, we begin to see that imagination—not factual access to indigenous wisdom—gave birth to neoshamanism and gives us our best access to what that movement might become for us. Sukenick knows this. And thus his writing, not widely known outside of avant-garde literary circles among readers who only fly with traditional narratives, can help us pursue further the possibilities Castaneda's trickery opens up. He even brings the idea of imagination itself into his shamanovelizing in a direct way. As in *98.6*'s theme of "Psychosynthesis."

BEYOND PSYCHOANALYSIS TO IMAGINATION

THE LAST SECTION of *98.6* (Part Three) explains why the California commune of Ron/Cloud fails to realize its ideals of entering the paradisal state of

Israel, a state of mind more than a geopolitical entity. Such an achievement, the novel says, requires "Psychosynthesis." Without ever citing the actual theory propounded under that name by Roberto Assagioli,[21] Sukenick has introduced the term earlier in *98.6*: "Psychosynthesis is the opposite of psychoanalysis but apart from that Cloud refuses to define it. Cloud feels that life is a lot like a novel you have to make it up. That's the point of psychosynthesis in his opinion to pick up the pieces and make something of them."[22] Psychosynthesis is Cloud's—and Sukenick's—way back to the Holy Land, to the source of fictive power, the springs of story.

In Part Three it is proclaimed that "only the imagination can deal with the imagination thus Psychosynthesis. A way of curing the disease without catching it. A way of things happening without happening. A way of dreaming without dreaming. A way of going mad without going mad."[23] Like Taussig's formulation, this is enigmatic, but it suggests what the radical deliteralizing brought by a focus on imagining might amount to.

Moreover, it hooks into the issue raised about indigenous shamans by numerous anthropologists with psychoanalytic leanings: is their shamanic ecstasy no more than schizophrenic possession? Sukenick suggests that it is nothing of the kind, though a different psychological theory, one based upon the validity of imagination, is required to assess what is actually going on. In this he extends don Juan's long course of instruction with Carlos in how he could "let go without losing his marbles," or even Taussig's preference for a shamanic (post)modernism that may be capable of "dismantling all fixed and fixing notions of identity."

The discussions of Psychosynthesis in *98.6* demonstrate with special clarity that the centrality of the imagination in the construction of shamanism is a deliberate article of faith in Sukenick's shamanovels. A closing monologue by a venerable sage at an Israeli commune called The Wave provides a further convincing example of how Sukenick's language draws the reader into his or her own pilgrimage to the Palestine of fictive power, there to become the author's kind of sorcerer. Yitshak Fawzi is ostensibly discoursing on the post-Newtonian idea in physics that particles and waves are complementary components of matter, though something nonscientific is at stake:

> The waves are the improbabilities of the unknown that one perceives through intuition. Introspection. Empathy. A sense of beauty. Through imagination in other words. . . . The waves are the spirit. The matter does not exist. That is the matter. That we imagine that it does and don't imagine that it doesn't do you follow. As if it exists without us without the imagination that is the matter. A loss of imagination.[24]

To anticipate our explorations in psychology later on, a loss of imagination is a loss of soul, a loss of relationship to psyche, and only a psychology of imagining—better still, an imaginal psychology—can offer the necessary shamanic healing.

As a writer and literary theorist rather than a psychologist, Sukenick was unaware in creating *98.6* of Assagioli's psychosynthesis approach or the Jungian movement I am calling imaginal psychology. He does imply in the novel that what he is after lies beyond Freudian psychoanalysis. But he tends to see all of psychology under that heading, and is therefore led to condemn it all: ". . . psychology was the trademark of a previous era," the narrator observes. Then he adds that "what we have instead of psychology is imagination. In any case psychology was always the science of imagination but as a medical science was obliged to treat it like a sickness."[25]

Certainly it is true that sometimes psychology has seen imagining as psychopathological. While acknowledging the use of personal dream material in his fictions, Sukenick emphasizes in a 1974 interview that he is not providing a mere safety valve for himself or the reader—or psychoanalytical raw material: "I don't want to use them as things to analyze. What I'm interested in them as is another level of reality, which we can make use of and include."[26] This "post-psychoanalytic" view largely accords with imaginal psychology, as we shall see, and with don Juan's shamanistic reliance on "a separate and pragmatic world of 'dreaming.'"[27]

BUT IT IS IMPORTANT to keep constantly in mind that don Juan is not a *literal* shaman any more than Sukenick is a *literal* psychologist. Both Castaneda's character and Sukenick's writing are literary, and as we Westerners move among the categories of shamanism, literature, and psychology we are finding, from Eliade to Castaneda to Sukenick, that literature is the primary perspective. *Its aesthetic priorities are the ones to look for in any psychology that can do justice to the quest for a Western version of shamanism: it will not be a scientific psychology.* Even anthropology as a resource, like Eliade's history of religions approach, turns out to have what we will find is a literary as much as a scientific basis.

So Sukenick's perspective as a shamanovelist is not just an interesting writer's angle, off to the side of shamanism's reality. It is central to how we in the West have constructed shamanism as a category, are fantasizing its return to us (or ours to it), and can have genuine access to through imagination.

Shamanovels, once seen as such, show us why the Castaneda controversy matters enough to learn from and, in so doing, also show us how to "become sorcerers." Any novel is a shamanovel in the sense of taking us on a magical flight. But if we are to learn from them how to become sorcerers their shamanic process of "lying" must be made conscious to us, and here novels with overtly shamanic themes, or scenes in which characters undergo ecstatic experiences of imagining or mythic visions, are needed. Beyond even these are fictions that are self-conscious about their own and their readers' processes of imagining. Such supreme shamanovels teach the art while they entertain with the usual immersion in the magical flight of novel-reading, even when teaching the art complicates the entertainment, "involving and disinvolving" us for a wilder ride than the simple pleasure trip we may have expected.

Literary lying like this initiates us into a new—and perhaps very old—way of knowing that can teach us, in ways we will examine, to live fictionally, work with waking dreams, imagine actively, and thereby, again, "become sorcerers." Sukenick's ambition for his own work is cognizant of such goals:

> I mean, my whole idea about fiction is that it's a normal, if I may use the word, epistemological procedure; that is, it is at the very center of everybody all the time at any period, and you don't have to search for psychological reasons, although they may be there too. But I think the epistemological ones are far more important and anterior. It's a way of making up the world and making sense of it.[28]

Sukenick's "normal epistemological procedure" is the functioning of fictive power in how we know. And although it may well operate at the center of everybody all the time at any period (as one psychologist, Carl Jung, would agree), such has been our modern loss of trust in the products of this procedure—the absence of powerful fictions in our lives, as Sukenick called them in his Castaneda essay—that it takes a new impetus, a sort of soul-recovery, to reassert it.

One of his commentators has explained this historical situation in the West with a remark by Wallace Stevens that Sukenick would know well: ". . . modern reality is a reality of decreation, in which our revelations are not the revelations of belief, but the precious portents of our own powers."[29] Even Stevens was not convinced that these powers were always or only "our own," but he was pointing to a way beyond the losses—the "reality of decreation"—suffered by Western modernity.

Like twentieth-century fiction writers from Samuel Beckett, Vladimir Nabokov, and Jorge Luis Borges to John Barth, Robert Coover, and Donald Barthelme, not to mention Vargas Llosa and Sukenick—all in various ways non-traditional storytellers—Stevens was teaching us to attune ourselves to the psychological and aesthetic *process* of imagining. This is in contrast to fixating on particular *products* of the process as objects of belief (often disconfirmed belief, as in biblical claims invalidated by modern science). Sukenick's commentator, Ihab Hassan, says something about the former's 1969 fiction collection *The Death of the Novel and Other Stories* that holds true for all of his work since then. He calls those stories "improvisations on an old question: how can the imagination take power again, pervade our lives, and alter the quality of existence?"[30]

It is an old question to which the best answer may be: by our reimagining a New Shamanism in the West.

IMAGINARY UNIVERSES

I HAVE MENTIONED that as a visiting faculty member at the University of Colorado in 1991 I was teaching a course on shamanism, and that one of my colleagues in the Religious Studies Department, David Carrasco, gave me a copy of a book he had co-edited about the life and work of his former teacher, Mircea Eliade. This book, *Waiting for the Dawn*, includes a lecture of the same title that Professor Eliade had given at the university in 1982—in the same auditorium, I imagined, where I heard Senor Vargas Llosa almost a decade later.

As his lecture title implies, Eliade's topic was the end of a world and the expectation of a new one, which is how he characterized the mood of the West since World War II. He felt that pessimistic visions of Apocalypse and optimistic hopes for a Golden Age were manifesting themselves in science, sociology, and economics, even if thinkers in these fields failed to realize they were expressing essentially religious expectations. His own focus, however, was on certain signs from more overtly religious directions: "the discovery of Asiatic and archaic religious spiritual traditions" by the West, which he saw as "the most significant event of our century."[31]

Even allowing for his preoccupation with the history of religions, the extent of Eliade's endorsement of this dual "cultural innovation" should startle us. I certainly found it arresting when I read it in 1991, and with my involvement in the study of shamanism and neoshamanism I was, if anything, even more struck by a section of the lecture entitled "Shamanism, Hallucinogens, Initiation." Here he begins with a paragraph that requires reviewing:

> Significantly, at least in the United States, the most creative encounter was with archaic—as a matter of fact, prehistoric—spiritual values. For the first time in his (not so long) history, modern man became contemporary with

his paleolithic and neolithic relatives, that is to say, he understood and reiterated their mode of being in the world. Indeed, the recent discovery of shamanism by artists and the youth-culture constitutes, in itself, a fascinating episode in the history of ideas. Only thirty years ago shamanism had a rather limited interest even for specialists—i.e., anthropologists and historians of religions. . . . A generation ago shamanism was considered to be either a psychopathic phenomenon, a primitive healing practice, or an archaic type of black magic, but contemporary scholarship has convincingly demonstrated the complexity, the rigor, and the rich spiritual meaning of shamanistic initiations and practices.[32]

Scholarship—often building on Eliade's big book first published in French in 1951, the "thirty years ago"—may have intellectually validated shamanism as an indigenous mode of spirituality worthy of respect in the modern West (or the post-war United States), as this strong statement stresses. But it does not acknowledge that the scholars alone could never have made "archaic" shamanism a part of the major cultural innovation Eliade was perceiving. This required Castaneda.

TO SOME DEGREE Eliade acknowledged Castaneda's indispensable role in his 1982 lecture, when he went on to say that "the 'existential' interest of American youth in shamanism and shamanistic techniques was abundantly illustrated by the reaction to Carlos Castenada's [sic] books. . . . These books not only became best sellers, but also created a 'para-shamanistic underground movement,' especially in California."[33] He does not supply any corroborating details about this movement, depending on our likely assumption that California probably did harbor such a youth counter-culture.

Nor does he seem aware of the beginnings of the more broadly based neoshamanism movement with Michael Harner's book *The Way of the Shaman*, which came out in 1980 bearing Castaneda's blessing. Part popular overview, part how-to handbook, Harner's bestseller accompanied his first workshops, appealing to seekers of various ages and originally based not in California but Connecticut, where he had established a Foundation for Shamanic Studies.[34]

A more important omission in Eliade's acknowledgement of Castaneda's role in the return of shamanism to the West is any engagement with the status of the latter's writings as fiction, as hoax. By 1982 de Mille had written not one but two debunking books, so Castaneda's sleight-of-hand was no longer secret. (Perhaps there is an unconscious admission of Castaneda's subterfuge in the frequent slip of the pen, evident here in *Waiting for the Dawn*, that misspells his name: "Castenada" suggests that he has indeed given us nothing—*nada*—at least nothing factual, however much he made marvels appear before our eyes.)

We have already seen that Eliade's own factual writing on shamanism was significantly driven by imaginative priorities revealed in his fictional work *The Forbidden Forest*. This was, indeed, secret in 1982; at least it seems to have been to Professor Eliade, and I am not aware of anyone else making that point about his work. In any case, the fictive basis of the neoshamanism for which his work laid a foundation may have been a blind spot for a man who, though a fiction writer upon occasion himself, even a shamanovelist, was so thoroughly devoted to the world of "objective scholarship."

Eliade's scholarship did, however, acknowledge the importance of what he called "creative imagination" even if he did not always see how deeply it informed that scholarship. For the most part he kept these two areas separate in his own conception of his work as both a novelist and scholar, while praising the process in which he participated when pursuing the former role.

In the full, unpublished version of his "Waiting for the Dawn" lecture (also made available to me by Professor Carrasco), he coupled this praise with his major stress on the yearning for spiritual initiation in post-war Western culture. He cites the appearance of initiatory scenarios in the work of a number of twentieth-century literary artists. "The creative imagination of the poet," Eliade claims, "grasped the meaning of initiatory ordeals . . . in a more profound sense than that presented by his literary sources."[35]

To see something as primordially mythic as the patterns of sacred initiation rituals in recent nonreligious literary works, he goes on, we have to practice a "demystification in reverse":

> . . . that is to say, we have to "demystify" the apparently profane worlds and languages of literature, plastic arts and cinema in order to disclose their "sacred" elements, although it is, of course, an ignored, disguised, or degraded "sacred." In a desacralized world such as ours, the "sacred" is present and active chiefly in the imaginary universes.[36]

The implication for us is that shamanism, with its initiatory emphasis, its magical flights and underworld journeys, its visionary healing practices, can only return to the modern West in imagination. Even if Eliade did not apply this to his own scholarly construction of "shamanism" as a Western category, it is noteworthy that he nonetheless endorsed the "imaginary universes," the unconscious worlds of imagination, made manifest by the creative process of the artist. There, he implied, are the secret rooms in which to seek the sacred forms of shamanism.

PROSPERO'S BOOKS, BOOKISH INITIATIONS

HOW DO THESE INSIGHTS square with the guidance we have drawn from Sukenick's example as an artist, a postmodern literary liar in search of persuasive stories—wisdom, religion, and philosophy—for our lives?

First of all, Sukenick searches not so much for vestiges of sacred traditions hidden in our secular texts like Eliade but for the very springs of story, the imagining process itself that might give rise to newly persuasive fictions. Even more radically, he seeks the *reader's* empowerment as a "sorcerer" capable of starting from the beleaguered ego of modernity and imagining upward, outward, downward, inward, and onward (if not "Juanward") toward a fresh sense of sacredness in life and in the world.

In a time, Sukenick says, when "mystiques . . . are laid bare"—not just by modern demystifiers like Marx and Freud but, we could add, by a contemporary debunker like de Mille—his strategy is to find, and have us find, what Stevens once called "the fecund minimum." Beginning there we may create a kind of *re*mystification that does not renege on Marxian or Freudian insights but that offers a modest reconnection to the sacred that Eliade might applaud. Sukenick usually refers to this goal less religiously than Eliade would, speaking, for instance, of "discontinuity and fragmentation reaching toward continuity and wholeness. . . ."[37] Repeatedly Sukenick reminds us that for him as a writer and for us as readers the minimum from which we begin is the blank page. Its fecundity is shown when words appear and are read, imagination ignited.

In other words, while Sukenick acknowledges, by implication, that we live in what Eliade called a "desacralized" world, where traditional systems of order—including traditional stories taken as persuasive—have broken down (here Sukenick again resonates with Taussig), he applies a different sort of "demystification in reverse" to this modern dilemma.

Although Eliade and Sukenick favor different sorts of literary texts and different strategies for seeking resacralization, this is finally less important, Sukenick goes on to imply, than a shared goal of their quite different literary involvements: "The question is not," he says, "the validity of this or that kind of fiction, but of the fictive process itself, which, far more than a literary matter, involves belief, myth, and the ways we understand experience."[38] And elsewhere Sukenick sounds even closer, from his postmodernist focus upon processes of fictional composition, to

Eliade's traditionalist concern for the sacred contents of secular novels and poems:

> In moving into areas associated with the sacred text, such as parable, prayer, incantation, magic, prophecy, and myth of origin, in becoming a medium between individual and collective experience opposing the manipulations of the media, a medium that might serve as an oracular bridge to reconnect the profane with a sense of the sacred, the narrative might once more authenticate fiction as having some urgency other than the commercial.[39]

The key ingredient is the activated imagination, a difficult achievement in an age of mass media, Sukenick feels, when we daily undergo "the manipulation of the imagination, a sellout of individual experience."[40] We could also see this as a species of soul-loss, requiring shamanic remedies.

In his 1985 collection of critical essays, *In Form*, from which I have been quoting, as well as in his 1987 study of the New York literary underground, *Down and In*, Sukenick calls Castaneda's don Juan a Prospero, Shakespeare's figure of occult sorcery in *The Tempest*. "The world of the sorcerer is a stage," Sukenick says in both nonfiction texts, "and Don Juan is the skillful stage manager."[41] In this desacralized culture, which tosses spiritual seekers in a tempest of deconstructed factual certitudes, where constructs of former sacredness are no longer credible, Sukenick wants each of us become his or her own Prospero, stage-managing imaginal realities. To understand this, it is helpful to look at his comic novel of 1986, *Blown Away*.

The novel is about the making of a Hollywood feature film, *Blown Away*, a bad remake of Shakespeare's play, toying with the urgency of a commercialized fiction. Sukenick's characters, however, often reflect critically upon such a debasement of imagining, acting out their misgivings. The screenwriter on the film project is named, appropriately enough, Plotz, Victor Plotz. He is also assigned to produce a "novelization" as well as a "*pren-ovelization*" of the screenplay. The omniscient narrator is Dr. Boris O. Ccrab—the two "c's" may refer to Carlos Castaneda. Carlos shows up in a Los Angeles restaurant at one point and tells Boris he's in Mexico,[42] just as the actual Castaneda had made the same statement to Sukenick in an actual LA restaurant.[43]

This strangely named narrator, Ccrab, is a psychic whose paranormal abilities are being studied by a young social scientist named Philitis:

> "I have a confession," I blurt. "It was all fake."
> "What was all fake?" Philitis is alarmed.
> "The so-called experiment. Telepathy. Telepathy is fake. I'm a fake.

This office is fake. You Philitis, . . . everything around us, all fake.". . .
"You don't have telepathic power?" asks Philitis.
"Yes I have telepathic power. But it's fake."
"I saw you with my own eyes Dr. Ccrab."
"What you see with your own eyes is fake."
"Sometimes I don't understand you."
"Understatement of the year. Did you ever read *The Tempest*, Philitis?"
"What's that?"
"'These topless towers, / These vast, insubstantial pageants rare, / All false, all clouds, / Players on a stage, which soon will be but bare.' A play by Shakespeare. It's about a sorcerer."[44]

Can this be Sukenick's sly reading of don Juan's teachings to the literal-minded young social scientist, Carlos ("Philitis" could mean an inflamed love of the literal), about the true nature of his sorcery, his shamanic power? Or even Sukenick's *version* of what a true teaching about becoming a sorcerer would amount to? How *would* the don Juan books have turned out if, at a certain point, the old sorcerer had said to his apprentice that he was a fake, the books had been fakes—but that he, and they, had had real power nonetheless, fictive power? And that readers, his other apprentices, should take the lesson of his fakery—and that of his author's—as their actual shamanic learning? Or that they should check out the Western literary sorcery of Will Shakespeare?

SUCH A SHARP TURN in the Castaneda production line might have put a crimp in his sales, but we know that Sukenick identifies with clouds, and might well have wished to cloud the minds of social-scientific philistines in search of clear and distinct occult abilities. Such literalism will not work for us any more than it worked for Philitis—unless our urgencies are as commercial as those of Castaneda, or his agent, or his editor, appear to be, in which case we may make some money off of other people's literalism. But is that all the shamanism we are seeking?

These issues are very much a part of *Blown Away*'s story of the commercialization of Shakespeare's sorcery. In the novel, Plotz, the screenwriter, dies in the effort to come up with a script for the monstrous movie producer Drackenstein, who has to deal with Plotz's burial:

It turns out that Plotz has no cemetary reservation in the book you're reading, and this is holding up the funeral. Drackenstein answers an ad for a plot in the [LA] *Times*: "good location, murmuring pines, moving, must sell. $450 or best offer." He concludes the deal, for cash, in a Hamburger Hamlet in West Hollywood, with a curious little man who advises him against cremation. "There's nothing like a good plot," he tells Drackenstein.[45]

Sukenick's punning on "plot" is outrageous, but could also be instructive. It could be referring to—and making light of—the literary-critical issue of "the death of the novel," which, like his fellow innovators in fiction Barth, Coover, and Barthelme, he felt was a boon to his form of novel writing, not a death-knell. Perhaps Sukenick feels there is no plot in which you can kill or bury a good plot. He did, after all, write a *story* called "The Death of the Novel."

But one of his biggest innovations, as we have aleady noted about his earlier novels, is to call frequent attention to the actuality of the reading process, to the act of imagining that the reader is presently undergoing. The phrase "in the book you're reading" recurs seven times in the last twelve pages of *Blown Away*. The contrast to Castaneda, maintaining his disguise, mystifying his readers, could not be sharper. Sukenick demystifies such fakery, bringing us back to the fecund minimum of the blank page. Then he remystifies our reading: the page is suddenly filled with his words which for the first time we *see* in full consciousness for the powerful peyote buttons they, or any words, can be.

Our magical flight begins, but we are awake for the trip now, controls in our hands (though maybe piloting a glider). Rather than demystifying in reverse to find a fantasied archaic shamanism, relying upon lingering traces of a bygone sacred in a profane landscape longing for spiritual renovation, we can seek a sacredness, Sukenick suggests, that may lie in a forward movement—what his poetic hero Stevens called "imagination's new beginning."

What Sukenick does to teach self-consciousness to his readers we can do, with a little help from our friend de Mille, to our reading of Castaneda, shifting the ground beneath our experience on the path to shamanic imagining. As *Blown Away*'s other psychic, Madame Lazonga, muses: "You know very well we're all living in a world of images to begin with. So stop whining and start using your imagination."[46]

We will want to know more about that world of images—and about what using our imagination might entail. For his part, Sukenick continues to foster its use in his innovative way, most recently publishing an interconnected collection of "hyperfictions" called *Doggy Bag*.[47] Annie Dillard, in her book with the shamanic title *Living by Fiction*, throws additional light on Sukenick's writing and our reading:

> On every continent, contemporary modernist fiction is written by educated and sophisticated writers. By no means all educated writers prefer it; but nowhere do uneducated writers produce it. . . . How could they? Borges is

> a library; Ronald Sukenick started as a Wallace Stevens critic. . . . It is a
> taste acquired through cheerful familiarity with the provisional nature of
> literary texts and the relative nature of historical values.[48]

In other words, it is a taste exactly in line with the intellectual circumstances of the educated seekers of neoshamanist wisdom, who ought, therefore, to find Sukenick's sort of sophisticated shamanovelizing an effective way to "become sorcerers" through acts of informed reading and the shamanic realities into which they can initiate us.

Given his own shamanovelistic aims, Sukenick would certainly concur with Eliade's cautionary conclusion to the 1982 Boulder lecture. After extolling the rediscovery of prehistoric and Asiatic religious traditions as the most significant cultural event of our century, he pointed out, almost at the close of his brilliant career, that "we must also keep in mind that modern man is *condemned to a literate culture.* By this I mean that oral tradition[s], upon which archaic and Oriental civilizations have until now been constructed, have all but disappeared . . . so that we are no longer able to acquire but a bookish initiation."[49]

A bookish initiation, however, an initiation in imagination, if it is mindfully experienced and includes something like the trials of a true initiation (with no assured outcome, as Taussig would insist), may be enough. Enough to turn the neoshamanism we have been sold by shamanthropologists into an authentic Western shamanic spirituality. For seekers and scholars alike, this can be a way to the soul of shamanism.

4

STUDYING WITH
SHAMANTHROPOLOGISTS

𝕴n a radio interview soon after his expose, *Castaneda's Journey*, was published in 1976, Richard de Mille said something that is pertinent to our reading of shamanovels while pointing us toward the final major factor in the creation of neoshamanism in the West. When the interviewer asks him what sort of person would doubt Carlos Castaneda's credibility upon reading the don Juan books, de Mille answers

> . . . a person with sufficient experience with literature to recognize fiction when he saw it. It's been very interesting to me that every fiction writer who has read Castaneda recognizes him as a fiction writer, but anthropologists and sociologists do not recognize this as fiction writing because they don't know much about fiction writing. They're not prepared to evaluate it; they don't have the feel of it. So they just say he fictionalized his report a little bit.[1]

The interviewer then asks de Mille if he can, as "a non-fiction writer as well as a fiction writer and a psychologist, maybe describe for us what in there would give us the impression why it's fiction rather than non-fiction." But de Mille's reply does not meet this request:

> No, I couldn't, because that would require a theory of fiction, and I'm not up on that sort of thing. But I imagine that a professor of literature could easily—or a literary critic could easily—give you a short theory that would distinguish, for example, the writing of the third to fifth books from the

writing of the first book, which is much more, which is a much better counterfeit of factual reporting. *The Teachings of Don Juan*—in many ways—is a very good imitation of factual reporting.[2]

De Mille's sharp distinction between the social sciences, including anthropology, and fiction writing, with literary critics and theorists supporting the latter, suggests several important ideas for our exploration. It also overlooks several things that may be just as important.

I have some training as a literary critic in my academic work of correlating literature with religion. But I am not a fiction writer, I also employ psychological approaches to interpreting religious phenomena, and I did not recognize Castaneda's writing as fiction at first. I was able to read Mircea Eliade's novel *The Forbidden Forest* as a literary critic as well as a psychologist of religion and see how its imagery expressed his spiritual predilections while constructing his interpretation of shamanism for the scholarly study he wrote at the same time.

But at least Eliade's two books came with clear and accurate labels: his shamanism study, though significantly shaped by subjective imaginings, is nevertheless a work of nonfiction scholarship, while his novel is just that, a novel. To make sense of Castaneda's work in birthing the new shamanism, however, I have had to draw on the views of Joyce Carol Oates and especially Ronald Sukenick, two card-carrying fiction writers who did see varying degrees of fictionalization in Castaneda's books, books which hid his novelistic process under the false label of anthropological fact. In particular I have adopted Sukenick's perspective, along with that of Mario Vargas Llosa, on the actual processes of writing and reading fiction. These theories of fiction from two fiction writers—two "liars"—have begun to show us how, as Western seekers after the wisdom of shamanic spirituality, we might all, in a real sense, "become sorcerers" in processes of reading and imagining which are sensitive to "shamanovels" of various sorts.

It is interesting that de Mille, himself mainly a social scientist despite his family heritage of fiction filmmaking, feels anthropologists and sociologists do not understand the fiction writing process that created Castaneda's mislabeled creations. And yet Castaneda himself was trained as an anthropologist. How did he cross over into the understanding—and the ability—of a novelist? The two creative-writing courses *Time* says he took at Los Angeles Community College in the late 1950s may have helped, though not enough to explain the creation of *The Teachings of Don Juan* a decade later.[3] The answer lies elsewhere.

Notwithstanding the anthropologist at the University of Colorado who was incensed at Vargas Llosa's literary lying, it turns out that the relationship between anthropology and fiction writing is closer and more complicated than is dreamed of in de Mille's debunking. That relationship requires our attention as we round out our careful review of how neoshamanism has come to birth in the West and what we can learn about its prospects for the future—and ours as its observers and possible participants.

THE ANTHROPOLOGIST AND THE FICTION WRITER

A FEW YEARS BEFORE de Mille's interview, around the time of Castaneda's first impact in the early '70s, an account was published of an anthropologist's apprenticeship that was strangely similar, but also intriguingly dissimilar, to that of Carlos with don Juan. The anthropologist in this other account was named Fred Murdock. Like Carlos he, too, was a graduate student:

> Among a few tribes of the Southwest, certain unexplained rites still survived; his adviser . . . suggested that he go to live on a reservation, where he might be initiated into tribal ceremonies, and try to uncover the medicine man's secret. On his return, he would prepare a thesis that the university press would undertake to publish.

Murdock takes this advice, and lives on a reservation for two years. "His palate became accustomed to new tastes, he dressed in strange clothes, he forgot his friends and the city, he came to see things in a way his reason rejected. . . . he took secret notes that later he was to burn—maybe not to arouse suspicion, maybe because he no longer needed them." The medicine man becomes his teacher and puts him through "certain exercises of a moral and physical nature," telling him to remember his dreams. On nights of the full moon he finds himself dreaming of mustangs. "He confided these repeated dreams to his teacher; in time, the teacher taught him the secret." Murdock leaves the reservation for the university.

There he decides not to reveal the secret, not to publish a book on his research, and when he announces this to his thesis adviser, he explains that "compared to it, science—our science—seems not much more than a trifle. . . . The secret, I should tell you, is not as valuable as the steps that brought me to it. Those steps have to be taken, not told." Murdock then adds that he won't necessarily be returning to the reservation: "What I learned there I can apply anyplace on earth and under any circumstances."

This was an intriguing account of a kind of anti-Castaneda, an anthropologist who apparently found real spiritual wisdom that he would not, like

Castaneda, turn into best-selling books. Murdock sounds like someone who has learned something even more valuable than Carlos, and his decision to keep the secret—with the steps taken to get to it—makes us want to know it all the more. We, too, might want to take those steps, if he would only tell us what they are.

About the same time the account of Fred's apprenticeship came out, another publication appeared that helps us see more deeply into a Castaneda–Murdock comparison. A box in the Boston *Phoenix* on March 29, 1972, contained what at first looked like a review of Castaneda's *A Separate Reality*, since it starts off with a heading containing the bibliographical information on that book. Quickly, however, it turns into a public airing of a curious correspondence between the author, Harvey Bialy, and Castaneda himself. "A short time ago," Bialy says, "I wrote the following letter to Carlos Casteneda [sic]." He begins with an odd salutation:

Monsieur,

Having read now both of your books dealing with Don Juan, I am struck by certain elements, both stylistic & formal, which lead me to the conclusion that you have created, quite intentionally, a new novel form, reminiscent to me of the prose of Mr. Borges. That is to say that Don Juan is essentially a creation of your imagination.

"Almost the mail," Bialy continues, apparently neglecting to include the usual word "next" before "mail" (or implying that the mail was not really involved), "brought the following reply":

Mr. Bialy,

I must confess, your deduction, by whatever means arrived at, is quite correct. Both *Conversations* and *A Separate Reality* are two parts of a possibly open-ended novel. My journals (which do in fact exist) allow the creation of an undetermined number of new books. Part of my method involved the creation, autonomously, of thousands of pages of field notes of real conversations with an imagined person. Only after these were completed could I begin the second stage of my work.

This is a remarkable statement. Written four or more years before de Mille's *Castaneda's Journey* blew the whistle on Carlos in 1976, it seems to confirm Castaneda's deliberate hoaxing involvement in the sort of fictive power-play Sukenick was about to suggest a year later and that I was able to infer thereafter. But there was more to this strange letter to Bialy:

I am telling you these things because the plan of the work also includes the eventuality of someone like yourself somehow tumbling on to me, and I ask you now to please see to it that both our letters are made public; thereby affording me the opportunity of publicly denying that I have ever written this letter to you at all.

—Carlos[4]

HOW DID HARVEY BIALY tumble to Carlos's *imaginative*, that is, fictional, creation of don Juan, something reminiscent of the work of the great Argentinian writer of short fiction—*ficciones*, as they are called—Jorge Luis Borges? To listen to de Mille, Bialy would have had to be a fiction writer himself to recognize Castaneda's writing as fiction. Was he? Not quite. Bialy was (and still is, I assume) a poet, and is identified as such at the bottom of the box. Moreover, as some of the oddities in this "correspondence" that starts out like a book review begin to add up, the entire thing reveals itself to the reader as an ingenious *poem*. And it is constructed to discount any denials Castaneda might publish if he is tricked into accepting the piece as a claimed factual correspondence between them!

To my knowledge Castaneda never did reply, nor did de Mille refer to Bialy's bizarre poem in either of his two books. The trick poem faded from public view after giving a chuckle—or a start—to readers of Castaneda, most of them still reading, like me, under a haze of credulity if not hallucinogens. In retrospect, almost twenty-five years later, I am impressed with Bialy's prescience in 1972. Not only did he see and enter into the sorcery of Castaneda's literary lying, imagining onward in his way the fictive power of the hoax. Beyond this, his reference to Jorge Luis Borges was a contribution to my thinking when I came upon the account of Murdock's anthropological apprenticeship.

Fred Murdock's story, almost a compressed commentary on Castaneda's fictive tutelage under his "medicine man," was just that: a story. In fact, it was one of the *ficciones* of Borges himself, a fictional sketch called, appropriately enough, "The Anthropologist."

How do we recognize it as fiction if we do not know its famous fiction writing author? The tone of the piece is, indeed, rather "literary," but it might be a "true story," an informal account of a factual sequence of events. I suppose it would also have been more difficult to accept as fact, however, had I not withheld certain parts of the plot, such as the ending:

That, substantially, is what was said.
Fred married, was divorced, and is now a librarian at Yale.[5]

That rather surprising outcome to an exotic anthropological adventure would probably have alerted us even if we did not know the author or the literary title of the "account." The point of this modest deception on my part is to suggest how close, even overlapping, the worlds of anthropology and literary fiction can be—as well as to reiterate that the library, at Yale or elsewhere, can be a site of shamanic fieldwork as long as imaginative writing and reading are happening. After all, another library a continent away at UCLA was most likely the secret room where don Juan—and with him, neoshamanism—was born from a lying anthropologist's pen.

How anthropology, in the improbable person of Castaneda, came to create this foundational body of fiction, and how his strange version of social science, along with that of several key successors, was sold to us as a new religious movement called neoshamanism are further questions in need of answers.

SELLING NEOSHAMANISM

"AS THE CULTURAL LANDSCAPE now lies, the reigning champions of religious salesmanship are the proponents of the New Age," wrote historian R. Laurence Moore in his 1994 study *Selling God: American Religion in the Marketplace of Culture.*[6] Although people drawn to neoshamanism may not all think of themselves as New Agers, surely neoshamanism itself was sold largely as part of the New Age movement that superceded the counter-culture in the 1970s and '80s. This association of neoshamanism with the New Age is also suggested by Marilyn Ferguson, whose 1980 book *The Aquarian Conspiracy* on "personal and social transformation" is the major document announcing—and thus selling—the beginnings of the New-Age subculture. She refers eight times to Castaneda and his writings, though she never mentions the hoax that de Mille had uncovered four years earlier.[7] Castaneda's work was given a New-Age stamp of approval. And perhaps the many New-Age authors since Ferguson who, not neoshamanists themselves, referred to Castaneda without discussing the controversy surrounding him played their unwitting part in selling neoshamanism.

We have seen that the publication of Castaneda's first book in 1968 by the University of California Press gave birth to what eventually acquired the name "neoshamanism." But actually it was the 1969 paperback edition of *The Teachings of Don Juan* that did most of this birthing, and its packaging was a major contributor to its success.

This began with a cover illustration of a peyote blossom in "Day-Glo" colors emerging from the juxtaposed heads of an elderly Native American and, apparently, an x-rayed Anglo—all of this overlaying a decuple rainbow. Here was an invitation to hallucinogenic reading, one that was soon heeded by thousands if not millions of people like my students and me who were turned off to church but turned on to what turning on with Carlos might show us about the spiritual meaning the larger culture seemed to lack.

Some of the book's cover blurbs helped the cause. There was a line from the *New York Times* on the front: "An extraordinary spiritual and psychological document . . . destined for fame." This was not the sort of thing the *Times* could say about most works of social-scientific discourse! Nor would one expect to find an endorsement like the following on the usual anthropological study: *Eye* magazine expanded upon the psychedelic signals of the cover art by calling Castaneda's text "the most remarkable documents to emerge from drug literature since Aldous Huxley's 'Doors of Perception.'" *The Los Angeles Times* agreed: "This is no ethnology text, with charts and footnotes, but the happenings themselves, told with such immediacy, honesty and clarity that the reader becomes a part of them, sharing Castaneda's exultations and bafflements and terrors. . . ."

Of course we now know that this immediacy was not so honest after all, but was a product of fictive power, Castaneda's brand of literary lying. The *Los Angeles Times* statement, seen with our improving hindsight, points to this power and how much it relied on our taking the book as fact. In either case something other than standard ethnology was involved. On the other hand, despite this last blurb, inside its covers the paperback also carried endorsements by the eminent anthropologists Edmund Carpenter and Walter Goldschmidt. And along with these the book contained acknowledgements from Castaneda to several other prominent anthropologists, an opening quotation from the pioneering social theorist Georg Simmel, a somewhat surrealistic but formally proper "Structural Analysis" of don Juan's teachings, and a set of scholarly appendices. Clearly, if strangely, this was a book with one foot in the world of ethnography and the other in the world of experiential shamanism, replete with hands-on hallucinogenizing.

During the next decade, as we know, Castaneda published—and his publisher marketed as nonfiction—four more of his enormously popular volumes about the character called don Juan. And he received, for reasons we still do not fully know, a Ph.D. in anthropology for the third, *Journey to Ixtlan*. De Mille has done his best to determine why UCLA awarded Castaneda his doctorate for work his committee must have known was largely or entirely fiction. Perhaps, to recall de Mille's interview, the committee members were, as anthropologists, unable to recognize fiction when they saw it. In any case, Walter Goldschmidt and Edmund Carpenter, who blurbed *Teachings*, and the UCLA anthropology department gave an anthropological seal of approval to work that others saw as "drug literature" outside the bounds of ethnology—even before it was seen through as a cross-cultural fairy tale, a Western fantasy.

If Castaneda was alone in redrawing the boundaries between fact and fiction, however, he had help in making the mysterious move from scholarship to shamanship that sold a sizeable subculture on the validity of a new psychospiritual option: neoshamanism. In 1976, Stephen Larsen, a psychotherapist and student of Joseph Campbell the comparative mythologist, published his book *The Shaman's Doorway*. This is an engagingly written work which refers approvingly to Castaneda before de Mille's debunking began. While he helped widen the reading public's interest in shamanism by his title alone, Larsen was more interested in exploring "the mythic imagination" more generally, and to my knowledge did not go on to offer workshops specifically focusing on neoshamanism.[8]

BUT BY 1979, an associate of Campbell's, Joan Halifax, another Ph.D. anthropologist (she specialized in medical anthropology), had published a popular book drawing on translated first-hand testimonies from indigenous practitioners entitled *Shamanic Voices: A Survey of Visionary Narratives*.[9] Although her bibliography cites mainly scholarly studies of shamanism and omits Castaneda's titles, her list of "Books of Related Interest" includes a category called "The Mystic Sciences." Here we find titles like *The I Ching and You, Self-Hypnosis in Two Days*, and *Do-It-Yourself-Shiatsu*, hardly books one would usually see as of related interest to a serious scholarly work. Anthropology was once more, as with Castaneda, merging into self-help healing from exotic directions. And again the publisher's packaging helped sell the bizarre blend.

The front cover of *Shamanic Voices* features an evocative collage of a coiled snake sleeping beneath either a full moon or a setting or rising sun, a picture inviting the buyer–reader to experience the kind of vision these "visionary narratives" promise to recount. He or she was less likely to notice the more ambivalent tone of the title of this collage by the art critic Suzi Gablik: "Simulation."

The back cover contains generalized praise from anthropologist Barbara Myerhoff, an authority on the peyote-focused practices of the Huichols of Mexico (who was also a friend and fellow graduate student of Castaneda whose work he may have borrowed, especially for the dramatic scene of don Genaro balancing at the top of the waterfall).[10] In addition the back cover has a laudatory reference by Claudio Naranjo, M.D., to Halifax's shamans being allowed to "speak for themselves about their experiences." Next it features poet-anthologist Jerome Rothenberg's avowal that the collection "makes immediate the experience of a once universal shamanism. . . ."

Rothenberg had already referred to the possibility of a kind of neoshamanism in his 1968 anthology of indigenous poetries, *Technicians of the Sacred*, a title adapted from Eliade's shamanism book. But despite being duped by Castaneda like the rest of us he had had something quite different in mind—for him poets were shamans and shamans were "proto-poets"—than the literalistic neoshamanism that began to be marketed in the wake of Castaneda's hoax.[11] Finally, to this stress upon the availability of direct shamanic experience is added the exclamation of R. Gordon Wasson, the world's leading researcher into indigenous uses of natural hallucinogens: "At last! Here is an anthropologist who lets the shamans tell us about shamanism."

Once again, as indicated by its verbal and visual packaging, we have a book that promises not only scholarly authority, by way of Halifax's credentials and those of her endorsers, but also something else. This something else is seemingly antithetical to social-scientific scholarship: experiential immersion in an alternative religious practice. Or at least the marketed simulation of such immersion, feeding fantasies that no doubt felt more literal to readers because of the same scholarly credentials they were finding unnecessary. Joan Halifax may have ingested peyote with the Huichols so that her interest would not remain academic, as she testifies.[12] But most of her readers had no access to Huichols and probably no peyote. All they had was her Dutton Paperback Original—and their manipulated imaginations in search of non-Western wisdom, or "power and healing," as it would soon be termed.

The year after Halifax's *Shamanic Voices* appeared, Michael Harner, a well-credentialed and well-published anthropologist, brought out his book called *The Way of the Shaman: A Guide to Power and Healing*, the major text of the movement after Castaneda's confabulations.

Harner had been on Castaneda's dissertation committee. Perhaps because of that he told an interviewer in the late 1970s that the latter's research was "110 per cent valid," angrily defending it as well against de Mille and poet Robert Bly in a letter to the *New York Times*.[13] We noted in Chapter 3 that his guidebook is partly an overview of anthropological theories and accounts of assorted shamanisms around the world, including his own fieldwork in South America. It also alludes approvingly to Eliade's comparativist approach to shamanism, an approach most other anthropologists resist because of its emphasis on shared traits between cultures rather than unique contexts. Harner assumes the validity of Eliade's stress on shamans' upwardly magical flights as accurately reflecting the data of the ethnographic accounts he drew on—instead of largely resulting, as we have found, from his own centered and celestial imagination.

Primarily, however, *The Way of the Shaman* is a handbook for neoshamanist practice. Indeed, it is almost a devotional tract for the new movement. Not surprisingly, given his defense of Castaneda, the 1982 Bantam paperback contains the founding father's glowing cover blurb: "Wonderful, fascinating. Harner really knows what he is talking about." This statement surmounts an illustration of a curiously Western sage or mage in meditation, a whitebearded Merlin encircled by a devilish gnome and several menacing animals.

A logo and some copy on the other cover informs consumers that the paperback in their hands is one of the "Bantam New Age Books" which pursue "A Search for Meaning, Growth and Change." Additionally, this back cover features an endorsement from Stewart Brand, editor of *The Whole Earth Catalog*, extolling Harner for transmitting "some safe basics on how to enter the shamanic state of consciousness," together with the publisher's description of how the author ". . . leads the reader through simple techniques and exercises to achieve altered states of consciousness without drugs. . . ." Despite this endorsement of the non-drug avenue to shamanic power and healing, the publisher also makes a claim just above it that is almost as suggestive of Huxley's prohallucinogen *Doors of Perception* as it is hard to deny: "CASTANEDA'S DON JUAN OPENED THE DOOR TO THE WAY OF THE SHAMAN."[14]

With such an emphatic pronouncement, and with transpersonal psychiatrist Stanislav Grof, onetime husband of Halifax, proclaiming inside the front cover that "Michael Harner is not just an anthropologist who has studied shamanism, he is an authentic white shaman," nothing was left in order to turn Castaneda's fictive power into a full-blown movement but to market workshops as well as books. Castaneda, protecting his trickery, did not do that, and Halifax, who later did, lacked Castaneda's *imprimatur*. Harner, however, who did have his support, soon established the Foundation for Shamanic Studies for exactly that purpose: not anthropology lectures or intellectual seminars but how-to workshops in becoming, more or less like him, a white shaman.

How could it happen that three scholars with Ph.D.s in anthropology, a field known for distanced observation and "value-free" objectivity, could start a new religious movement? How could such a *shamanthropology* come to pass? Apparently not all anthropologists were as orthodox as the one who wondered how Vargas Llosa, writing as a novelist, could lie about the Machiguenga.

How the New Ethnography Explains Shamanthropology

ALONG WITH THE AGGRESSIVE sales techniques of the trade publishers who promoted neoshamanism through the writings of our three shamanthropologists, the academic field of anthropology itself may have been ripe for contributing to this most unexpected and unacademic by-product, as literary and religious as it is social-scientific.

Neoshamanism could even be called, in part, an unintended (and no doubt unwelcome) side effect of a certain development within anthropology. It was a development of theory and method which departed from social-science traditions of literalistic factuality to embrace the literary lying we have found so central to Castaneda's writing and to our undeluded learning of its main lesson: how to "become sorcerers" ourselves.

This development is called the new, or postmodernist, ethnography. We need to survey it briefly to see what has been happening to the field from which Castaneda, Halifax, and Harner saw fit to depart in founding neoshamanism, if only to discern some of the forces that pushed them out—and perhaps produced them. We will want to be alert as well for any comments the new ethnography has made about these or other neoshamanists.

To take our point of departure from the term itself, "ethnography" is of Greek derivation and means "writing culture." The use of this exact term as the title of a key work in the new ethnography, a 1986 collection edited by James Clifford and George E. Marcus, signals the literary drift of this theorizing, as does its subtitle, "the poetics and politics of ethnography." Clifford puts this quite directly in his important introduction: "No longer a marginal . . . dimension, writing has emerged as central to what anthropologists do both in the field and thereafter."[15] He then adds that "the making of ethnography is artisanal, tied to the worldly work of writing."[16]

Ethnographers, in other words, are workers, artisans, and their work is primarily writing, first in taking field notes and later in crafting these into more formal narratives. This worldly work may make them less different from novelists or poets—or from Castaneda—than we, or de Mille, might have supposed. It is beginning to be clear that a certain kind of anthropologist might not only recognize but appreciate fiction writing. Clifford goes on to clarify this possibility:

> In anthropology influential writers such as Clifford Geertz, Victor Turner, Mary Douglas, Claude Levi-Strauss, Jean Duvignaud, and Edmund Leach, to mention only a few, have shown an interest in literary theory and practice. In their quite different ways they have blurred the boundary separating art from science.

The last sentence, which could just as well refer to the boundary between the nonliteral and the literal, imagination and fact, borrows the metaphor of "blurring" from a groundbreaking 1980 essay of Geertz's, "Blurred Genres," which had made a similar point. For his part, Clifford continues by saying

> ... the notion that literary procedures pervade any work of cultural representation is a recent idea in the discipline. To a growing number, however, the "literariness" of anthropology—and especially of ethnography—appears as much more than a matter of good writing or distinctive style. Literary processes—metaphor, figuration, narrative—affect the ways cultural phenomena are registered, from the first jotted "observations," to the completed book, to the ways these configurations "make sense" in determined acts of reading.[17]

Clifford's comments are surprising to the nonanthropologist, just as, with Clifford Geertz's essay six years earlier, they were disturbing to those in his field who held to an older, more "scientific," model of ethnography. But Clifford's and Geertz's views were increasingly shared by other anthropologists like Steven Tyler, who goes so far as to call the new ethnography poetry. This radical remark is reported by an observer from my field of religious studies, William Doty, who also contributes his own helpful reaction: "But to make such a statement surely implies an ending to a particular period of upholding sharp genre boundaries. . . ."[18]

PERHAPS 1980 IS THE BEST date for the ending and new beginning Doty indicates. That was the year, we recall, of Harner's *Way of the Shaman* and, with it and with Harner's marketing of workshops, the emergence of neoshamanism as a movement birthed by Castaneda and nurtured by Halifax. It was also the year when Ferguson's *Aquarian Conspiracy* spread the word to an overlapping New-Age movement.

Of most immediate relevance, however, is the fact that it was the year of Geertz's "Blurred Genres" essay, in which he explained that this genre-blurring is best exemplified by the following:

> ... philosophical inquiries looking like literary criticism . . . scientific discussions looking like belles lettres . . . baroque fantasies presented as deadpan empirical observations (Borges, Barthelme) . . . documentaries that read like true confessions . . . parables posing as ethnographies (Carlos Castenada [*sic*]). . . .[19]

We are familiar with some if not all of these examples of blurred genres or border crossings. We have already seen how Borges could compose a *ficcion* that read like an account of an anthropologist's apprenticeship. And the

"Barthelme" Geertz refers to is Donald Barthelme, one of Sukenick's experimental fiction writing colleagues.

As it happens, this same Barthelme once wrote a spoof of Castaneda for the *New York Times* entitled "The Teachings of Don B: A Yankee Way of Knowledge," offering data for de Mille's thesis that every fiction writer could see through nonfiction disguises.[20] When I sought permission to reprint this delicious satire—itself genre-blurring if you did not get the spoof—in my *Seeing Castaneda* anthology his response was, more or less, "You don't take that clown seriously, do you?" Despite his trickster antics, I did. So, partly as a joke for Barthelme, I entitled my introduction in the anthology "Taking Castaneda Seriously."

I am still not certain that many people are taking him seriously in the way I would hope. But Geertz's inclusion of his hoax as the main instance of blurred genres in ethnography certainly helps. It indicates that to take Castaneda's writing seriously—which is to say, not literally, but as a parable about fictive power—it is necessary to understand how the new ethnography perceives as well as participates in the blurring of boundaries. For it is a blurring that is also implied by the two words I have coined to suggest something of the lesson we can learn about the soul of shamanism from figures like Eliade and Castaneda: shamanovels and shamanthropology. At the very least Geertz's metaphor raises some good questions for us to explore in connection with the latter.

If Castaneda's writings are deemed fiction, or fictional parables, how different is that from the new assessment of ethnography as the making of literary art as much as science, ethnographic writing as a kind of poetry, perhaps even fiction? Reminding us of Sukenick, the anthropologist Marilyn Strathern has indeed used the term "persuasive fictions" to characterize such writing. This prompts William Doty to observe that "in recognizing the fictive imagination of the ethnographic specialist as both . . . a type of imaginative poesis and as a sort of revelation, Strathern represents an approach to the history of scholarship that is not as unusual today as it was earlier."[21]

If scholarship in anthropology can now be construed as art, can it also be construed as shamanship, as a religious expression? Does the new ethnography, in implying that the distance from anthropology to Castaneda's fiction writing is not so great as de Mille imagined, also explain how the former could have initiated a shamanthropology of such improbably unscientific beliefs and practices? For instance, beyond Geertz's valuable but brief indication, what have the new ethnographers had to say about Castaneda and company?

CASTANEDAN NARRATIVES IN THE NEW ETHNOGRAPHY

WRITING CULTURE, the definitive new ethnography collection edited by Clifford and Marcus, contains an essay by Mary Louise Pratt called "Fieldwork in Common Places" that provides important clues to possible answers. It does this by emphasizing the role of personal narratives in ethnography. These would go from first-person accounts in its historical predecessor, travel writing, to personal elements in field reports starting with the pioneer anthropologist Malinowski, and then on to the role of such narratives in current anthropology. Here is a potential insight into how our shamanthropologists could incorporate not only fiction writing but also personal spiritual practice into their books and workshop presentations.

For decades exiled to separate books by authors of more objective reports or relegated to brief framing anecdotes within the latter, personal narratives comprise a feature, Pratt recounts, that has refused to be "killed by science." This is because it mediates, she claims, "a contradiction within the discipline between personal and scientific authority."[22] Most significantly for our purposes, she uses the example of Florinda Donner's 1982 book *Shabono* to illustrate the terms of this contradiction.[23]

She notes, for one thing, that the book's subtitle was definitely problematic for any scientific conception of anthropology: "a visit to a remote and magical world in the South American Rainforest." For another, *Shabono* carried a cover blurb by none other than Carlos Castaneda, who decisively blurs, if not obliterates, several genre boundaries. He calls the book "at once art, magic and superb social science." This no doubt damned the work in the eyes of most orthodox anthropologists. However, it surely sold more copies to the early followers of neoshamanism.

Pratt's article then goes on to refer to a reviewer who complained that the Donner book was "a kind of melange of fact and fantasy for which Castaneda is so famous,"[24] and another which decried what it called *Shabono*'s "narcissistic focus" on Donner's "personal growth in the field." This latter reviewer insisted that "to confine anthropology to the personal experiences of specific anthropologists is to deny its status as a social science."[25] Having examined these critiques of Donner's book, Pratt asks two questions: ". . . though it is not written in the standard idiom of ethnographic description, what places her personal narrative within anthropology's purview? Once there, why is there such confusion about how it should be evaluated?"[26]

She has no ready answers to these questions. But her puzzlement can serve our exploration. For Castaneda, in having fused or confused shamanism with anthropology through his autobiographical fiction—fictionalized personal narratives employing what seem to be borrowed ethnographic details—may be seen to encompass all the issues and ills presented by the writing of Donner (to whom he has a continuing relationship as a fellow shamanthropologist). That is, the disturbances of ethnography that perplex Pratt in considering *Shabono*—not to mention the related disruptions of theory and method represented by the new ethnography of Geertz, Clifford, Marcus, Tyler, and Strathern—may have given rise to Castaneda's shamanthropology.

And by the latter term I mean not only the "sham anthropology" of his hoax, but beyond this the entire blurry hybrid of neoshamanism he has concocted, passing it on to other shamanthropologists like Halifax and Harner to preach to a public of spiritual seekers.

WE COULD LOOK STILL further at how the new ethnography evaluates personal narratives to find more "placements" of Castaneda's writing. For example, George E. Marcus and Michael M. J. Fischer, in their co-authored volume from 1986, *Anthropology as Cultural Critique*, inspect "'dialogic' interchange" between ethnographer and informant, deciding that this sort of personal narrative belongs in the finished ethnographic text. Within this category they place Castaneda's books as "'sorcerer's apprentice' ethnographies."[27] They even maintain that his works, "along with many other examples of fictive writing, have served as one of several stimuli for thinking about alternative textual strategies within the tradition of ethnography."[28]

It seems that for new ethnographers like Marcus and Fischer, unlike the traditionalist reviewers of Donner's *Shabono*, Castaneda's work, even understood as "fictive writing," is just within the far boundary of the field of anthropology. *But the field has been redefined by the new ethnography to include fiction, presumably like Sukenick's and Borges's as well as like Castaneda's.* Seen from the standpoint of the new ethnography, the *anthropological* basis of neoshamanism as a Western idea is no less aesthetic, no less imaginative, than is its prehistory in Eliade's comparative religions approach. Most readers of Castaneda and colleagues, however, knew nothing about the new ethnography. So to them (and here is an irony we should ponder) the anthropological credentials of these founders seemed rather to ratify the *factual* grounding of what their books were putting forth, supporting Castaneda's scam and fueling our fantasies.

The lesson of the new ethnography for neoshamanist seekers is nevertheless clear once we have uncovered it. Admittedly, for neoshamanism as a socially embodied phenomenon to have come about and sustained itself in the 1980s and '90s, more was required than the conflict between "sorcerer's apprentice" ethnographies open to fiction writing and the exclusivism of a strictly scientific notion of scholarship. Not even with the paradoxical credibility, for a science-driven culture, that was given to shamanthropology by its residue of scholarly legitimacy, could intellectual or psychological factors alone have carried neoshamanism as a social movement as well as a personal interest, even a personal spiritual path. A gospel needed proclaiming—or needed selling—that would lead to practice, perhaps to a sort of worship, within a community, however loosely structured. But with the workshops of the post-Castaneda shamanthropologists burgeoning in the United States and other Western countries, and the emergence of related "drumming circles," this ingredient for social embodiment was to some extent supplied.

Still, without Castaneda and his hoax there would have been no neoshamanism, private or public. And without the new ethnography—in a struggle for the defining control of anthropology against a prior scientific model of objective representation—there would probably not have been a popular author named Castaneda. Or he may have simply become a novelist who never pretended to be anything else and never prompted anyone like Michael Harner to leave an academic career in anthropology and begin leading workshops in neoshamanism.

At a Journey Workshop

I AM SITTING CROSSLEGGED on a polished hardwood floor in one of two concentric circles of fellow participants. There are upwards of a hundred of us. We have come to this lecture hall at a workshop center in the Hudson River Valley in July of 1990 with our cushions, bandannas, and drums to learn, over a weekend, the basics of the "power and healing" Harner's neoshamanism has been teaching for ten years. Harner walks to the center to speak. He is a stocky man, mostly bald, with a bushy salt-and-pepper beard and rather thick glasses. He also has a somewhat laconic style of speaking and a ready wit, a surprising cackle of a laugh. After considerable experience in the field, well-received academic publications, and teaching in several prestigious institutions, he knows his anthropology. When Carlos supposedly first met don Juan in the early 1960s, Harner was in the South American jungle with people like the Jivaro and the Conibo, learning first-hand their versions of shamanism. Although two decades later he left academe to start his Foundation for Shamanic Studies and began to offer workshops related to his popular guidebook, *The Way of the Shaman*, he carries the credibility of scholarly expertise as well as of direct contact with indigenous wisdom. I get the impression that he has led this particular basic workshop on "The Shamanic Journey, Power, and Healing" so many times that, without notes, he knows exactly what he wants to say and how he wants the participants to receive it.

His emphasis this weekend, he begins, is not on academic ideas about the meaning of shamanism: "this is an *experiential* weekend," he insists. However, he has a few points to make before we can partake of the exercises in "journeying" that have drawn us here.

Harner's first point is a major one. He grants that different cultures have different versions of the basic practices. But there *are* "basic practices," so he intends to eliminate "a lot of culture-specific things." Instead we will get "core shamanism," the pure essence without cultural trappings. Because of this, "we are not playing Indian; we're playing human."

This sounds to me a lot like an academic idea about shamanism. As mentioned above, it is closer to Eliade's comparativism—the emphasis on shared cross-cultural "patterns"—than to the usual anthropologist's reluctance to depart from "local knowledge," the specific contexts of each culture. Comparisons are indispensable, illuminating phenomena that may not reveal all their facets in their local context alone. The danger is that when overly decontextualized they become merely the least common denominator, an imagined abstraction that then bears little resemblance to any actuality they may have had in their specific occurrences.

I do appreciate his impulse to avoid having us "play Indian." Certainly that is a temptation of too much neoshamanism, and for Stanislav Grof to call Harner a "white shaman" recalls the Native American use of that term to indicate a fraudulent appropriation of their culture and spirituality by non-Indians—non-Indians whom they also deride as "plastic medicine men."[29]

But could a genuine form of shamanism be based on a sanitized abstraction (from a non-Indian's imagination) which appeared to jettison Harner's own richly specific fieldwork in South America? Could this form of shamanism—neoshamanism—be seen instead as *based on* acts of imagining, in this case the *creation* of a "core" of shamanism that, consciously understood as a Western product, might provide for a different sort of shamanic opportunity?

These are issues I cannot wish away. Still, the workshop situation and Harner's professions that we are not here to discuss theory make it inappropriate to raise them in the group. I realize my academic questions are out of bounds here, and I keep them to myself. I have come to the weekend in an attitude of openness to experiencing the Harner brand of neoshamanism I have read about in his book and seen advertised in New Age magazines. ("Neoshamanism" is a term, by the way, that he does not use—perhaps he feels it is a put-down or an inaccurate pigeon-holing of what he is attempting to do—though I continue to find it a necessary name, since his positing of a "core" to shamanism is a *new* maneuver.)

OUR ROUTE AS "JOURNEYERS," despite my misgivings, will not be through any one culture: we will have "direct communication with the spirits," and it does not seem to matter "whose" spirits they are. This suits our individualism, I surmise, and maybe that *is* our culture. Going home to the ancient spiritual practices of the planet, the entire planet, Harner indicates, is the aim of core shamanism. Or what that concept makes possible when coupled with techniques we will soon be sampling.

Before this can happen he cautions that such methods are no more than that: techniques, like yoga, which are not a religion, and we are not worshipping. This is debatable, I think, knowing there will be no debate. While shamanism is often described as a set of practices originally within a cosmology or religion—Eliade at least implies this—the practices in particular cultures were dependent upon the larger prevailing religious system. Furthermore, neoshamanism can definitely be understood, by 1990, as a new religious movement of nontraditional spirituality. Again I feel Harner is insuring that the constraints of context, religious or cultural, do not hamper what his core shamanism claims to offer: access to "power and healing."

As he proceeds with his introductory talk I am happy to hear that he is respectful of Jung—he calls him a shaman—notwithstanding a suspicious posture toward psychology in general. He goes on to say that Jung's term "archetypes" was a product of his wish to remain scientific when dealing with phenomena more forthrightly called "spirits" (and at this point he does refer to the Conibos' belief in entities translated by the latter term). I have my doubts about whether Jung or Harner is more beholden to scientific restrictions in interpreting spiritual experiences. This is something I will explore long after the weekend.

For now I am pleased that Harner can say something that Jung would applaud: "some people might call it [a spirit encountered in shamanic practice] an image, but those images have power." Is he aware that post-Jungian imaginal psychology is *based on* this power?

Harner next turns to Eliade to define a shaman. At least he takes the element of Eliade's definition that is most pertinent to his own needs in workshops like this. The shaman, in contrast to the medicine man or the trance medium, Harner asserts, makes journeys into other worlds in search of "miraculous solutions to human problems." The reference to problem solving sounds more modern and American than shamanic, although admittedly shamans served practical functions within their communities. Does a problem solving focus mean the same thing for understanding shamanism when it is applied in a context of individualism? Remaining positive, I leave that question unanswered. And I have no problem with the shaman being seen as one who travels to other worlds of some kind—Eliade's "ecstasy" and "magical flight" come to mind—even if there are other aspects of the shaman's role that may have been neglected in this definition.

Having gestured approvingly to Jung and Eliade, Harner now makes his first comment about Castaneda. In public statements he had strongly supported the validity—the factual validity, unless Harner were secretly a new ethnographer—of the latter's writings. I, on the other hand, had felt this support was unwarranted given de Mille's persuasive evidence of the don Juan hoax. I am anxious to hear how he justifies his defense of Castaneda, knowing that it plays its own role in sustaining neoshamanism as a Western fantasy derived from believing in the factuality of the don Juan fairy tale. Unfortunately, this, too, is a theoretical discussion Harner has ruled out. His statement is limited to giving credit to Castaneda for having invented the terms "ordinary reality" and "nonordinary reality." These are terms which, he acknowledges, "I find useful."

He finds them useful, it turns out, in framing his own distinction between the "ordinary state of consciousness" (or "OSC") and the "shamanic state of consciousness" (or "SSC"). This is an interestingly psychological translation of Castaneda's more cosmological terminology. The OSC, he goes on, is "the reality we vote on," consensual reality. The SSC, on the other hand, affirms isolated subjectivity. No enemy of subjectivity myself, I nevertheless worry again about an overemphasis on individualism.

Just about now, however, I am put in my professorial place. Harner reiterates that we are not here to argue. We're here as open experimenters, "to see if I, Michael Harner, have anything for you." Who can argue with that? I am ready to journey.

There is one last warning, meant, I nervously worry, especially for me. We are going to have a "*direct experience*," Harner insists, and "the terms imagination and fantasy, as something created in and by our own mind, are only *theories* of what's happening." Was this not also a theory? Apparently not: "leave the baggage of theory behind," he suggests. Where those two terms were concerned, I had a lot to leave behind, and I would be sure to pick it up when we finished.

NEOSHAMANISM NOW

MOST OF THE POINTS Harner made in his introductory remarks at the workshop he had made ten years earlier in *The Way of the Shaman*. But I had wanted to see what shamanic studies with the author himself felt like, to see how shamanthropology presented itself in performance, as it were. I hoped thereby to gain further insight into the nature of the neoshamanism it had created through its imaginative maneuvers, including imaginative marketing.

Knowing about the new ethnography helped explain academic anthropology's role in producing shamanthropology. Still, this bookish understanding of one source of neoshamanism needed to be supplemented with a concrete involvement in its cutting edge and future prospects. A dose of "direct experience"—however much this, too, might be an act of imagining—seemed a good idea.

Perhaps above all I wanted to gain a sense of how neoshamanism understood itself, how conscious it was about its involvement in a Western fantasy that Castaneda's hoax had focused into an unlikely spiritual movement for modern seekers, supported by affable ex-academics like Halifax and my workshop leader. His book may have outlined how one can make a journey to a lowerworld or upperworld to find power animals and celestial teachers, but I could not fully assess this central experience of neoshamanism until Harner himself had led me there.

What I encountered on my journeys during that July weekend, and what they taught me, are topics for the second half of the book, where we turn from Western fantasies to imaginal realities.

As for the more recent exploits of the shamanthropologists, Castaneda's ninth book, *The Art of Dreaming*, came out in 1993 and he continues to maintain his writing is nonfiction.[30] He has never offered workshops, but various neoshamanists who claim to be apprentices with him or to him have begun to do so as well as publishing their own books.[31] Among these is another shamanthropologist, Florinda Donner, Ph.D. After publishing *Shabono* in 1982 to a cool academic reception and some commercial success, she wrote two more books, *The Witch's Dream* in 1985 and *Being-in-Dreaming* in 1991, each with kind words from Castaneda.[32]

Then, in 1993, the Rim Institute in Arizona and Pacific Artist Releasing in Hawaii each announced a workshop entitled "Toltec Dreaming: The

Legacy of Don Juan." Donner, now Donner-Grau, was joined in these two events by Taisha Abelar, who had published *The Sorcerers' Crossing* in 1992, again with Castaneda's shamanthropological *imprimatur.*[33] The workshop brochures describe her as "a martial artist and scholar who also apprenticed with Don Juan." But they do not say what field her scholarship is in or what her academic credentials are. New-Age magazines like *Magical Blend* and *Body Mind Spirit* regularly carry updates on the activities of these and other henchwomen of Castaneda.

Harner's workshops, now often led by a cadre of trainees as well as by Harner himself, seem to be proliferating, judging by the schedules I frequently receive from his Foundation for Shamanic Studies. One of these trainees, Sandra Ingerman, has by now come out with her own neoshamanistic self-help books.[34] Another, a Norwegian poet named Ailo Gaup, is employing Harner's methods to rekindle the indigenous shamanism of his native Lapp (Sami) cultural heritage, as I learned from a conversation with him in Vermont in 1990. This attempt of "*core* shamanism" to revive Europe's last *native* shamanism is a fascinating twist in the short history of neoshamanism. Either it is a feather in Harner's cap—his foundation does involve itself in projects to assist tribal cultures—or a highly strange moment in the modern West when cultural simulation thinks itself cultural stimulation.

In either case Gaup has published his first book in English, a translation of a 1988 novel in Norwegian, *In Search of the Drum.*[35] The drum has become the major sacred object of neoshamanism, at once communal focus, holy implement, and symbol of the journey. It is no accident that the leading periodical of the subculture is called *Shaman's Drum*. Neoshamanism nevertheless remains a religion of the book—and the magazine—even more than of the drum. As a maker of Irish drums once said in an ad I received, "in some ways, drumming transports me to another world just like reading does."

MICHAEL HARNER HAS PRODUCED no more books since *The Way of the Shaman*, although that neoshamanist scripture was reissued in 1990 and a new book has been rumored for several years. I have never been able to find a copy of what the front-matter to the 1980 book calls his "recent novel, *Cannibal*, which he co-authored." Workshops similar to Harner's but offered independently from his foundation are also appearing in increasing numbers. The most prominent of these are probably the ones devised by another shamanthropologist, Felicitas Goodman, a retired academic who established the Cuyamungue Institute in New Mexico. There, her brochure says, she "conducts research into the use of ritual posture to mediate trance experience." If the mantle of serious researcher makes her closer to scholarship than to shamanship, she nevertheless markets worldwide workshops. There one can employ postures culled from iconographies of various religious traditions, as well as Harner-style percussive "driving" with drum or rattle, to induce what her 1990 book *Where the Spirits Ride the Wind* calls, in its subtitle, "trance journeys and other ecstatic experiences."[36]

Lynn Andrews keeps turning out her shamanovels ceaselessly, but she is not a shamanthropologist. Or, as she put it in a 1991 letter: "If you want to be an anthropologist, then study anthropology. I am a woman who is learning one way of experiencing the world of power. That is all." Her return address is "Lynn Andrews Productions" in Los Angeles.

Meanwhile, Joan Halifax, who *is* a shamanthropologist, continues to contribute to neoshamanism in her own way. Since the appearance of *Shamanic Voices* in 1979, she has published a second book, *Shaman: The Wounded Healer*, in 1982;[37] has done research for Joseph Campbell's lavish 1983 work *The Way of the Animal Powers*, the volume in his *Historical Atlas of World Mythology* series that deals with shamanism;[38] has continued to its conclusion her leadership of a spiritual-educational community, the Ojai Foundation, in California; has begun an involvement with a similar community in Santa Fe; and has produced a third book, *The Fruitful Darkness*, in 1993.[39]

At different times during these years, she has led tours and workshops, including one on "The Teachings of the Shields." Judging by an audiotape, this workshop qualifies as a neoshamanist experience, combining "borrowings" from Native American spiritual imagery and rituals such as medicine wheels and the "stone people lodge" (sweat lodge) with her own practice of Buddhist meditation, her ecological convictions, and anecdotes from her wide travels to seek out shamans, Buddhist teachers, and places of solitude.

The Fruitful Darkness shares some of this eclectic "Bodhishamanism" in a book marketed within HarperSanFrancisco's "Nature/Anthropology" category. After silence on the matter of neoshamanism's hoax-driven birth in her first two books, her epilogue to this one quotes uncritically from Castaneda's fourth volume, *Tales of Power*.[40] At a book signing for *The Fruitful Darkness* in July of 1993, she told the assembled signees that for her the academic world was "absurd." She had gone into the exploration of shamanism "not to study shamanism but to study with shamans" in order to heal herself. Moreover, she felt, as she put it, that it was "same same" for Carlos and for Harner.[41]

It was not same same for me. I was studying, instead, with shaman-thropologists, those anthropologists who preferred—or pretended—to study with shamans and pass their learning—approximately—along to us. Their workshops were valuable as long as you did not take them literally. Like the trip to Oaxaca or the trip on *ayahuasca*, they could be helpful, on this basis, to Western seekers after shamanic wisdom. Other fantasies are fine, too, for the shamanizing likes of us, if we are mindful of them as fantasies, as fictions in line with the literary lying that can teach us to "become sorcerers." We simply need to realize that all these important imaginings are caught up with the writing and reading of books—the works of shamanovelists and shaman-thropologists, who are sometimes the same person.

Such imaginings do not need to *end* there, on the other hand, as this book will go on to show. With the help of an appropriately attuned psychology, deliteralizing our Western fantasies, as we have done in the careful reimaginings of these first chapters, can lead us on to imaginal realities—realities akin to those encountered in what we have called "shamanism."

ENTERING JUNG'S HOUSE

WHERE A MODERN MAN
REDISCOVERED THE SOUL

Before Michael Harner, before Carlos Castaneda, even before Mircea Eliade, there was another figure who needs to be consulted for his contribution to a New Shamanism in the West. He never promoted shamanism, hardly used the word, and while he respected— even envied—non-Western spiritual traditions including those of the primal peoples he met in the American Southwest and the African bush, his dream was a Western one. Trained in medical science, he was fascinated by phenomena science discounted—the occult, the paranormal, we would say today—and he saw such things as relevant to the sufferings of the patients he treated as a psychiatrist.

Above all he was open to the unscientific implications of his own experience of the reality of the psyche and the images which constitute it. He gave us words with which to honor these imaginal realities of the soul, making possible another New Shamanism hidden and unrealized in the fantasized neoshamanism we have had thus far. He was a flawed man, sometimes lacking in judgment about his personal relationships and the political realities of his day. But he was also a courageous man of enormous imagination who gives us guidance to our inner depths—the *inner depths, the interiority of an ensouled self and world—even when we do not idealize him. He taught us how central fantasy and imagining are to our mental life, and thereby became the closest thing we have to an authentic shaman in the modern West: heir to Merlin, progenitor to a lineage of imaginal psychologists who can lead us toward shamanic imagining.*

His career is much debated to this day; his name is well known. It is Carl Gustav Jung. He lived by a lake.

The driveway slopes downward toward the front door. It is flanked by tall shrubs to form almost a tunnel, with the formal dark door beckoning at the end. The day is cloudless, the sun high over the lake. As I descend the cobblestones and concrete, the door becomes more distinct, preceded by a small gravel circle where the shrubs end and cars can turn around. I am tempted to turn around, too. This is Jung's house, 228 Seestrasse on Lake Zurich in the town of Kusnacht, Switzerland, and above the door, carved in Latin, it says *Vocatus Atque Non Vocatus Deus Aderit.* I do not read Latin, but from my bookish initiation into Jung's life and work over the past ten years I know what its daunting message is: "Called or not called, the god will be present."

It is 1973, before my Castaneda book has been killed, before the phone calls from Carlos, before my *Seeing Castaneda* anthology or de Mille's exposé. I am newly into the don Juan books during a time frame that is still, effectively, the '60s. Trained to be skeptical, I am nevertheless mainly credulous about these books. I have signed the contract with Warner to do the doomed book, and I am in transition professionally from Pennsylvania to Vermont, where Goddard College preserves the 1960s throughout the 1970s.

My 1967 dissertation on Melville had drawn on Jungian perspectives, and some graduate school cronies with whom I have stayed in touch have engineered my participation in a conference on "Jung, Hesse, and Comparative Religion" in southern Switzerland near where Herman Hesse, a favored novelist of the counter-culture, is buried. I will be speaking on my early Castaneda work.

I have written to Jung's son Franz, an architect who occupies the family house with his wife Lily, for permission to visit on my way to the conference. I am told by those acquainted with him that he is a formidable man, not disposed to indulge romantic pilgrims. He has sent me a chilly acceptance to bear this out, insisting that the ghost of his father does not stalk the halls of 228 Seestrasse, which he calls a simple Swiss family home, not a shrine.

In addition to my beginning work on Castaneda, I am preparing a biographical article on Jung which will appear a year later in the journal *Spring.*

I have told Franz Jung that a visit to the house will serve my biographical interests as a scholar, which is more or less true. I am, nonetheless, a romantic pilgrim approaching a shrine, and I am very nervous. I have never been to Europe before, let alone been in a decidedly upper-class European home. I feel distinctly inadequate—and not less so for knowing "the god will be there." Perspiring in an absurd red and white-checked summer sport jacket, I press the doorbell.

If the god will be there, it also appears that the gods are with me. Franz is away on business and Lily answers the door and shows me in. She is gracious and relaxed, pointing to Jung family portraits as we ascend the broad stairway to the second floor where we will sit in Jung's study to talk.

I have seen pictures and read descriptions of this room, and, suspiciously shrinelike, it seems to have been preserved untouched. Jung's desk is here, with his photograph of the carving he had done on the block of stone delivered in error to his retreat tower at Bollingen, down the lake. Here also are alchemical texts and Tibetan tangka hangings with their mandala designs. I can almost smell his pipe smoke. For anyone steeped in Jung it is like stepping into a myth, his "personal myth" as he referred to his life in writing his autobiography, *Memories, Dreams, Reflections*, with the help of his assistant Aniela Jaffe.[1]

As this work makes clear, the personal myth always surrounded the psychological ideas he developed from within it. Nowhere is this more the case than in his "confrontation with the unconscious," as the autobiography calls it: the inner turmoil that followed his stormy break from Freud in 1913 and that eventually led, he felt, to all his later theories.

Science had brought him, the son of a Swiss pastor, to prominence as a psychiatrist, a medical doctor specializing in the new clinical approach known as "psycho-analysis." After severing connections with Freud he had resigned his university position, and the concepts he developed out of the initiatory confusions of his "confrontation" he renamed "analytical psychology," a reversal signaling that something besides Freudian ideals of scientific fact had begun to drive his theoretical work.

Somewhere in the study where I am sitting he sat, sixty years ago, recording his disturbing fantasies and dreams, even painting them in "The Red Book" that all Jungians know about. Some of its pictures and calligraphy can be seen in Aniela Jaffe's compilation, *C. G. Jung: Word and Image*; in a 1972 article, she notes that a chapter of this journal of his was entitled "The Rediscovery of the Soul."[2] In this room he probably also took down an atlas and told Gerhard Adler, training under him to be an analyst, to show him where on the coast of India he had landed in the dream Adler had just recounted—and insisted to another trainee, Marie-Louise von Franz, that a schizophrenic young woman really was on the moon, where she said she was.[3]

The theories, late as well as early, are set forth in the twenty or so volumes of Jung's *Collected Works*. Even now, a dozen years after his death, the German-language edition is still being edited. She is involved in this project, Lily tells me as she invites me to sign the guest book in the great man's study. But she is also reading someone else's work. She is fascinated by Castaneda's writing, and wants to hear my views.

WE ARE OUT in the garden now. She has just pointed out an enormous coiled ammonite fossil in the first floor solarium, saying that Jung had gotten it transported down from the Alps. She calls it a "foundling stone." His love for stones intrigued me, since I had written about "sacred stones" from Eliade's perspective and had just made my first visit to Stonehenge and Avebury, megalithic complexes in England. The garden, overlooking Lake Zurich, has a stone wall with carvings, presumably Jung's. As much tourist as pilgrim, I have brought my camera along. But Lily cautions that photographs may not be taken in the garden as we stand before a sort of headstone under a ginkgo tree. I later hear the speculation that some of these carvings may refer to Jung's long-term relationship with Toni Wolff, something the children and grandchildren of Emma Jung, his wife, and of Carl, would prefer not to have anyone probe.

I cannot recall the other carvings, but the one on the headstone is of a Chinese sage, looking up to the branch of a tree—perhaps this ginkgo tree—where there are several leaves. One leaf, however, is in the air between the sage and the branch, falling. Lily explains that the tree, or its seeds, was sent to Jung from China. The leaves represent Jung and his children as of 1955, when Emma died. She is the falling leaf.

Now, of course, Jung's leaf has fallen as well, and as we say our good-byes Lily asks me if I would like to take one from the tree as a memento. I am touched by the story of the carving and readily accept her offer. It is something I will keep for years in a little metal container that had held small cigars called "Tom Thumbs." The symbolism of this name relates to my article on Jung's life.[4] The leaf, I realize, is a religious relic.

I walk up the long driveway and make my way to the churchyard cemetary in Kusnacht where Jung is buried. On his headstone is another inscription in Latin, this one biblical, saying something like "the man of the earth earthy, the man of the heavens heavenly"—an appropriate graveside sentiment, I suppose, though Jung's relationship to biblical teachings was far from orthodox. Certainly he was earthy, by all accounts, including some of his own, even underworldly. The English writer Colin Wilson has called him "the lord of the underworld."[5]

Next to the headstone, lying flat on the flowery grave, is what I take to be another foundling stone, perhaps dropped somewhere in the Alps when the Ice Age ended. Uncannily similar to a stone on Hesse's grave on the other side of the Alps to the south, it has a hollow depression to collect rainwater. Before I disturb it a bird is drinking there, drinking at Jung's grave.

The train ride back to Zurich is brief, especially since my head is swimming with the symbolism of my visit. More than anything else, it had seemed a sort of underworld journey. It was a mostly pleasant one, I had to admit, but a nervous pilgrimage to the home of a dead man nevertheless, and one who had come to occupy a large place in my own psyche. There had even been a few moments at the grave where he himself, mentor to much of my learning, lies under the actual ground.

I am one year younger, on this journey, than Jung was when he left the world of Freudian psychology and its scientific aims to plunge into his unconscious and produce, out of this confrontation, a new possibility for Western sufferers and seekers. I had just left the world of conventional academe to take on the joys and terrors of counter-cultural teaching in remote Vermont. What had I confronted at the house and grave of Carl Gustav Jung—or avoided? And what would I encounter in the years to come as I entered the journey of middle age, a married man with four young children, and tried to make sense of Castaneda? What initiations awaited? How could Jung's underworld journey be a guide?

DESCENT TO THE OBJECTIVE PSYCHE

In order to seize hold of the fantasies, I frequently imagined a steep descent. I even made attempts to get to the very bottom. The first time I reached, as it were, a depth of about a thousand feet; the next time I found myself at the edge of a cosmic abyss. It was like a voyage to the moon, or a descent into empty space. First came the image of a crater, and I had the feeling that I was in the land of the dead. The atmosphere was that of the other world. Near the steep slope of a rock I caught sight of two figures, an old man with a white beard and a beautiful young girl. I summoned up my courage and approached them as if they were real people, and listened attentively to what they told me. . . . They had a black serpent living with them. . . .[6]

James Hillman, the editor of *Spring* for whom I was preparing my article in 1973, makes a crucial point about this passage from the "Confrontation with the Unconscious" chapter of Jung's autobiography. Jung was "spiritually alone" after the end of his friendship with Freud, Hillman says. "But in this isolation he turned neither to a new group, nor to organized religion, nor to refuge in psychosis, nor to security in conventional activities, work, or family; he turned to his images."[7]

Hillman, too, turned to images, for on this priority he has based the imaginal psychology he has developed out of Jung's thought. Not only a psychology *of* imagination, or a psychology just *about* images, Hillman's post-Jungian thought thinks *with* images as it approaches the self and the world. His brand of imaginative psychologizing will be our major resource as we continue to seek a shamanic spirituality for Westerners.

But this search begins with Jung's descent to the images of what he called "the objective psyche"—the soul as a dimension or world standing over against the ego, independent and often subversive of the ego's wants and demands, not a matter of the ego's subjectivity, not something only "all in our head," not something we "make up." The objective psyche—of which we, as egos, are largely unconscious—feels like an "inner" realm, but not one only within us: "The unconscious of man can reach—God knows where," Jung once told an interviewer.[8] It is more as if soul is the interiority of everything, anywhere.

Little of this was obvious to Jung until the confrontation forced upon him in 1913. His was not exactly a bookish initiation, but figures from books nonetheless peopled visions it brought, and books were to come that share its message for *our* initiation. The theories that explained it, however, not to mention Hillman's extension of those theories, awaited this experiential descent, Jung's direct experience of images as independent beings. Hillman's commentary continues, and we need to track it closely:

> When there was nothing else to hold to, Jung turned to the personified images of interior vision. He entered into an interior drama, took himself into an imaginative fiction and then, perhaps, began his healing—even if it has been called his breakdown. There he found a place to go that was no longer Vienna, figures to communicate with who were no longer the psychoanalytic circle of colleagues, and a counsellor who was no longer Freud. . . . It is from this point onward that Jung becomes that extraordinary pioneering advocate of the reality of the psyche.[9]

The reality of the psyche: it is with this radical idea, born out of Jung's radical experience of initiatory trauma, that Western culture, beyond its scientific skepticism and its scientific literalism, becomes open once again to its own form of shamanism.

All it takes is for people to see how very radical this idea indeed is, and that is very hard for most of us. It was hard for Gerhard Adler and for Marie-Louise von Franz—and they were students of Jung! But he taught with radical maneuvers: he took the reality of the psychic India that Adler had dreamed about so seriously that he wanted to find it on a map, knowing it was not literally there. Likewise he sided with a schizophrenic girl who said she was on the moon, prompting von Franz at first to think, "That old man is crazy or I am stupid."[10] Eventually she came to understand the psychic reality of the moon for the girl, a reality whose force Jung could only convey by saying she *was* on the moon.

IT IS EASY, in a psychological age such as ours, to say that unconscious contents can make an impact upon our dreams, our moods and neuroses, even our bodies and behavior. Jung went farther than that, and Hillman has followed him as few other Jungians have.

This may be why Hillman says *perhaps* Jung began his healing with his descent to the underworld, and notes that the experience is usually seen as a breakdown. "Healing" is too often an affair of the ego only, a symptomatic "solution" to the surface of a mystery that we shallowly perceive as a problem. In its depths is the mysterious psyche, where healing that deals with its reality, its "objectivity," may look like, and feel like, a breakdown to the ego. Indeed, the ego may need to break, as in depression, for consciousness to go down into the psychic underworld where a shamanic dismemberment of some sort might be required. To this topic, too—the suffering of soul work—we will want to return.

Our lack of control over a *real* psychic Other is at the very least an inconvenience to the ego. Hence its resistance to understanding the radical extent of Jung's concept. To enter Jung's house, however, his "secret room," you must pass through the door that says "Called *or not called*, the god *will be present*."

It was in that house, of course, that Jung made his initiatory descent and met his inner figures. The old man was first Elijah, then Philemon, the young girl Salome. The snake had no name, but seemed fond of Jung, perhaps as a guardian animal, though Jung did not develop the shamanic parallels in 1913. However, the conclusion he did draw in retrospect allows us to do so eight decades later: "Philemon and other figures of my fantasies brought home to me the crucial insight that there are things in the psyche which I do not produce, but which produce themselves and have their own life."[11] It is certainly a crucial insight for us if we want to reimagine shamanism for the modern West.

And notice that Jung does not even say "my psyche"; he says "the psyche." We do not possess it. Our imagining does not invent it. "Our" imagining takes us there, where *its* imagining has equal reality and rights. Just as our imagining takes us into a novel—or a shamanovel—though we know we did not write it, or onto a stage to play a part we did not create. These are the parallels Hillman draws when trying to honor and understand Jung's journey: an interior drama, an imaginative fiction. As Hillman elaborates:

> Entering one's interior story takes a courage similar to starting a novel. We have to engage with persons whose autonomy may radically alter, even dominate, our thoughts and feelings, neither ordering these persons about nor yielding to them full sway. Fictional and factual, they and we, are drawn together like threads into a mythos, a plot, until death do us part. It is a rare courage that submits to this middle region of psychic reality where the supposed surety of fact and illusion of fiction exchange their clothes.[12]

All our careful probing of the literary sources of the New Shamanism—Eliade's soaring novelistic imagination of scholarship, Castaneda's instructive trickery, Ronald Sukenick's self-conscious literary lying, even the new ethnographers' attempt to bring the anthropology which has researched indigenous shamanism for the West into collusion with the fiction writing that neoshamanism has fed on—all of this patient exploration helps us to use Hillman's writing about Jung's writing for envisioning what a truly imaginal shamanism would entail. Not literalistic but literary. Not scientific but artistic.

Only by taking with utter seriousness the sort of knowing made possible in novels and plays, Hillman is saying, can we gather what Jung's descent might mean for us as a resource. Only by valuing such expressions of imagination can we learn the lesson of what Hillman has called the poetic basis of mind.

Hillman also speaks of a "middle region" in regard to Jung's confrontation with the objective psyche, using the Greek word *metaxy*. He says Jung's inner persons were "figures of the middle realm, neither quite transcendent Gods nor quite physical humans."[13] Borrowing another term from ancient Greek thought, he calls such psychic figures *daimons*—partly to point up Jung's courage in dealing with them on equal terms. For such inner imaginings, like the daimons, had been reviled and repressed for centuries by the

Church, which changed the name of unauthorized images which were allowed their autonomy by seekers such as Jung, calling them "demons." "Thus Jung's move which turned directly to the images and figures of the middle realm was a heretical, demonic move."[14]

Moreover, since science saw demons as nonexistent, Jung's was a drastically unscientific maneuver as well—not one for which a medical doctor was trained. Even worse, as a psychiatrist he was choosing what was defined "in our clinical language as multiple personality or as schizophrenia."[15] He was in good company, we might say today: shamans were routinely seen as suffering from acute schizophrenia by Western observers. In the culture of European medicine in 1913, of course, the experience must have been terrifying and must have been a step taken out of desperation and an adventurousness few of us could have mustered in his place.

Hillman's assessment, though, goes beyond seeing this as an act of merely personal import, however great, in Jung's private life. Out of the initiation came psychological theories and methods for all of us—and the possibility of finding from within the West's own resources a shamanism to match our seeking. Hillman never mentions this possibility in underscoring the vast ramifications of Jung's breakdown, but we can now begin to make the connections for ourselves:

> His move between the two orthodoxies of theological religion and clinical scientism re-established in experience the middle realm which he was to call "psychic reality." This psychic reality discovered by Jung consists in fictive figures. It is poetic, dramatic, literary in nature. . . . What we learn from Jung is that this literary imagination goes on in the midst of ourselves. Poetic, dramatic fictions are what actually people our psychic life. Our life in soul is a life in imagination.[16]

CROSSING JUNG'S BRIDGE TO THE METAXY

WHAT WE NEED is not a Jungian interpretation of the various symbolic motifs of the New Shamanism stemming from Eliade and Castaneda. Our emphasis is more on the processes of experiencing and imagining, for one thing, than on particular contents interpreted as symbols. What I am suggesting that we seek is rather a sense, made possible by Jung and successors like Hillman, that *there is a shamanic underworld or otherworld for Western seekers— and Western methods for approaching it.*

These methods cannot be understood, let alone used, without the radical shift in our attitude toward imaginal realities that Jung's legacy requires.

This is mainly because we live in a modern culture driven by scientific literalism, a rigid reliance upon factuality which serves science and technology well, and thereby serves many of our genuine needs in areas such as medical care. Jung was a medical doctor who never fully shed his scientific mantle, what Hillman has called his empirical disguise. But Jung knew—his underworld journey helped teach him—that applied to matters of spirituality and imagination, this literalism was thoroughly inappropriate.

He also knew that divesting ourselves of science's literalism in these matters was a delicate operation as well as a tremendous struggle. This is even reflected in his language, as he wrestled with his rigorous scientific training while learning from his subtle experience of psychic reality. He thereby offers us an indispensable bridge, for we cannot just wish away our imbeddedness in this scientific culture with its "scientism" or, as Theodore Roszak somewhere calls this misapplication of literalism, its "myth of objective consciousness." This is where we begin, and it is from here that we must cross over to a more appropriate attitude.

The bridge Jung provides is his language, his writing, which allows us to reimagine neoshamanism—already *has* allowed us to do so, since it schooled my reimagining efforts (and thus yours) in the first half of this book: to see through the literalism and move out of the unconscious fantasies into a conscious imagining that can be shamanic. Jung's psychology of imagination brings passive fantasies to conscious awareness *and* promotes an active participation in the imagining process, the fictive power, that produced them. Now known as fantasies, they are no longer taken literally but point toward a new relationship with the imagination.

The service that a post-Jungian psychology like Hillman's performs here is to help us with the words of Jung, insuring that we grasp their legacy for our specific purposes. We need not walk Jung's bridge backwards into the science that trained him. A post-Jungian imaginal perspective equips us to leave behind the literalism, the reliance on factuality, with which he struggled.

For example, when he sometimes called the phenomena of the unconscious "psychic facts," we can see that this is how, out of his scientific background, he felt he needed to speak in order to indicate the reality of the psyche. He also presumed a fact-focused readership, even while developing the ideas that could counter the misapplication of such an attitude. In his autobiography he tells us that early on he realized the difficulty of talking to "one's fellows about anything that is unknown to them. They pardon such ruthless behavior," he added sardonically, "only in a writer, journalist, or poet. I came to see that a new idea, or even just an unusual aspect of an old one, can be communicated only by facts."[17] We need to move ahead from where such rhetoric leaves off, however, respecting his struggle and searching out worthier words to honor imaginal realities—words he also provided, words a writer, journalist, or poet might use.

It is this latter bridge, from science through art to a soulful spirituality, that Hillman helps us walk. Having already said, in response to Jung's descent to the objective psyche, that "our life in soul is a life in imagination," he goes on to term Jung's account "an instructor's manual." He could as easily have called it a bridge of words, since he finds that it is certain bridging words which are crucial:

> We have already been given the clue in the instructor's manual as to how this third realm traditionally called "soul" can be re-established—and by anyone. Jung says he treated the figures whom he met "as though they were real people." The key is that *as though*, the metaphorical, as-if reality, neither literally real (hallucinations or people in the street) or irreal/unreal ("mere" fictions, projections which "I" make up as parts of "me," auto-suggestive illusions). In an "as-if" consciousness they are powers with voice, body, motion, and mind, fully felt but wholly imaginary. This is psychic reality, and it comes in the shape of daimons. By means of these daimonic realities, Jung confirmed the autonomy of the soul.[18]

PERHAPS, GIVEN THE SUBTLETIES of Jung's struggle, his bridge is a tightrope, or the slippery brink of a waterfall we need to traverse as did Castaneda's don Genaro. Surely, as Hillman's acrobatics with Jung's words demonstrate, we will need great agility to deliteralize our attitude toward the imaginal daimons of the soul without devaluing their reality in the bargain.

What is not a fact is deemed "unreal" in our culture, and imagination is considered a childish affair—or a wholly owned subsidiary of the Disney Corporation. If we do not outgrow it, we have a developmental problem of mental health. So staying in Jung's and Hillman's *metaxy*, psyche's middle realm, is a difficult balancing act for adults who want to take imagining seriously as a shamanic reality. But Jung's legacy demands no less of those in search of the soul of shamanism.

Finding or inferring the places in Jung's writing that point to aesthetic rather than scientific understandings is a step in the right direction for such seekers and the scholars who would join them. This is why Hillman's imaginal psychology extends Jung's own ideas for us most helpfully. It realizes his radical legacy as art, as literary rather than literal, as closer to Sukenick's shamanovels in its evolution than to its origins in medical psychiatry. "As Philemon taught Jung," says Hillman, "you are not the author of the play of the psyche."[19] But you can be one of the characters in the drama, and images from the theater are frequent in Jung's and Hillman's formulations about our relationship to the psyche.

To understand the wide variety of arts media honored by his psychology it is also helpful to recall those pictures Jung painted for his Red Book: "I took great care to try to understand every single image . . . and, above all, to realize them in actual life."[20] While Jung's attempt to interact with his underworld images was still strongly shaped by the science that had shaped him, it is noteworthy that his "realizations" were aesthetic expressions, and the method this led to, art therapy, is another bridging maneuver to shamanic imagining we will need to revisit.

Jung's wrestlings with words as well as images for psychological experience continued throughout the years after his confrontation with the unconscious. If "modern man," as he wrote, was in search of soul, this modern man, a Merlin of sorts, had rediscovered it, if only by recognizing it when he fell into it in a shamanic descent. Jung himself survived his ordeal with the objective psyche to share the healing wisdom with us, but he feared at the end of his life that the psychology he fashioned to do so went unheeded, uncomprehended, like Merlin's cry in the fairy forest. There may have been some petulance in his worry, a bit of bruised ego that wanted wider acceptance for its views. But who can say that postmodern persons are any less bereft of soul than modern men? Jung's Merlin cry does deserve our greater attentiveness.

Just as Jung realized his personal daimons in art, so his psychological legacy must be realized by successors whose words are never far from the arts of imagination, which are Merlin's bardic media today and the channels of our attunement. It is such post-Jungian successors who make Jung's rediscovery, his attentiveness, our resource in the search for an imaginal shamanism.

We have already met one of these successors, James Hillman, and we will want to follow his extensions of Jung's thought very closely. But he is not alone in seeking to realize the radical legacy of the man who lived by a lake.

As Part One has suggested, there is another New Shamanism available to Western seekers. In patiently reimagining the passive fantasies fueled by our initial reading of the first neoshamanism that has been offered to us, we have seen the possibility of a mindful interaction with such fantasies, a bookish initiation into an imaginal shamanism. We have begun to learn what "becoming sorcerers" in the modern West requires: a new or renewed relationship to the imagination in our actual lives of suffering and celebration—including our lives as readers whose imagining has been inevitably literary. Now we need to gather the resources with which to meet that requirement. The Jungian tradition in psychology uniquely offers such resources. Not only are there elements of the life and work of Carl Jung himself that can empower our understanding and participation as Western seekers of shamanic healing, but he has fostered successors who can take us even further toward a soulful spirituality of shamanic imagining.

As Part Two will show, the work of imaginal psychologists like James Hillman, Thomas Moore, and Mary Watkins, among others, explores this needed new relationship to imagining. With their help we can make a truly shamanic recovery of soul, for as Jung said, "Image is psyche." Their guidance, as applied in these next chapters, can teach us to attend with heartfelt respect to the autonomy of inner images, their movements in our dreams and miseries, reveries and regrets. In so doing we serve psyche, the soul of self and world, and make our own lives more soulful. For Westerners attracted to the healing power of shamanic wisdom, this is the New Shamanism that is now to be studied and sought.

5

REALIZING THE RADICAL
LEGACY OF JUNG

*F*or James Hillman, the implications of what Carl Jung said about the descent to the daimons—especially Jung's own descent to the daimons—were aesthetic: imaginal, fictive, mythic. In his book with the radical title *The Myth of Analysis*, Hillman says that the psychoanalytic tradition in general "has replaced the imaginal power of the psyche with the concept of the unconscious."[1] However, in the essay on Jung from which I have been quoting, "The Pandaemonium of Images," a chapter of his *Healing Fiction*, Hillman adds that for him

> both daimon and unconscious are modes of imagining, modes of writing fictions, and both have their healing efficacy as the case may be. Imagination goes on in the commonplace and in everyday "unimaginative" language, providing we hear into it for its images or look with an imagining eye.[2]

This is the attitude, or the ear and eye, we must develop for our Western soul-recovery through shamanic imagining, the legacy of Jung we most need to realize. It is an attitude Hillman certainly learned from Jung, a scientific psychoanalyst who nevertheless built a bridge *from* the concept of the unconscious over *to* the imaginal power of the psyche. Hillman extends that bridge even further in the direction of the arts, by means of the arts, in this case re-visioning the scientific as well as the unscientific terminology as different ways of imagining, but more specifically as different modes of "writing fictions."

In another chapter of *Healing Fiction*, "The Fiction of Case History," Hillman actually calls Jung a "writer on fictions," and goes on to observe that

> for Jung, the more fictitious and far-out the better (hence, alchemy, Tibet, Zarathustra, astrological aeons, schizophrenia, parapsychology) for such "materials" obliged him to meet them on an equally imaginative level. But—both Freud and Jung assumed an empirical posture, subjected themselves to empirical criticisms, and attempted to reply with empirical defenses. They would have been better served had they turned for help to the field in which they were themselves working, the field of the literary imagination.[3]

This means the fictive power of the literary imagination that has secretly fostered neoshamanism is also the imaginal power of the psyche, the lost "soul" of the West and of its modern seekers, to be rediscovered and recovered in acts and arts of shamanic imagining. By aestheticizing Jung, Hillman brings psychology into contact with the aesthetic core of neoshamanism, a movement prepared for by the novelistic imagining of a historian of religions and created by an anthropologist operating as a literary artist. For instance, post-Jungian psychology like that of Hillman, crossing the bridge, meets shamanovels like those of Ronald Sukenick—and sees through to those of Carlos Castaneda, too.

Hillman's writings contain very few direct or indirect references to Castaneda. But the imaginal psychology he has initiated out of Jung's most important legacy reveals significant connections to the don Juan writings—with the crucial proviso that Hillman's psychological moves in favor of fictive or imaginal power operate openly and mindfully, while Castaneda's neoshamanist moves do so under the cover of his hoax.

However, once having uncovered and acknowledged the reality of Castaneda's writings as we experienced them—that they were neoshamanist fictions unconsciously driving our Western fantasies—we can make use of the "echo effect" I have referred to earlier and can explore these connections to Hillman's work. Thus we will be weaving together in another way the rise of neoshamanism with the resources of post-Jungian imaginal psychology.

What is this echo effect? To clarify it further we must reiterate a major point of Part One. While most of Castaneda's fans, and many of his commentators, presume that "the controversy" does not matter, that the issue of whether he has tricked us is irrelevant given the supposed transcendent truth or timeless meaning of the don Juan teachings themselves (teachings which, it is said, are there to be learned and lived, fact *or* fiction, like their ancient and Asian parallels), we cannot, as I have said, leave it at that. Although I was an early defender of Castaneda and I scarcely shared Richard de Mille's later fixation on proving conclusively that his work is a hoax, I find the very strong likelihood that it is just that to be central to the learning of a long literary apprenticeship: ours as well as Carlos's. The larger ramifications of this trickster teaching for our lives and culture—the possibility of a genuinely Western imaginal shamanism—will never be understood or enacted by shrugging aside the fact–fiction issue. It is the single issue through which all the teachings in and of the Castaneda books are filtered. Confronting this issue, we can see through our literalized fantasy of the wise old Yaqui sorcerer who was teaching us through Carlos's factual account.

This confrontation with our unconscious fantasizing—fantasizing controlled by Castaneda the trickster—allows us to see that the trickery *in* the don Juan fairy tale is also the trickery *of* its telling. Only such a confrontation allows us to see through *our* literalism as readers just as Carlos was led by don Juan to see through his. This is the echo effect, and this is what I tried to tell Lily Jung as we discussed Castaneda during my visit to Jung's house in Kusnacht in 1973.

Sukenick's "Upward and Juanward" piece had just come out in the *Village Voice*, but Richard de Mille's expose was three years away, and I was just beginning to formulate these ideas about Castaneda. I was also just beginning to read Hillman. Not much later, however, I had made enough progress in both areas—Hillman actually helping me to see through Castaneda's disguise as much as de Mille did—that I could understand that once you achieved awareness of your reader's role as an apprentice to writings that were fictions, not factual reports, you could revisit major themes of don Juan's teachings without taking them literally. It was in doing so on this basis that I could see instructive connections to Hillman's post-Jungianism.

THE HILLMAN-CASTANEDA CONNECTIONS

IN *THE MYTH OF ANALYSIS*, which appeared the year before I got to Jung's house, Hillman does not discredit psychoanalysis, as the title might imply. But he points out the mythic, fictive ingredients in its supposedly scientific approach—just as we are doing for the neoshamanism Castaneda the shamanthropologist founded—and seeks to resituate it on a deliberately imaginal basis—just as we are doing by moving his neoshamanism toward an active imagining that is shamanic. For Hillman the work of psychoanalysis must be shifted toward what he calls, after the Romantic poet John Keats, "soul-making." This process, he says, is "not treatment, not therapy, not even a process of self-realization but is essentially an imaginative activity or an activity of the imaginal realm as it plays through all of life everywhere."[4]

The word "imaginal," it should be obvious by now, is chosen for a reason. I learned it from Hillman, probably from this book in 1972, and he derives it from Henry Corbin, a scholar of Islamic mysticism. Rather than drawing a firm distinction between the *real* as factual and the *imaginary* as unreal, Hillman usually employs the adjective "imaginal," just as "fictive" does not have the connotation of unreality that "fictional"—or, even more so, "fictitious"—has.

Much of what Carlos encounters under don Juan's tutelage in the Castaneda books could be called imaginal rather than imaginary: realities the author calls "nonordinary." Even the "seeing" discussed in the early stories could be called imaginal perception. Of course, don Juan and Carlos themselves can now be seen as imaginal, or fictive, as well, in that not even exposing Castaneda's hoax—showing his books are fictional, his characters fictitious or imaginary—has rolled back their reality as inhabitants of our imagination.

Time and time again in Hillman's work focused on imaginal realities —in dealing with historical research, say, or when he discusses research into creativity—he stresses that "we examine this research, not for its positivistic, objective, scientific 'facts,' but for the fantasies expressed in it."[5] Seen from Hillman's perspective, emphasizing the fictive or the mythic, "analysis now points beyond itself."[6]

This statement, in turn, points back to a declaration in Sukenick's *98.6* about "Psychosynthesis": "Psychosynthesis is the opposite of psychoanalysis but apart from that Cloud refuses to define it."[7] Hillman's psychology, moving from scientific psychoanalysis to its imaginal core, implicitly provides the missing definition for Sukenick's Psychosynthesis, of which Cloud says "only the imagination can deal with the imagination thus Psychosynthesis."[8]

So Sukenick, who has helped us toward "becoming sorcerers" by meditating on the implications of our reading of Castaneda, assists us as well in seeing the Hillman–Castaneda connections. And if Psychosynthesis is also "a way of going mad without going mad,"[9] it points not only to don Juan's advice to Carlos that he should "let go without losing his marbles" but also to Jung's descent to the objective psyche, the underworld of daimonic images. This was a journey which some have seen as Jung's lapse into madness but which Hillman has built on as Jung's courageous venture to recover the lost soul of Western culture, with Jung's methods of journeying constituting an instruction manual for the rest of us.

Meanwhile, we have found that acts of writing and reading are much more central to the rise and future possibilities of neoshamanism than we had probably realized. We likewise have discovered that what is being written and read—words, language—can be crucial; in Jung's case such writing offers a bridge between scientific literalism and what Hillman refers to as the middle region of soulful imagining, closer to the arts than to science. This discovery continues in the comparison of Hillman and Castaneda, for Part Two of *The Myth of Analysis* deals with "psychological language" and takes up a term Castaneda helped to make culturally significant: "hallucination."

Hillman ponders this term in a way that indicates the deeper meanings of hallucinogenic experience as courted by the counter-culture and dramatized but then transcended in the don Juan books. He looks at the history of how the word has been applied to devalue private experiencing that was threatening to the prevailing worldview of the modern West:

> Hallucinations put in question the materialist theory of sense perceptions; they are indeed dangerous phenomena. . . . The soul lost its conviction in itself as a timeless intangible in vivid touch with timeless intangibles. In 1817 the evidence for such convictions became "hallucinatory." Public reality encroached upon private reality. The key word is "convincing": one could have these intimate experiences providing one did not give them real faith.[10]

It should be clear from our discussion of Castaneda in Chapter 2 how similar this is to the issues raised, for instance, by don Juan and Carlos conversing, in *The Teachings of Don Juan*, about whether Carlos "really flew." But Hillman, writing in the early 1970s, adds a footnote on hallucinations which makes even more telling connections to Castaneda:

> Perhaps [the use of hallucinogens in the 1960s] signifies a desire to "save the phenomena" that have long been declared aberrations and to readmit the banished modes of perception and, with them, another *Weltanschauung* and theory of the real based on a new theory of perception. . . . It is a pity that this essential issue of metaphysics must be obfuscated by parent–child complexes and the . . . fight over legality, authority, and order. The issue at the deepest level is not drugs. The issue is the admission of a nonmaterialistic view of the real, the reality of private knowledge, and, ultimately, the reality of the soul.[11]

IN THE PREFACE to another major book, *Re-Visioning Psychology*, from 1975, Hillman announces that he is "working toward a psychology of soul that is based in a psychology of image."[12] Far from advocating drug use—which, in addition to its well-advertised dangers, can substitute a kind of chemical literalism for a truly changed worldview—Hillman wants a new psychology, following Jung's, that can teach us how to understand and honor the reality of the soul by attending to its images everywhere. That is, he wants psychology (ideally, *all* of psychology should become "post-Jungian") to be "radical" by remaining true to the roots of its defining name: the *logos* of *psyche*, the meaning of soul.

In exploring how this imaginal psychology can supply a Western shamanism, we have pursued connections to Castaneda's accounts of a shamanic apprenticeship, re-visioned as imaginal or fictive tales, a bookish initiation. While preparing *Re-Visioning Psychology*, Hillman did not have the benefit of de Mille's debunking of Castaneda's literalistic texts. No doubt he knew about his books mainly as a counter-cultural and cross-cultural fad distracting psychologists from the necessary task of attending to the lost soul of Western culture. Accordingly Hillman's allusion to Castaneda in 1975 is a negative one: "Psychology senses its failure and gropes around for new modes of re-visioning itself by means of new religious reflection. But Yaqui hunting wisdom. . . [is] no less simplistic than psychology's former favorite mirrors—machines, monkeys, and infants."[13] But since it is really Castaneda's wisdom that is at issue, the fact that he as well as his character don Juan is a product of Latin-American culture provides a "mirror" or model for psychology that is actually in close accord with Hillman's advice in *Re-Visioning Psychology*.

There he counsels us to abandon the northern European, Reformation origins of conventional psychology and "venture South" as part of a Renaissance emphasis for post-Jungian psychology. This "return of the Renaissance into our Northern Consciousness," says Hillman, "comes from the other side of any mountain, across any border, as Italian, Arab, Mexican, Jew, Caribbean, or as Renaissance moor."[14] Perhaps it can come as Prospero, Shakespeare's Renaissance imagining of the Mediterranean sorcerer and Sukenick's stand-in for don Juan? Or can it come as that personification of the psychologizing process, the very act of "seeing through," proposed by Hillman himself: the Knight Errant? If so, is he so far from a disreputable old Yaqui *brujo* or his trickster author? Hillman refers to "the psychological mirror that walks down the road, the Knight Errant on his adventure, the scrounging rogue. . . . And leaving, before completion, suggestion hanging in the air, an indirection, an open phrase."[15]

At any rate, three years after *Re-Visioning Psychology*, the journal under Hillman's editorship, *Spring*, published Michael Whan's essay, "'Don Juan,' Trickster, and Hermeneutic Understanding."[16] Presumably, since Hillman published Whan's article, which has a closing section on "Trickster psychology and the fact/fiction controversy," this meant Hillman was aware of

Castaneda's hoax and open to the value of considering his trickster tales from the perspective of post-Jungian psychology.

It also meant, for me, as I have recounted, the beginning of a new friendship: I corresponded with and later met Whan in England as a fellow Castaneda fan who was also a fellow student of Hillman's realizations of the psychology of Jung. Certainly I was a fan of Whan's post-Jungian characterization of the don Juan books:

> Castaneda's accounts offer a literature of fascination and enchantment for the reader: the basis for a psychedelic cult with the authentification and authority of an anthropological field report. However, this literal reading of the sorcerer's magical world is repudiated within the story itself. The author addresses himself *to the reader* through don Juan, speaking against a literal interpretation of the sorcerer's description.[17]

SOULFUL SPIRITUALITY

MICHAEL WHAN AND I were not the only students of Hillman's post-Jungianism. There was no "movement"—Hillman's writings are not always easy to read, and his radical message is not necessarily welcomed by psychologists, even some Jungian psychologists. But *Spring*, of which Hillman took over the editorship in 1970, has had a steady readership, and Hillman has held a respectable position of authority as former Director of Studies at the Jung Institute in Zurich. The sales of Hillman's books also have been solid, if not spectacular. Through the 1970s and 1980s other writers, inside and outside of psychology, published in *Spring* and associated themselves with Hillman's ideas.

First were the Jungians Patricia Berry and Rafael Lopez-Pedraza, who had helped Hillman to get things going in Zurich; then David Miller, a religious studies colleague of mine who re-visioned Christian theology in Hillman's direction; and Robert Sardello, a therapist who was associated with Hillman when he moved from Zurich to Dallas, and Mary Watkins, a developmental psychologist trained in both Jungian and phenomenological thought. Paul Kugler and Edward Casey lent philosophical depth to the Hillman circle, while art therapists Howard McConeghey and Shaun McNiff nurtured the crucial aesthetic interest Hillman had revealed for a psychology of soul. Supporters from abroad—Wolfgang Giegerich and Noel Cobb and Alan Bleakley from psychotherapy, Peter Bishop from cultural geography—came on board.

Others appeared, too: Ginette Paris, a communications scholar and "psychological feminist"; Michael Perlman, re-visioning ideas about nuclear and ecological threats; Robert Bosnak, an unusually thoughtful therapist of dreams; Russell Lockhart, showing how an imaginal therapy would work; Michael Vannoy Adams, a postmodernist literary critic; Charles Boer, an irreverent classics professor; and even a Chicago lawyer, Benjamin Sells. Many more writers appeared in *Spring*: less prolific contributors like me and Michael Whan, as well as prominent figures from the Jungian world who did not identify themselves so much as co-conspirators with Hillman.

There were several conferences, at Notre Dame University in Indiana and in Dallas, and twice there were remarkable gatherings at a small college in Newport, Rhode Island, on the theme of "Facing Apocalypse." I attended these latter events myself, and heard about the others, and in 1992 I presented some of my correlations between imaginal psychology and shamanism at a "Festival of Archetypal Psychology" in honor of Hillman, again at Notre Dame. None of this would have made much of an impact on the larger public of readers and seekers, however, had it not been for one other name within the Hillman camp: Thomas Moore.

Moore is the author of two bestsellers, with another in the making, the first ones by a post-Jungian of the Hillman variety, realizing Jung's legacy of unscientific soul psychology. Before we can assess them, however, and see how they may apply to our search for a Western shamanism involved with imaginal realities, we need a bit of background.

A holistic view of the person generally has included "body, mind, and spirit," particularly in New-Age contexts—which, as we have seen, overlap with neoshamanism and help make possible its marketing. But this holism, when seen from a post-Jungian vantage point, does not seem whole at all, but limited or partial, for where is soul?

Soul, from this angle, is *distinct* from spirit, which is seen as closer to mind, as the German word for both, *Geist*, suggests. Spirit, like mind, favors detached abstractness, purity, and unity, all characteristics that transcend earth and body and their sensuous imagery. Soul, on the other hand, thrives on attachments and imaginings, the concrete and sensual, immanent rather than transcendent meaning, emphasizing the multiplicity and imperfection that cling to earth and body.

Hillman, in a key essay, distinguishes soul from spirit by way of the imagery of heights and depths.[18] He contrasts the "peaks" of spirit, as in the icy clarity of a Himalayan enlightenment, with the entangling, mist-shrouded "vales," or valleys, of soul, with its perplexity and moodiness, the matted undergrowth of dappled everydayness. One implication of this is that Hillman takes very seriously the term "depth psychology," for depth is, to him, the inherent direction of soul or psyche (about which psychology should be concerning itself).

It was Jung, though, who preceded Hillman into the vale of soul, not only with his underworld descent but by way of the three little words he put together: "Image *is* psyche."[19]

By "image" Jung meant the autonomy of inner images instead of images as copies of outer objects perceived by the senses—let alone the images of the media, advertising, or politics. He tied this sense of the imagination to the soul-dimension that the ancient Greeks expressed in the word *psyche*. Implicitly in Jung and more openly in Hillman's provocative writings, psychology is not the science of behavior (an empirical endeavor focused upon bodily activities), or even the scientific study of the mind (a cognitive operation confined mainly to the spiritual or *geistige* domain), but an essentially aesthetic meditation on the mysteries of soul. Similarly, psychotherapy, from this standpoint, is service to soul more than a repair of the ego's complaints.

Meanwhile, we have moved through several decades of "humanistic," "transpersonal," and New-Age psychologies and therapies with what looks like a *soul-less* holism, despite the best efforts of Hillman.[20] (We will want to wonder whether the same can be said for the evolution of neoshamanism in the most recent decades.) To become truly "whole," in other words, our holism needs its own healing, but lacks soul, and lacks the poetic imagination to "make" soul out of our lives in the world. For all its lofty harmonizing goals, holism as we have had it thus far could not care for the soul.

AT LEAST IT COULD not do so until Moore came along in 1992 with his bestseller *Care of the Soul*, and then a second one, *Soul Mates*, two years later (and a new offering, *The Re-Enchantment of Everyday Life*, has just been published).[21] Moore had trained to join a Roman Catholic monastic order but left it for the academic study of religion. He gained a doctorate from Syracuse University, where he studied with Hillman's theological colleague David Miller, and taught at several institutions. These included Southern Methodist University in Dallas, where he met Hillman himself and eventually apprenticed under him as a psychotherapist. Moore then left Dallas and the academic world in the mid-1980s, entering the practice of psychotherapy in Massachusetts.

Along the way, imbibing Hillman's rich brew of radically revisionist Jungianism and learning from his own work with patients, Moore began to write in behalf of a soul-based psychology. *The Planets Within*, his revised dissertation on the Renaissance astrology of Marsilio Ficino, begins with an introduction entitled "The Recovery of the Soul." *Rituals of the Imagination*, a small collection of essays on ritual, mythic sensitivity, and dreams of urban life, grew out of his work with the Dallas Institute of Humanities and Culture. And *Dark Eros*, an exploration of the strange life and ideas of the infamous Marquis de Sade, unflinchingly champions the need for "perverse" imaginings (but not sadistic acts) in our process of soul-making.[22]

These three books demonstrated the range of Moore's influences and interests. He also has a degree in musicology, and helped start an organization called the Institute for the Study of Imagination, inspired by Chopin's *Études* as an imaginative model of study, not as analysis but attention.

In 1989 Moore made contact with a larger audience when he compiled an anthology of Hillman's writings for Harper and Row, *A Blue Fire*.[23] Reading this book in particular, one can begin to see Moore's great skill in communicating ideas that in Hillman's hands are sometimes difficult to decipher. For example, Hillman's usual name for his brand of thought is "archetypal psychology," a seeming endorsement of Jung's debatable notion of the archetype as a transcendent essence or universal idea determining the patterns of our perception and behavior through clusters of similar images. But this would hardly fit with Hillman's emphasis on the primacy of the individual image as it shows itself.

Moore cuts through the confusion in *A Blue Fire* by stating bluntly that "archetypal psychology is not a psychology of archetypes. . . . This work is called *archetypal*, the adjective . . . because it seeks out the images in events that give rise to meaningfulness, value, and the full range of experience. It strives for depth, resonance, and texture in all that it considers."[24] Moreover, archetypes are explained not as metaphysical facts but as "fundamental fantasies," so that, in Moore's phrasing, "*archetypal* means 'fundamentally imaginal.'"[25]

This last phrase indicates very pointedly why I prefer the term "imaginal psychology" to describe the radical realization of Jung's legacy Hillman has made possible. And it is precisely the psychology that can redirect us toward a consciously Western shamanism whose re-visioned fantasies have led to imaginal realities, whose literalized fictions have been seen through to reveal the fictive power we need to "become sorcerers."

Of course the most crucial term of all continues to be "soul," which Moore, following Hillman, says "eludes reductionistic definition; it expresses the mystery of human life; and it connects psychology to religion, love, death, and destiny. It suggests depth. . . ."[26] In other words, soul, about which I will have even more to say, displays the very qualities Moore conveys to a wider audience in *Care of the Soul* and *Soul Mates*. In *A Blue Fire* he concluded his editorial prologue with a declaration about Hillman that points straight to his own subsequent success in breaking through a society of soullessness with a well-received message in his two enormously popular books:

> Hillman rarely writes about practice, yet his theory offers the basis for a radical approach to psychotherapy. . . . The great secret of archetypal psychotherapy is a love for what the soul presents, even those things the therapist and patient would love to make vanish. This love comes in many forms: interest, acceptance, faithfulness, desire, attachment, friendship, and endurance.[27]

The word "care," as Moore uses it, could sum up all these soul-loving nouns, and with his unusually sensitive—we could as well say loving—self-help books, the great secret of archetypal, or imaginal, psychotherapy is out: he has given Hillman's immensely important theory a practice ordinary people can follow without falling into a delusory step-by-step formula for perfect health or assured spiritual perfection. In this accomplishment Moore contributes something that extends significantly beyond (while not at all contradicting) what he has applied from Hillman: the possibility of a soulful spirituality.

It should be noted that Hillman, in his major work *Re-Visioning Psychology*, says that soul has "a religious concern."[28] Additionally, his article on the peaks of spirit and the vales of soul, which concentrates on the related distinction between spiritual disciplines and psychotherapy, includes a section on "the puer-psyche marriage." The Latin *puer* denotes the flighty youthful spirit in need of soul's grounding, the reflection brought to the puer by psyche's wounding, worrying, winding ways.

Although this "marriage" within the personality could involve a soulful form of spirituality—and it is also true that Hillman's passion for ideas could be seen as spiritual—it must finally be said that so staunch is his advocacy for soul in a soul-starved world that spirit seems to come off as the villain, threatening once more the wholeness of our holism. Moore puts this diplomatically in *A Blue Fire* when he says that his mentor "often takes a position that is sharply critical of spirituality, especially the kind of spirituality that seeks to escape or transcend the pleasures and demands of ordinary earthly life."[29]

And yet ordinary earthly life is exactly where Moore wants spirituality to be rooted, thus giving priority to a downward movement while not denying the value of the "magical flights" of spirituality—this vertical imagery very much recalling the legacy not only of Jung's descent but of Eliade's ascensional yearnings and their effect upon his definitive view of shamanism. It is an ironic likelihood, given the aim of "soul retrieval" surrounding neoshamanism, that it has inherited a tendency to a soulless spirituality. Certainly Moore shares Hillman's impatience with such an ungrounded spiritual practice, but more than Hillman he seeks to remedy it by exploring down-to-earth sacredness.

In *Care of the Soul* the central statement on this possibility is found in a section called "Spiritual Practice and Psychological Depth." Here Moore says that "the soul also needs spirituality, and as Ficino advises, a particular kind of spirituality: one that is not at odds with the everyday and the lowly."[30] As a concrete example of this soulfully spiritual practice, Moore refers to Jung's retreat tower at Bollingen on Lake Zurich and speaks of the importance of such retreats to spiritual practice. He suggests that retreats can be especially valuable in a modernist culture that is little concerned, in its manic technology and literalistic modes of knowing, with fostering the slower reflections of soulfulness. He also warns that "retreat itself can be either soulful or escapist. Some concrete, physical expressions of retreat, however, could be the beginning of a spiritual life that would nourish the soul."[31]

From Jung's Retreat to Hillman's Festival

Jung's Bollingen Tower, like the house I visited in Kusnacht with its book-lined study, may comprise another "secret room" where shamanism was born. In Jung's secret room, however, it was not so much a scholarly construct that was imagined, with magical flights upward, as with Eliade, or an abstracted universal essence, as with Harner and other comparativists. What was born with Jung was instead the possibility of turning this cross-cultural fantasy into a reality of the objective psyche—an underworld of daimonic images to which Western seekers could journey.

At Bollingen he had carved his block of stone, and wanted to inscribe "Le Cri de Merlin" on the back. In his Kusnacht study a photograph of the stone adorned his desk. Now he lies, like Merlin, invisible as in a tower of mist, his radical message perhaps imprisoned in that stone. But his calls sound still, awaiting our comprehension, challenging our imagination in such a way that only the emergence of a mindfully Western shamanism will suffice as a response. His calls "call the question" for a culture that seems virtually driven by a war against imagining.

How would a Western shamanism, conscious of its imaginal basis, care for the soul? That will be the focus of the balance of this book. But we have already learned that Jung's experience of the images of the objective psyche—of the images that *are* the objective psyche—together with the insights he drew from that experience and the elaborations of those insights made by successors like Hillman and Moore, is a crucial resource.

Jung definitely concerned himself with the phenomenon of soul-loss in indigenous cultures and in ours: one of his most popular books is entitled *Modern Man in Search of a Soul.* As someone whose psychology attempted to recover the lost souls of modern men and women, to honor radically the reality of the psyche in self and world, he is probably the closest example we have of a Western shaman in this century. He was not without his faults, and not all of his ideas are equally applicable to deconstructing the literalistic forms of neoshamanism *and* reconstituting the imaginal shamanism hidden in its core. However, without the life and thought of Jung, there would be no imaginal psychology of the sort Hillman, Moore, and others are so brilliantly building. But he did live and leave his legacy, which they have realized so that we can draw upon it as Western seekers after the soul of a shamanic spirituality.

I AM ON THE CAMPUS of Notre Dame University with Howard McConeghey, the art therapist who has become my friend in Albuquerque. We are walking to the building where the opening session of the Festival of Archetypal Psychology will be held. The July sun is oppressive, even at twilight, but we are both excited to be here, a strange Catholic setting, as it seems, to honor a secular Jew whose psychology speaks of inner daimons, Greek gods and goddesses as guides to understanding a multiplex psyche, and, occasionally, "Christianism" (Hillman's sarcastic reference to aspects of a religion he feels has monopolized the imagination of the West).

Howard has known Hillman for years, having been his host in Albuquerque at various times and having applied his ideas to the art therapy program he has run at the University of New Mexico. But Howard may have been as great an influence on Hillman as the other way around, at least in one crucial area.

A student of Fernand Léger who sought out Picasso and Gertrude Stein when he was a young GI shortly after the liberation of Paris in 1944, Howard is serious about art, and his large paintings testify that for him art therapy is not standard psychotherapy with expressive arts as a diagnostic adjunct. For him, art therapy is first and foremost about making art, a serious attempt beyond self-expression alone, and making art is about making soul. This means that art is at the center of imaginal psychotherapy, not on the periphery; art therapy is the true basis of any psychotherapy that seeks, as the name demands, to nurture psyche, to serve soul. The likely impact of these views on Hillman is shown by his new 1992 preface to his first book, *Emotion*, written thirty years earlier. In the new preface, he makes the very points about art therapy that Howard has been stressing and implementing with his students for years in New Mexico.[32]

Howard has a bushy white beard, a gravelly voice, and a fierce loyalty to Hillman. He is hard to miss in a crowd, even a crowd of several hundred, which is what we find when we enter the auditorium. It is 1992, a year after my experience in the auditorium at the University of Colorado hearing Mario Vargas Llosa talk about the power, positive as well as negative, of lies. Here at Notre Dame the topic will not be lying as such, but the fictive power of the imagination will be the subtext of every talk. Most of the post-Jungians I have mentioned are here, including Thomas Moore. Or rather, Moore will be here in a night or two, at Hillman's celebratory "roast," and will give a talk the next day.

The first night is given over to welcomes and introductions, and to the only presentation of the festival by Hillman himself. The expectation is that he will stun us with another unexpected salvo in behalf of soul, upsetting standardized psychological concepts—and conventional intellectual opinions—that depend upon a stable and single ego in charge of every self, an ego well-defended against the deeper needs of imaginal realities. He relishes the role of gadfly and does not disappoint on this night.

Hillman is tallish and slim, or he seems tall because he is slim. He has a sharp face, a prominent nose, and quick eyes—not unlike my father, I nervously realize, wondering about the personal basis of my attraction to his ideas. He could be a praying mantis, or a dancer. I am told that at his sixtieth birthday party in 1986 he donned a top hat and tails and did a Fred Astaire tapdance. He is only ten years older than I, and our direct interactions have been infrequent, but through his work he is very much another mentor, and I relish hearing his latest irreverent observations.

Howard and I are settled into our seats after greeting assorted post-Jungian cronies, some of whom, like Michael Whan and Alan Bleakley, Peter Bishop and Wolfgang Giegerich, have traveled here from overseas. What could Hillman talk about, we wonder, that would be upsetting at a Roman Catholic institution like Notre Dame? We have heard that he left the University of Dallas, another Catholic school, in part because of a controversy over inviting a speaker who had once written in behalf of euthanasia; the university had canceled the speaker's contract and Hillman had quit in protest. Would he revisit the issue of mercy-killing? Abortion? Birth Control? Pornography?

Pornography—and he is for it.

The Art of Uninhibited Imagining

I do not take notes on the wicked details of Hillman's talk, but the overall message is once again clear: the soul's imaginings have no regard for the ego's inhibitions, and the inhibiting of sexual fantasies is a cultural as well as personal loss. Furthermore, a psychology of soul can only attend appropriately to its imaginings by abandoning—Jung would have said relativizing—the exclusive concerns of the ego. Whatever the objective psyche, in its autonomy, presents is taken to have a necessity we do well to take seriously, despite any moral misgivings we may also harbor.

As with Moore's argument in *Dark Eros*, Hillman's defense of pornography is a plea for the power of fantasy, underscoring a point about imaginal psychology it is easy to neglect as we confuse it politely with other versions of Jungian thought or with assorted transpersonal views of "growth" that speak otherwise of "soul" or "creative visualization."

No images that come to us can be forbidden—though none need be acted upon. Indeed, it is a tenet of imaginal psychology that by remaining open to all forms of imagining, depressive and tormented (or salacious) images along with the uplifting ones, we reduce the need to act out what we are ashamed to imagine. This *radical* honoring of soul's expressions remains in force on the opening night of Hillman's festival. And it is *only* this radicalism of the image that makes imaginal psychology a resource for realizing a truly shamanic imagining.

However, the temptation to harmonize and sweeten, diluting the radicalism Hillman's talk reflects, is ever present. The wider culture of personal growth promotes it, and that culture is within most of us. It also dilutes imaginal psychology by disdaining intellectual activity. While post-Jungian psychology is not primarily a movement of the academic world—certainly not in psychology departments, or areas of cultural studies where neo-Freudianism is more in favor—it can nonetheless be intellectually demanding. Its initiations are definitely bookish; a space in theory must be cleared for imagination to be fully honored where conventional theories deflect or oppose such honoring. Nowhere is this more the case than in Hillman's difficult writings, despite his endorsement of hands-on art-making as soul-making.

BUT HOWARD, the artist and art therapist, has no problem with Hillman's intellectuality. Howard's paper, a day or so after the first evening's session, makes the point that both modern art and imaginal psychology represent a radical break with tradition. He also emphasizes that "psyche" and "aesthetics," in their original Greek meanings, come together around the central importance of a sense—and a sensing—of beauty, despite the afflicted images with which the soul must force our attention in the twentieth century as did the extreme expressions of modern art. He goes on to say that art and imaginal psychology are joined by their close attention to the world of things through imagination.

Howard's own personal bias among the various art media, he tells us, is toward the visual arts, which he feels are importantly continuous with the visual quality of dreams. On the other hand, he quotes from several poets and various theorists. Above all he stresses how Hillman's ideas are congruent with his way of teaching and doing art therapy.

Surely shamanism under any definition has its ties not only with the literary arts, as it does most dramatically in Western attempts at neoshamanism, but with the visual arts as well. As early as 1967 a book by Andreas Lommel appeared with the same encompassing title as Eliade's, which had been published in English only three years before: *Shamanism*. Lommel's subtitle is more interesting: *The Beginnings of Art*.[33]

The book is filled with evocative pictures of shamans' costumes and implements. These pictorial images have their own power, if only to provoke Western fantasies. Nevertheless, even where the latter is the case, their exoticism contains a secret magic from which an imaginal shamanism mindful of its fantasies can learn. Perhaps their power lies in echoing the otherness, the dangerously desirable alien reality, of the psyche itself. If engaging that inner otherness directly is too much for us, maybe aesthetic material—imaginal material—from other cultures, the more remote and "primitive" the better, must substitute.[34]

Unfortunately, this cross-cultural fascination has inevitably been accompanied by colonialism, and often still is, notwithstanding our best intentions and protestations of respect as heirs of a Western heritage that has been rapacious toward non-Western peoples. Fortunately, the psychoanalytic tradition, in particular its Jungian and post-Jungian stream, allows Westerners to find and be fascinated by their own strangeness—and to seek their shamanism there.

Shamans of some description, sometimes called the first psychoanalysts, may indeed have been the first artists; a strange figure on the Ice Age cave wall at Lascaux suggests as much. Some modern artists may feel their role follows these forebears: the "eye of the artist," Maureen Korp demonstrates, is some-times informed by the shamanlike "seeing" in the self-understanding of con-temporary painters and sculptors, especially those producing site-specific works.[35] Or the art works themselves may embody shamanic themes, as Michael Tucker states the same year as the festival in his 1992 book, *Dreaming with Open Eyes*.[36]

But whether psychoanalyst or artist, performer or curer, the shaman (recalling especially the culture of the Siberian Tungus people who gave us the term) has always also been a religious figure, a religious specialist. Admit-tedly what the scholars have imagined as "shamanism" has seldom been seen as a religion in itself, yet it never exists—at least until the advent of neoshamanism—outside of an explicitly religious context. Generally there has been some kind of animistic system, a "nature religion," within which shamanism operates as a set of spiritual healing practices.

THE ARRIVAL OF THOMAS MOORE

THE PERSON AT THE FESTIVAL who best represents a concern for spiritual practice—while not separating it from either psychotherapy or an aesthetic sense—is Thomas Moore, who arrives the evening of Hillman's roast. Every-one is buzzing about Patricia Berry's absence from the dais at the roast. Not only was she involved with whatever "founding" imaginal psychology can be said to have had in Zurich several decades ago, but Hillman was married to her for a time, and she has stories to tell. Hillman will be royally roasted by Berry the next day in her scheduled talk, but on this night even the sharpest barbs against him are uttered in great good humor.

And into this lively ambience, in a room full of tables of people half-full of dinner wine, saunters Moore. He is carrying his new baby daughter Siobhan, who has the red hair of her mother, Joan Hanley, an art therapist. Joan is a product, professionally, of Shaun McNiff's program at Lesley Col-lege in Cambridge, where I assume they met after Tom's move to Massachu-setts from Dallas almost a decade ago. I remember his phone call to me in Vermont asking my advice about where to settle in New England, and I have enjoyed being involved with him in programs of the Institute for the Study of Imagination he helped to start once he relocated to Massachusetts.

I have actually known Tom since the 1970s, and I greet him now dur-ing what is not a little like a triumphal entrance. *Care of the Soul* has appeared just this year. While it has not yet hit the bestseller lists, I know about the large advance Tom got for it from HarperCollins and the initial positive response it has received. The signs are that it will be a big hit.

Knowing this I also know the subtle or not-so-subtle pressures there must have been to make the book bland, sanitized, and sweetly inclusive rather than hard-edged in Hillman's way. When I sit down with Howard to listen to Tom the next morning, I am interested to hear how he has managed to market imaginal psychology without succumbing to the tug to harmonize soul with, say, New-Age notions of spiritual betterment.

FOR HIS PART, Tom is relaxed, articulate in a casual fashion, his considerable erudition worn very lightly. Although he does not discuss the actual machinations of working on the manuscript in relation to his editor's (and agent's) feedback, his manner appears to reflect the tone of the book. One of his greatest skills, I have already noticed over the years, is a graceful thought-style, flexible rather than formulaic.

In his remarks this morning on the care of the soul, Tom reminds us of the advice of his fifteenth-century guide Marsilio Ficino: when you are presented with two alternatives, choose both. He also grants that his psychology in the new book is in a sense sentimental, adding that he thinks he has some consciousness about it. He feels there is a place for an ennobling version of imaginal psychology, especially since he has already written in favor of the Marquis de Sade—if you consult de Sade's writings, he tells an inquirer, "your darkness might pick up some imagination." Darkly or sentimentally, he is absolutely serious about applying imaginal psychology to the everyday ways we actually live our lives. And this, too, lends a legitimate simplicity to his literary efforts.

I find his comments encouraging and persuasive. Indeed, I find them impressive; I am envious of his deeply irenic style, not oversimplifying or papering over differences. It becomes clear to me—and I have not yet read the new book—that Tom knows all about the differences, the oppositions, in which Hillman's thought places such great stock. In the case of the most consequential one, the opposition between spirit and soul, he has shown me the possibility of a truly soulful spirituality. (Later, reading his text, I will detect beneath his pleasant narrative that he wants a spirituality dependent upon soul more than the reverse, an agreeable nod in Hillman's direction.) At every point, though usually with little fanfare, he privileges the imagination.

His substantive ideas in the talk concern spiritual practice as a soulfully grounded activity that can learn much from formal religion, once the latter is re-visioned out of its contentiousness over the factual truth of its beliefs and seen more as powerful sets of images and stories. Tom makes no bones about his Roman Catholic monastic training or the fact that the title of his book is taken from the Catholic tradition. That tradition refers to the *cura animarum*, the care of souls, and a priest is also referred to, he points out, as a "curate" who nurtures the spiritual needs of parishioners. But there is a Protestant tilt to his Catholicism: a "priesthood of all believers" in a therapeutic culture.

Nonetheless, his preoccupation with spiritual practice is real enough, and, as with Howard's talk on art therapy, I am again curious, here at the end of the festival, about the connections there might be to shamanism.

I have already given my paper, and the people who were there seemed to like what I said. But no one else has presented on my topic. No one else has been directly working on shamanism in relation to post-Jungian psychology, nor had I heard of such work in writing my paper, though I later learn that Shaun McNiff's book *Art as Medicine* comments on this relationship.[37] I had not, of course, heard either Tom's or Howard's presentations when I wrote it. Having now had a chance to see how their ideas could inform mine, I realize there are further points to be made about how an imaginal shamanism is possible, how it can be a spiritual practice for the West, both artful and soulful.

I will have to write a book, I decide, beginning with an assessment, based on Jung's legacy in imaginal psychology, of neoshamanism from Eliade to Castaneda to its current shamanthropologists and workshop leaders. Once having demonstrated the centrality of imagining to that short history, I will need to gather the resources for not only understanding this imagining but showing how it can be the basis for a Western shamanism in practice as well as theory, in dreams and reveries, suffering and healing, as well as in the words and thoughts that support them. Indeed, I will have to write a book about the soul of such a shamanism.

6

DREAMING THE UNDERWORLD JOURNEY

Every night we dream, scientists say in their sleep labs, with their ideas about Rapid Eye Movements and EEGs and brain scans. They tell us we simply do not always recall the experience, though other observers suggest the dreams we "recall" are the only ones we have. Either way, when we do remember or record, we say "I had a dream last night," thus in one innocent phrase shrinking and seizing possession of something that has had *us*. For we know that when we dream we are in the dream, it surrounds us, not vice versa. So is this way of speaking already a resistance, an initial defense against the reality of dreaming? Is it the verbal equivalent of the caffeine with which, each morning, we crush the images of the dream in preparation for a workaday world, the shared world of the modern West, that wants nothing to do with that other world, the otherworld or underworld where dreaming happens?

The first principle of work with dreams should be: "Do no harm to the dream." But immediately upon awakening there is a danger of harm being done, whether with words or chemicals. The war against the underworld begins with these intimate errors.

More insidiously, though just as innocently, we harm the dream by interpreting it in the ways our culture has taught. The dream may be an endangered habitat or species—like an indigenous tribe seen as "savages" to be wiped out by Western colonial powers—that we are killing with concepts, meeting its wild images with our attempts to control and domesticate, if not destroy.

None of our common Western interpretive maneuvers with dreaming serves an imaginal shamanism, so in seeking the latter we must realize such innocent moves as dangers. We must go in another direction, downward into the underworld, as respectful travelers on a shamanic journey not of conquest—Freud called himself a "conquistador" in *The Interpretation of Dreams*—but of attentive conversation, equal dialogue, perhaps even apprenticeship.

What Freud started Carl Jung continued, though with a less colonialist ideal to subdue and enslave. But if Jung opened a different avenue to dream workers, most have not taken it. The conquering ego with its self-serving concepts continues to dominate the dream, whatever school of psychological interpretation is employed, a century after Freud, to do the dirty work. Just as the main varieties of contemporary psychology have forgotten their field's obligation, inscribed in its name, to understand soul (or in psychotherapy to serve soul), so the ruling approaches in the field resist the reality of a phenomenon which, after all, remains stubbornly irrational in the face of our sophisticated science.

To the extent that psychology has styled itself a science, turning away from Hillman's idea of the poetic basis of mind, it has turned itself into an enemy of the dream, whose phenomenology rebukes the methods modern psychologies use to interpret it. This is most obvious in the most scientific versions of psychology, where the dream is seen as the brain's nightly biochemical voiding of meaningless waste products. It is easy for those of us who value our dreams to look askance at—or simply look away from—such hard-nosed dismissals that master the dream by redefining it out of existence (once again, as with caffeine ingestion, chemicals are used to conquer dreams).

We are less aware that our well-intentioned analyses wield just as sharp a sword against the poor savage dream. The possibility of a shamanic imagining for Western seekers depends upon opposing this war on the underworld, the West's oppression of the Southern unconscious by the Northern ego.

THE WESTERN WAR AGAINST THE UNDERWORLD

LIAM HUDSON, neither a Jungian nor a post-Jungian, but a wise and even-handed English observer of dream theories, concurs with me in making the same claim. In his book *Night Life: The Interpretation of Dreams* he begins by noting on the first page that, in the years since Freud opened the century with his great dream book, "our very access to our dream experience has at times been threatened" and that the field of dream research "is one in which, amidst the clamour, the vigour of the dream itself is at risk."[1] He characterizes the field as divided between those in the psychoanalytic tradition who see dreams as encoded messages from the unconscious and those with more scientific training who view dreams as nonsense, the clap-trap of soft computers getting rid of their garbage. His aim is to chart a middle course between these contrasting approaches, exploring the overlap of dreams, dream language, with poetry—and thus with the ambiguity of poetry.

Hudson suggests that as ambiguous messages, dreams accord with both psychoanalytic and brain biochemistry approaches. While he scarcely seems to allow that dreams admit us to an underworld that might be shamanic, his appeal to poetry as a means of explanation sounds like James Hillman, and the audience he intends to address could include those of us who have an imaginal shamanism in mind:

> . . . to those for whom the dream is inherently an object of fascination; to those eager to know how the imagination manages, against all odds, to subvert the dull tramp of habit; and to the conceptually alert—those who realise that psychological explanation, the business of setting a thought to catch a thought, constitutes a mystery as strange in its way as dreaming itself.[2]

Hudson's book does not cite Hillman's work, and *Night Life* does not follow a post-Jungian path. Still, its sense of the mystery of psychological thought is in line with Hillman's concern for a soul psychology and leads toward a shamanic relationship with dreams in the modern West. Hudson even acknowledges that dream theories are themselves a species of dream, "often true in the sense that they are compelling or fertile, without necessarily being true at the level of fact. . . ."[3]

He reminds us, for instance, that Freud's dream interpretation scheme was revealed to him, or so he thought, by a specific dream on the night of July 24, 1895.[4] Jung had his own "theoretical dream" that suggested the idea of levels of consciousness and the unconscious, personal and collective, an idea from which his psychological theory, including his theory of dreams, derived.[5] The psychoanalytic tradition in psychology, in valuing dreams as expressions of the unconscious, threatens the dream less with its theories than do more scientific sorts of psychology. The scientists think *their* dream theories are "true at the level of fact." Thus they can dispense with actual dreams since their concepts, they presume, are free of dream qualities.

NEVERTHELESS, BOTH STREAMS of psychology pose threats to the dream, as Hudson concludes in attempting to reconcile them by building his own theory of dreams as poetic statements. We could say more specifically that for Hudson the very danger of the dream—its wildness, its radical independence from ego concerns—is what is endangered.

Maybe that is why analogies from ecology and ethnography suggest themselves to Hudson as ways to grasp the extent of the threat to dreaming posed by modern behavioral science and even by psychoanalysis (or by Hudson's own position in between). We may be killing the dream, he fears, as we are killing the cultures which gave us what we have fantasized as shamanism—while thinking that such fantasies are "true at the level of fact," since part of our warfare is directed against the value of acknowledged fantasies. It is all the same attack, and we are victims *and* perpetrators.

"The dream is of its essence feral," Liam Hudson concludes, "and the attempt to impose *any* matrix of schemes and procedures could constitute a form of domestication."[6] The feral dream, wild imagining—like those wild lands and wild people south of the border that Freud's image of the conquistador would colonize and control for king (the ego) and country (Western science)—is at risk from the same forces in our culture that suppressed as superstition the shamanism now sought by the same culture through literalized fantasies. It will require a revolution in dream work to prevent what has happened to many indigenous peoples, wild habitats, and undomesticated species from happening to the dream.

James Hillman is a psychological revolutionary who can help us make this refusal. His theory, or anti-theory, about dreams is strikingly different from all but the most imaginal aspects of Jung's legacy in being *deliberately* dreamlike if not from a single dream such as the ones that shaped Freud's and Jung's concepts. Understanding Hillman's radical attitude toward dream work will necessitate painstaking attention to his book from 1979, *The Dream and the Underworld*, for that understanding is not easily acquired. But in gaining it we are already being initiated into the underworld journey as Westerners mindful of our shamanic fantasies.

AGAINST DREAM INTERPRETATION

I SUPPOSE HILLMAN'S approach to working with dreams could be called anti-Western as well as an anti-theory, since he opposes so much of what the modern West has done with dreams. But he does follow in the tradition of Freud and Jung, developing the latter's radical legacy of respect for the imagining soul. And he draws deeply from older Western resources, underground springs of shamanic possibility, starting with the image of the underworld.

This metaphor, a way of honoring the imaginal environment of dreams as a separate reality, is deliberately far from modern models of the mind such as the machine or computer that insult the dream, promising impossibly automatic "access" to unambiguous "information." The underworld of Greek myth, on the other hand, allows us as Westerners to meet dreaming on its own metaphoric ground—to go, for once, in the direction of the dream, to see without evasion what and how it is saying. A theory of dreams that is guided by this metaphor is already a vehicle for a journey.

Hillman's book about this gives no simple steps to unlocking dream messages for fun and profit, or even for clear-cut meanings. As we have seen with Hudson, the act of dream analysis or interpretation itself subtly wrongs the dream, substituting a well-ordered conceptual singleness for the feral independence of its elusive and multiplex dream images. Hillman therefore attempts something that is as necessary as it is inconvenient, and absolutely indispensable for an imaginal shamanism: he tries in his book to set forth an approach that does not interpret dreams.

That is, while he imagines a theoretical perspective that attempts to see the phenomenon of the dream as we actually experience it, he does not advance a symbology, an interpretive scheme for assigning symbolic meanings to particular dream images. For Hillman the tangled and elusive quality of the imagining soul is something to which he gives full priority in his overall psychology. It is also something he practices unapologetically in his writing style, including the writing of his dream book. The literalist in us may not like his wordplay—and it may not always work—but it is also necessary to realize how revolutionary he *has* to be with words to serve soul and honor its dreaming.

Hillman's suggestions about how to relate to the imagery of dreams are difficult to follow—as obscure, sometimes, as the dreams themselves. It is out of respect for the integrity of inner images that he resists the usual interpretive move, nowhere more evident than when we work with dream material, of translating from the soul language of imagination to the spirit language of conceptualization. This is a move of the colonizing Western ego to exploit the wilderness of the psyche. It is a move we should join him in opposing if we want to find our way to shamanic imagining and journey to the underworld.

The question then becomes: how can we avoid conceptual interpretation—images translated as symbols for concepts—and do justice to the dream?

In *The Dream and the Underworld* , the answer to this question is complex and subtle because it is radical, going to the deep roots of dreaming as an expression of soul's imagining. As dream workers we need to approach the dream's imaginal depth with a suitably deep imagining on our own part, with a "container" that is not conceptual, not scientific, not materialistic or physiological, let alone technological. We need to hold the reality of the dream in waking consciousness without resorting to any of these literalisms. And for Hillman, as we have anticipated, the container that meets this criterion is the ancient Greek mythology of Hades, which matches in *its* nonliteralistic depth the nonliteralistic depth of the dream, likewise evoking endless mystery and poetic ambiguity and coming from the depths of the West's own cultural memory.

To make possible a journey to this underworld, a re-visioning of Western dream theory that re-visions the dream and re-visions in behalf of the endangered dream, Hillman offers three metaphoric bridges. By traversing these as we traversed Jung's bridge to the objective psyche, we make a modern or postmodern reconnection to dream realities paralleling shamanic realms of initiation. Hillman provides a "bridge backward" into the historical past, including the history of psychology along with that of Greek mythology; a "bridge downward" of delving deeply, sticking to the image of depth that is inherent in the post-Jungian sense of soul; and a "bridge inward" to the psyche of the Western individual, the storytellers, scholars, and seekers who populate this book on the soul of shamanism and for whom it is written.[7] But Hillman cautions that

> it is [the] dayworld style of thinking—literal realities, natural comparisons, contrary opposites, processional steps—that must be set aside in order to pursue the dream into its home territory. There thinking moves in images, resemblances, correspondences. To go in this direction, we must sever the link with the dayworld, foregoing all ideas that originate there—translation, reclamation, compensation. We must go over the bridge and let it fall behind us, and if it will not fall, then let it burn.[8]

THESE ARE REVOLUTIONARY words indeed, equal to the requirements of a shamanic dream journey for people in a culture that has tried to wipe out both shamans and dreams—even while idealizing each. Perhaps *by means of* idealizing each, in fantasies that, so long as they are blind, serve mainly the desires and conveniences of ego.

While Freud's interpretive direction was, from Hillman's standpoint, away from the dream, he did refer to the ancient underworld in a line from Virgil's *Aeneid* about moving the underworld river Acheron that he chose for the motto of *The Interpretation of Dreams*. This leads Hillman to an important observation. "Mythology," he says, "is a psychology of antiquity. Psychology is a mythology of modernity."[9] This reiterates his message about modern psychology in *The Myth of Analysis*, but underscores as well the psychological contribution of ancient mythology, suggesting from another angle the pertinence of the Greek realm of Hades to a modern psychology of the dream.

The difference between Hillman's dream psychology and Freud's, then, and to some extent Jung's, is that Hillman's is, again, *intentionally* mythic in its style and language. It mindfully acknowledges its own imaginal status, as we must do with any form of shamanism we can claim as Westerners.

With his various assertions and the very rhetoric of his writing, Hillman attempts, through this deliberate mythologizing, to render a respectful service to the dream. And this is assuredly reflected in his open emphasis upon the underworld as the mythic "place," the appropriate placement, of our dreaming. Having positioned dreams there in our thinking about them, we Westerners are given the best possible perspective from which to see their significance. "Underworld," he indicates, "is the mythological style of describing a psychological cosmos."[10] Since psychology, in his view, is ultimately mythological in modern culture, this style is entirely fitting.

Dreams and their underworld, it should not surprise us, are also linked by Hillman to depression, as even the word itself implies: "the dream takes us downward,"[11] he repeatedly stresses. A therapy that reflects the depths of the dream world will therefore underscore what he calls "the disintegrative effects of the dream."[12] This is the process he elsewhere calls "pathologizing," or "falling apart," the sacred wounding by which soul is made and which we will explore further in Chapter 8 as a version of shamanic initiatory dismemberment. Here it can be said, as Mircea Eliade says of the shaman, that suffering is given a spiritual value,[13] and that healing must go beyond band-aid cures.

Indeed, healing with Hillman is more than anything a deep change of attitude, including a change of attitude toward our dreams. This in turn involves an adjustment, if not an abandonment, of what he terms "ego-heroics."

It is the ego, as we have already glimpsed, that wants to interpret dream images so that they "mean" concepts satisfying to its well-ordered view of itself and the world. (It is the ego that tells us when we awaken that we "had" a dream and rushes us to the coffee-maker to forget.) Like Hercules the hero, entering the underworld to overcome it, clean it out, and shape it up—a Western colonizer subduing the species of the South—the ego's dominance wrongs the dream, wrongs its images, and thereby wrongs the soul. But a psychotherapy true to its name, we have learned, will serve psyche or soul. And this means that its dream work will not translate the soul's images in the service of the ego. And so continually in *The Dream and the Underworld*, Hillman denounces interpretation itself mainly in the sense of an ego manipulation of the soul images of dreaming.

To guard against drifting into an *ego*therapy in our approach to dreaming, Hillman provides his elusive shift of attitude or perspective—itself a journey with shamanic ramifications, maybe all the underworld journey there is to make—in place of conceptual interpretation schemes. In this respect he counsels that "because the dream speaks in images, or even *is* images . . . because dreaming is imaging, our instrument for undistorted listening can only be the imagination."[14]

SOUL WORK WITH DREAMS AS THE WAY TO THE UNDERWORLD

THE SECOND HALF of *The Dream and the Underworld* consists only of two long chapters, one simply entitled "Dream," the other called "Praxis"—a hint that there will be some advice about how to practice Hillman's shift to noninterpretation. There are indeed some specifics in these chapters that are worth exploring as signposts on the underworld journey.

For instance, Hillman says,

> the right work with dreams parallels what the dream is already doing . . . dying to the dayworld by ruminating [digesting] it from literal realities into metaphorical realities. The more I dream of my mother and father, brother and sister, son and daughter, the less these actual persons are as I perceive them in my naive and literal naturalism and the more they become psychic inhabitants of the underworld.[15]

This is a striking insight, opposite to our usual certainty that if I have seen my uncle the day before the dream, or the week before, and he appears in the dream, that is "why" I dreamed about him. Hillman's move makes power animals out of my friends and relatives: once they are in my dream, they are figures of imagining, not a comforting link to dayworld issues that my ego wants explained.

In 1974, five years before Hillman's dream book, Patricia Berry published a long article in *Spring* that surely must have influenced her colleague and then husband (and he does refer to it in *The Dream and the Underworld*). It was called "An Approach to the Dream," and it presses the idea that a dream is more than anything an image. What she and Hillman mean by this, and what an imaginal shamanism must learn, is very precise, and comes from Jung. "Following Jung, by image we '. . . do not mean the psychic reflection of an external object, but a concept derived from poetic usage, namely, a figure of fantasy or *fantasy-image*. . . .'"[16] As ever, even in its early years, post-Jungian imaginal psychology cultivates its connections, and those of Jung, to the arts, to poetry and fiction, paintings and plays.

Here the aesthetic sense of image is reiterated in order to emphasize a crucial point about the difference between my day-uncle and my dream-uncle that can return us to Hillman. Unlike hallucinations, whether psychotic or psychedelic, which claim external perceptual reality, "with imagination any question of objective referent is irrelevant," Berry insists. "The imaginal is quite real in its own way, but never *because* it corresponds to something outer."[17]

But does not my day-uncle in the dream contradict this important principle of the nonfactual reality of the imaginal? Berry is aware of this objection and meets it: "Certainly the familiar figure must be some sort of afterimage or *Tagesrest* [day-residue]." As a Jungian analyst she has a way of countering this approach to the dream, and then worries that a more radical, post-Jungian strategy may be required. Most Jungians

> . . . call them products of the personal unconscious and then seek to sort out the projections they carry for us. So far, so good, for it seems what we're really doing is attempting to redeem these images from their perceptual imprisonment and to reclaim them as psychic, thereby shifting our standpoint from the perceptual to the imaginal.

> But this cannot take place, our exit from this perceptual world becomes blocked, our movement stuck, when we deal with these so-called personal figures on a personal level, forgetting that they are fundamentally fantasy-images *cloaked* in after-images. . . . When my spouse, children, or friend appear in my dream, they have become to some extent removed from the 'reality' of the perceptual world with which they are so closely associated. The dream offers the opportunity to make metaphorical these figures, and thus the psyche may be seen as working toward the imaginal, away from the perceptual—repetitively and insistently.[18]

LIKE HILLMAN AFTER HER, Berry speaks of shifting our standpoint: it is this shift that allows for an imaginal shamanism in regard to the underworld journey of dreaming. It allows that world to be truly "other," a nonordinary realm beyond the ego's control. And perhaps it is even parallel to the shift from ordinary perception to "seeing" in the Castaneda stories.

However, as Berry warns, our exit from this perceptual world—in effect, our shamanic dream journey as the soul's repetitive and insistent work—can be thwarted at the outset if we literally take personal figures, like my day-uncle, only as representatives of our ordinary waking life. Even the ego, as a participant in the dream, our "I" as a dreamer or dream ego, is not to be taken literally as our waking ego, but becomes another image of the dreaming soul, a "shade" in terms of the ancient Greek underworld, dying to its dayworld identity. Hillman underscores this difficult aspect of his revolutionary dream theory by saying that ". . . the first move in teaching the ego how to dream is to teach it about itself, that it too is an image. . . . The dream is not 'mine,' but the psyche's, and the dream-ego merely plays one of the roles in the theatre, subjected to what the 'others' want, subject to the necessities staged by the dream."[19]

Day-residues from our familiar lives offer themselves as matter to be made into soul through imagining. They thus stand as guardians of the gate as we embark on the underworld journey of dreaming. They can block our way if we take them as literal figures pointing us back to the dayworld; or they can provide a portal if we see them, see through them, as fantasy images from the underworld, inviting our descent.

Hillman's work with dreams, perhaps because it is so impossible to pin down, invites the altered consciousness—and, maddeningly, requires the ordeal for consciousness—that can initiate an underworld journey not just as an intellectual concept but, admitting its obvious intellectuality, a felt experience of mind. What it takes, as traditional shamans may agree, is a surrender of ego expectations of clear-cut explanation. This is a discipline of soulful spirituality that workshop neoshamanism, for all its declarations of experiential immediacy, seldom demands.

Still, something in us—Hillman would say our dayworld ego— wants to know exactly how to work with the dream experience, wants steps to a clear-cut practice, and resists the slow apprenticeship that the underworld journey requires if we would honor it fully and find its shamanic elements. Like a shamanic calling, however, not a set of unambiguous instructions is necessary, but an initiation.

Certainly, as we have already seen, Hillman offers no such step-by-step instructions, and it is the ego which wants them that must be initiated out of its attitude, taught to exit from its dayworld agenda. The ability to work with the deliteralizations of dreaming depends upon this sort of shift, as was also implied above. Nevertheless, we do not start out as initiated travelers, so we want to know just how this shift will be brought about.

WORK ON DREAMS FOLLOWS THE WORK OF DREAMS

HILLMAN WILL NOT cooperate, giving us more mythic images instead, including the figure of Hermes as our teacher, our guide, and Hercules as the imaginal stand-in for the heroic ego in each of us. But we are, or can be, Hermes as well in our work with dreams.

The dream worker's role is to guide the ego to the underworld like Hermes. He "takes souls down" as a psychopomp or conductor of souls, whereas "the hero standing behind the ego tries to bring them back up again."[20] We could also say the conventional dream interpreter is this same kind of hero who wants to drag dream images "back up again" by explaining them with conclusive concepts. "For us," Hillman continues, "this means that our heroic ego is uninitiated and that our nightly descent into dreaming is a mode of initiation. This means a radical reversal of theory. . . . [The dream] does not complete ego-consciousness, but voids it. So it matters very much the way we descend."[21]

To make dreaming a shamanic journey we must not go down, as we are inclined to do, in the way of Hercules. Hercules descends in resistance to the initiation of the dream, storming the underworld to take rather than to learn like Ulysses or Aeneas. Unlike these more respectful visitors who have their dayworld lives changed by the descent, Hercules needs Hermes' assistance because he meets the shades of the underworld as though they were literal realities. Consequently, "the shades themselves had fled on his arrival, like dreams that disappear from the daylight mind,"[22] and Hermes had to tell him that a vision he drew his sword at was actually an image.

Hercules, says Hillman, "seems unable to imagine (he has already slain the imaginary beasts, the animal powers of imagination, and washed away the shit of the animals' home where imagination breeds in putrefaction)."[23] Imagination, we might say, *happens*, as in the dreams that come to us unbidden—we can do nothing about it, really. Once it does happen, however, it matters very much how we "deal with it," and Hercules' way is not how.

The shamanic journey, especially as Mircea Eliade has classically described it, might seem to be a heroic one such as Hercules made, or such as our egos make each night, but Hermes is a far better model for an imaginal shamanism. Uninitiated Hercules does not know how to interact with the images of the underworld: his goal is total control or mastery. No shamanic healing wisdom can come from such a failed encounter. If we follow Hercules, we do not even try the journey, for we have not left behind our dayworld attitudes.

With a respectful theory, or anti-theory, of the dream, on the other hand, we can let the dreaming experience itself be our Hermes, seeing not symbols for dayworld meanings but lessons in how we can enter fully into the journey calling us as we "fall" asleep. Hillman advises, "we can discover the hero in ourselves when in a dream the ego acts aggressively toward what it suspects, what is unfamiliar, and what is autonomous (animals). Also, heightened activity gives us away—rushing, change of scene, leaving for the next task, and speeding through space in chariots of locomotion."[24]

Now, short of controlled lucid dreaming (which can be even more the work of the dayworld ego), we cannot dictate what our dream ego does in the dream, whether it is acting heroic or learning its lessons from Hermes. However, as dayworld dream workers we can withhold our encouragement from herculean maneuvers in the underworld, refusing to adopt the dream ego perspective—especially when it is performing like Hercules—as the defining way to interact with the figures and events of the dream, the defining way to descend. The apprenticeship we must serve is to learn how the dream initiates the ego and to support that process.

It could be said that our underworld journey starts with our work in the day, with a dream attitude that lets us work interactively with the phenomenon, but such work is instructed by attending to what the dream itself has to teach. Here is where Hillman is at his most passionate:

> The initiation of the heroic ego—learning the metaphorical understanding of the dream—is not only a "psychological problem," only for the sophistication of the therapy session. It is cultural, and it is vast and crucial. The culture-hero Hercules as well as our mini-herculean egos . . . is a killer among images. The image makes it mad, or rather evokes its madness, because heroic sanity insists on a reality that it can grapple with, aim an arrow at, or bash with a club. . . . The heroic ego literalizes the imaginal. Because it lacks the metaphorical understanding that comes with image-work, it makes wrong moves, and these violently.[25]

In statements such as this Hillman indicates in the strongest possible terms—here from the standpoint of the history as well as the psychology of Western culture—the extent of the barriers to truly imaginal work with dreams, and to a truly imaginal shamanism. His fervent denunciation of the herculean ego laying waste to the underworld jibes with Hudson's quieter fears about the endangerment of the dream.

And yet Jung has opened a door for both imaginal dream work and imaginal shamanism. And Hillman with his colleagues is leading us through it, showing with the greatest care what dreaming the underworld journey entails.

BECAUSE THE EGO is so opposed to the images of the dream underworld, our conscious dream work must assist in initiating it, converting it, teaching it, while keeping the experience of the dream alive. "Like Hermes with Hercules, we take the dream-ego as an apprentice, learning to familiarize itself with the underworld by learning how to dream and learning how to die."[26]

The shamanic parallels are especially strong here, since the picture we have of the shaman's initiatory ordeal typically includes some kind of death or dismemberment during the ecstatic trance-journey. By having visited death, having been broken down to basic elements, and then having been reconstructed and returned, the shaman acquires the secret of life, the power of healing. But there is no round-trip ticket for the journey if truly taken: the return, as Michael Taussig reminds us, is never guaranteed.

Unless we make contact with our wounding—Hillman's "pathologizing"—the imaginal journey will prove superficial. We wish each other "pleasant dreams" because they usually are not pleasant, but this is exactly the hard schooling we have to have for any hope of healing power to be realized. Our dream work can teach us the "death" we must face for shamanic rebirth to happen. Every night this difficult lesson is taught in many big and little ways to the resistant ego; with the help of dayworld work this hero can die to his or her literalism in the dreamworld down below.

But how does this initiatory apprenticeship proceed, we still may ask, if the ego, like Hercules, is indeed violently resistant to the underworld images of the dream? Once again Hillman provides no simple method, and those psychologists who might do so do not help us toward the soulful spirituality of an imaginal shamanism.

Nevertheless, we have earlier had some guidance about how to regard "day-residues," those familiar figures from our lives who become images in the underworld. We have also seen from several angles how the ego in the dream is an obstacle to the journey. We have even found how recourse to mythic models—starting with the Greek underworld itself—is more helpful to our interactions with dreaming than scientific research or conceptual interpretation.

In addition, there are intimations in *The Dream and the Underworld* about how Hillman's recommended attitude shift might be put into practice. Just keeping the dream itself alive, for instance, by avoiding interpretations that kill its images, is a crucial idea that is really the first piece of "practical advice" Hillman hands to the dream worker.

> It is not what is said about the dream after the dream, but the experience of the dream after dream. . . . The dream is effective as long as it remains alive.
> . . . It is better to keep the dream's black dog before your inner sense all day than to "know" its meaning (sexual impulses, mother complex, devilish

aggression, guardian, or what have you). . . . For a dream image to work in life it must . . . be experienced as fully real.[27]

Here a colleague like Robert Bosnak, whose book *A Little Course in Dreams* spends an unusual effort on the process of dream recall, can supplement Hillman's perspective. For Bosnak, memory is deeply intertwined with imagination, and can be enticed toward the imaginings of the dream through exercises his book describes.

Seeing a dream as "a happening in space, an articulation of space," which we may later misrepresent as a completed story, he begins with a view not very far from Hillman's reliance on the mythic image of the underworld (and close to Taussig's idea about shamanic narratives). Bosnak then observes that "we find ourselves in a space called 'dream' upon awakening. . . . During the dream we believe we are awake, in the same way that we believe we are awake when we truly are. That's why it is important to remember dreams as spatial structures, so that our experiences in dream space can be most adequately recalled."[28]

Although Hillman insists that "the forgotten dream is the dream resisting to be remembered," apparently contradicting Bosnak, he goes on to speculate that this is "perhaps because memory has been put into the yoke of the dayworld and the forgotten dream refuses this service."[29] Clearly Bosnak's exercises in dream recall have to do with imaginal memory, remembering in service to the underworld. His book provides a practice for keeping the dream alive, and he combines his emphasis on recall with Jung's process of "active imagination" in a way that we will want to consult.

DYING TO THE DAYWORLD

IT OUGHT TO BE made clear that with Bosnak as with Hillman the term "dream work" is not used to refer to what Freud saw as the dream's own mechanisms for disguising the expression of repressed wishes. However, with Hillman, as has already been hinted, "the work on dreams follows the work of dreams."[30] He would have us all be teacher's aides to our or others' dreams. And in "following" its work we do not unravel or reverse that work as Freud did in interpreting dreams. Rather, we are to "respond to its work with the likeness of our work, all the while aiming to speak like the dream, imagine like the dream."[31]

Even the concept of "work" is re-visioned here from its own herculean associations, and once more the dream teaches us how. We should, says Hillman, "return the idea of work to the example of the dream, where work is an imaginative activity, a work of imagination such as takes place in painters and writers."[32]

This journey may not be a labor of Hercules, but it bears repeating that such work, even when playful, is by no means easy, as artists know very well. According to Hillman, "Each dream is practice in entering the underworld, a preparation of the psyche for death."[33] In one sense, then, experiencing the dream fully is itself the "praxis" that imaginal dream workers must engage in.

The emphasis on death, again, as in the underworld being the house or land of the dead, is a constant in Hillman's writing. It has to do with enriching life through soul-making. Like the shaman, we have said, we must in some way be dismembered, must fall apart, to be healed—or perhaps it is *in* disintegration, the difficult demotion of the ego as only and eternal authority for the self, that healing happens, almost as a by-product. The riches that Greek myth attributes to Hades, otherwise known as Pluto, may only be available by adopting his deathly perspective, seeing his dark "night-residues" in our days.

Along with death and the imagery of wounding we are counseled as dream workers to "pay special attention to *whatever is below*." Especially valued in Hillman's practice of dream work are "the emotions that go with these images of bottoming . . . [namely:] reluctance, loathing, sadness, mourning, inhibition, enclosure, lethargy, or that sense of depth that presses on us as depression, oppression, suppression. Our downward imagination has entered the earth."[34] To be a journey that truly goes to a world that is *under* involves alertness to the dream's depressions.

Now that we are down in the underworld with an imaginal attitude, avoiding literal perspectives and heroic projects, initiating the ego and attending to the emotional bottoming brought by the dream images we keep alive in the day, what might a closing chapter on practice ("Praxis") possibly add to a book that exemplifies the idea that "what we practice is theory"?[35] What might it teach us about an imaginal shamanism that can provide Westerners with a soulful spirituality?

Let us try to find out by starting, finally, with a dream:

I am on top of a high cliff overlooking the ocean, perhaps in Cornwall, England, near Penzance. Below, all alone, is my boat, a white, long, narrow rowboat. I know I have to retrieve it. It is early morning and I am waiting until it's warmer. I'm on a perch or ledge or pole, and I realize there's no way to get down except to jump, and I wonder why I didn't plan this retrieval better. But then I am at a tiny beach with a sort of surfboard and realize I can try to paddle out to get the boat. The only problem is when I start to do so I find myself in a crowded harbor and I know this isn't where the boat is. So I start walking to my left to get beyond the harbor, but there are many necks or inlets. A male friend—unidentified—accompanies me as we try to work our way to the left through the neighborhoods of the harbor town. At one point I realize I'd forgotten that what I'm trying to get to is a boat and had been confusing it with the surfboard. We go through some sort of fish-processing plant where there is a guy with a map of the town which he shows us and which my friend later snatches away from him. We continue on and meet a woman, youngish, who takes us in this lit-tle room to meet an older man whom she says she's divorcing. The man looks familiar from television: a lined face, blond-mixed-with-grey curly hair. He says he knows my book and plays a little record of him discussing it. The alarm wakes me up and the name Carl Nielsen comes to me, though I know that's the name of a big-shot classical composer from Scandinavia.

This seems a fairly ordinary dream, my dream, not a particularly "big" or archetypal one full of overtly mythic images. The feeling-tone was first fear-ful on the high cliff, but merely "concerned" thereafter, though in waking life I cannot swim, do not surf, have never had a boat, and cannot recall being in one alone.

In addition to being concerned rather than panicky during most of the dream I also felt "frustrated" by not being able to get past the busy harbor town to retrieve my boat. Another "P.S." during dream recall is that at one point in the dream I refer to "Gweek," or point it out on a map, probably to the fish-processing guy who had had one. I realize in the dream that the town of Gweek is near, or almost to, or on the way to, another town called "Mousehole," pronounced "Mowzel," in the opposite direction from where I want to go. Both towns are in southwestern Cornwall, and Mousehole is in fact to the right of Penzance if you were standing in the latter town facing out to its harbor. In between there is a feature called Merlin's Rock, though it is not in the dream.

But this is beginning to sound like day-residue, hunting for familiar figures or places from my waking life to give some reassuring sense to the dream: "Oh, I know why I dreamed *that*," as we all too frequently say, initi-ating a conceptual interpretation instead of initiating ourselves into the underworld's strangeness.

There are, in this dream, various sorts of day-residue, principally geo-graphical and topographical—I *have* stood on the cliffs of Cornwall more than once, and visited the town of Penzance, most recently in the summer of 1995, less than a year before the dream—but also in the associations I have to the people involved: the male friend, I want to think, is my dayworld friend John, the youngish woman my ex-partner, from whom I have parted disastrously in this past year, the older man me.

But they are not these dayworld figures. Better to work backward, allowing the latter to be more dreamlike in my emotional connection to them, understanding their role as participants in the soul-making process of my life. Even the Cornish landscape and the map of it can be deliteralized while taken as totally real. Like dayworld Jung asking Gerhard Adler to point out on a map where he landed on the coast of India in his dream, we can simultaneously validate the dream's reality and turn the map—and the land-scape it describes—into an imaginal text. The map can become, for instance, a Rorschach design, a projective diagram: what do these places mean to me, to soul in me? Or perhaps "Gweek" is the dream's wordplay for "Greek."

UNDERMINING THE DREAM-EGO

ANOTHER AXIOM OF HILLMAN'S dream work—letting the dream take the lead—could be implemented by having the dream comment on other dreams, or they on it, so that an underworld conversation is heard that gives us a wider sense of that world's reality. (Always the prerequisite for a shaman-ic journey in anyone's version is that the otherworld destination be honored as real.) My dream was followed eleven nights later by one which contains some shared imagery with the first but different activities:

> I am on a trip in England with my friend John (?). We are in rowboats which capsize in a storm. There are two very thin sculls (or kayaks?) to continue in. I take off in one, leaving my wallet behind, possibly on the floor of the capsized rowboat. It's night; I'm making my way up the east coast of England to Scotland. I have two little paddles. I use both, one in each hand, to propel myself along. At some point, having avoided some rocks or shoals, I get back on dry land, possibly in Scotland.

Again there are boats, of course, and my starting to paddle out on the surfboard with my arms in the first dream has become an odd two-paddle operation in the scull or kayak. Now I have retrieved my long narrow row-boat: it has divided into two boats, the capsizing rowboat and the slender scull. This time my male friend has accompanied me out onto the water, but I leave him behind, along with my wallet. And although the journey is imperiled, I make it to dry land, possibly at my destination.

Is all this questing and paddling, this restless retrieval, a calling card of the heroic ego? Does his achievement of the Scottish coast detract from the underworld needs of the soul? Is the lofty overview at the outset of the original dream—I initially mistyped "overlooking the see"—a tip-off that we are dealing with the unengaged distance of the hero as Hillman critiques him? How about the time of day, near to dawn, a most heroic hour?

At least my dream ego lost his wallet, an interesting failure if the boats are life-vehicles, carriers of my livelihood, my financial and emotional vitality, after the emotionally and financially ruinous end of a ten-year relationship. Or are the boats the soul I am trying to retrieve, shamanlike, and does the treasure, the riches, rest with the capsized one? Or is it that in order to proceed on the journey I am obliged to leave behind the wallet, let go of the financial losses, let that sink and be forgotten with the storms of the past?

Many possibilities—these are but a few—present themselves when ambiguity is allowed to be a guide, duplicitous Hermes initiating us into soul's uncertainty so that even the hero's victories are undercut, thrown into question.

The extreme unlikelihood, given my dayworld uninvolvement in water sports, that I would own any sort of boat, let alone propel it, is a constant reminder that this is the underworld: things go differently here, soul's imaginings confront the ego as other, and "familiar" elements must be seen from that alien perspective.

I have said that the first dream did not seem especially "big" or archetypal, but with the second dream all those boats do add up to something— or would, if we were symbol hunting. In the west of Ireland a few years ago, I saw a little boat drawn up on the shore of an estuary. Its name was "Memory." I took a slide of it, and wonder when I show it how different this boat, evocatively named and now a photographic memory image or imaginal memory, is from a dream image, particularly of the boats I have encountered more recently in dreams. My former partner, I should say, was a canoeist, a kayaker, and owned at least one of each, keeping them at the house we owned in Albuquerque. So there's some more day-residue to reverse. The youngish woman in the dream takes no notice of my boat-retrieval ambition (she does not feel I am trying to steal *her* boat), but is intent upon informing me of her own agenda to divorce the older man who knows about my work.

WITH ALL THIS THEORY and a case study of sorts behind us, what does Hillman end up saying about "praxis" that can insure we see our dreaming as an underworld journey, an imaginal parallel to the shaman's search for soul?

He begins his last chapter by issuing two cautions. He warns the reader, first, that to do work with images we cannot ever be content with generalities, "and even specific examples of dreams, when presented as illustrations for practice, become generalities."[36] Thus my dream, or my tentative work with it, is worthless advice about how to give specific attention to each image in my dream. At least it is worthless for anyone but me, since anyone else would have to take my images out of the concrete context in which they exist in the underworld in order to apply my work to their versions of those images.

Hillman does grant, however, that generalities can deepen our perspective: in the case of his chapter on practice this would be our perspective on the specific groups of images he discusses. In the case of my dream, presumably with sensitive enough discussion we could be deepened in our viewing of boats and their retrieval—at any rate our viewing of *those* boats and *that* retrieval. The exercise might lower our sights for other dreams, others' dreams.

Hillman's second warning concerns the nature of the underworld itself, this shamanic realm we inherit from ancient Greece in our modern psychology. It is a far-reaching warning:

> . . . *underworld* refers to the psychic perspective, the attitude of the soul that cannot be said to have a praxis in the dayworld sense. To put the underworld into practice betrays the dream, which is not practical, as we have learned. The previous chapters you have troubled to go through were intended to lower you to soul and soul to underworld. . . . What follows are not even imageries of the underworld, since any dream and any God, including the hero, has a style of leading us there—once we assume the underworld perspective. That is the key. We are not presenting images *of* the underworld. . . . No, the underworld is a perspective within the image by means of which our consciousness enters or is initiated into the underworld viewpoint.[37]

In addition to these strong cautions against the kind of practice that might *prevent* the underworld journey, "seducing the whole book back up and over the bridge into the dayworld,"[38] Hillman does to the word "practice" itself what he did to the word "work" (and did at a workshop, if truth be told, to the word "journey": he feels it is overused, but we have need of it for drawing shamanic parallels). He reminds us that even the taken-for-granted term "practice" must be re-visioned in the radical shift toward soulmaking that imaginal psychology seeks. Rather than taking it in the usual sense of action or application—which says Hillman, "could be more dayworld, more ego"—practice is seen as athletic or, especially, aesthetic: ". . . what we do at the piano, in the gym, on the stage: a workout, a trial run for refining skills. We practice in order to notice little things that might otherwise escape. . . . not to become practical, but to become practiced."[39]

And so, with warnings and terminology in place, Hillman gives us his imageries, fifteen of them, in order to deepen our perspective on the dream, and thereby already to guide us on the journey to underworld depths. We will not go through each of these sets of images. The entirety of *The Dream and the Underworld* is there to be read and pondered, and the close consulting of it here is also meant to encourage that experience of bookish initiation. But there are two of his imageries we ought to inspect, both to see how he works with them and to discover how they relate back to my own dream.

WATERS OF DREAMS, DREAMS OF ANIMALS

WE WILL TAKE them in reverse order to Hillman's sequence, exploring what he says about bodies of water in dreams and then animals. My dream took place next to the ocean/(sea)see—really, if not literally, the English Channel coast of southwestern Cornwall. The associated dream fragment was set on the North Sea, and there were the memory boat's Irish estuary and even my ex's wild rivers. And then there were also the fish at the processing plant and maybe a mouse hole.

For Hillman, not surprisingly, water is not automatically about the unconscious mind in some vast general sense. On a true underworld journey of dream work the details of water dreams would always be more important than such a generality, and the processes water helps us imagine are more significant than any static symbolic content we might assign to water images. Those processes are ones that draw us down, below sea level, perhaps below "see level," to where dayworld meanings are indistinct and the submarine environment can drown and dissolve us, submerging the ego, no longer dominant, with the other figures of the objective psyche.

Again we encounter the ending that authentic shamanism of any sort knows must precede new beginnings. Bodies of water can embody the flow and flux that soul would substitute for rigid control. The underworld perspective, Hillman is suggesting, and the journey that adopting it entails, has the qualities of water: it produces reflections; it "moistens" the dry ego (as does the shedding of tears); it breaks down and carries down into depths that are invisible to the literalism of our landbased consciousness. Herman Melville knew this: "water and meditation are wedded forever," he said in *Moby Dick*, and "in landlessness alone resides the highest truth, shoreless, indefinite as God."

Can we give up, give way, to a watery grave, a shamanic dismemberment among the fishes? My dream seems to resist this. My boat was a way to
avoid being in the water, and even when I tried to paddle out to retrieve it, I
had the surfboard to prevent me from immersing. Then the second dream
jumps impatiently from capsizing to a successful sculling, resulting in arrival
on dry land. The water was surmounted, mastered. But realizing this, feeling
how depths were refused, can itself be a work of underworld journeying,
sensing the down side of every positive achievement.

*Dreaming the underworld journey is a radically imaginal way of working
in cooperation with the workings of dreams.* Sometimes a dream can be a fish-
processing plant, doing something with denizens of the waters—not necessarily killing and canning them: any process might be meant by the dream.
Perhaps any plant, too, like the palmetto trees that grow in Penzance's salty
Gulf Stream breezes. Or my dream could be a fishing process, for the dream
does love punning and reversal and plays on words of whatever kind.

The fish also figure in Hillman's second set of images, those regarding
animals, and here there are two crucial implications of Hillman's work with
dream animals that we need to understand.

First there is the word itself: "animal" contains and is derived from the
smaller word "anima," which is Latin for soul, just as "psyche" is Greek for
soul. Since, to recall Jung's motto, "Image *is* psyche," image is also anima,
and animal images in dreams are, as Hillman says, "carriers of soul . . . there
to help us see in the dark."[40] When such images come we must pay close
attention to them rather than to our reactions in the dream. This is partly
Hillman's way of emphasizing the autonomy, the independence, of soul's
images, just as Jung did in working with the objectivity of the psychic figures
he confronted in 1913.

"As from a duck blind," Hillman urges,

> or when downwind stalking a deer, our focus is on the image, acute to its
> appearance, ourselves abashed, eclipsed in that intensity in order to follow
> the precise movement of its spontaneity. Then we might be able to under-
> stand what it means with us in the dream. But no animal ever means one
> thing only, and no animal simply means death.[41]

Since he says that in some fairy tales death comes as a fish, it is important to
note that my fish are not necessarily or only about death. However, by having the fish on dry land, possibly dead and under human control, their
autonomy as images seems compromised, perhaps another refusal of imaginal depths. But by the same token it could be a bit of underhanded wisdom
once we see it, realizing how soul wants an opposite attitude.

The second implication I want to point out about animal images in dreams will require quoting a long paragraph in its entirety. Such images in our dreams support the case I am making in this book that imaginal dream work like that of Hillman amounts to a Western shamanism, as does imaginal work more generally.

HILLMAN'S PARAGRAPH BEGINS with an idea—really another image—that may bring to mind the painting on the Ice Age cave wall at Lascaux that some commentators call the first image of the shaman: a birdheaded male figure with a staff or wand topped by a bird shape, facing an enormous bison. Hillman, however, connects his cave painter with Adam: "The appearance of an animal restores us to Adam. We recover the first man in the cave, tracing out the animal soul on the underground walls of the imagination."

He then reiterates his critical post-Jungian insistence upon the independent reality of animal images and, indeed, of all dream images (which makes them equivalent to the "spirits" with whom shamans have been said to consort):

> Of course, the different animals present styles and shapes of vitality, so one tends to say, "Animals in dreams represent instincts. They stand for our bestiality and primitivity." No, they do not; first, because they are not ours or us; second, because they are not images *of* animals, but images *as* animals. These animals show us that the underworld has jaws and paws, opening our awareness to the fact that images are demonic forces.[42]

By "demonic," of course, he means "daimonic," as we noted earlier. He uses the more common spelling here, I would imagine, in order to indicate the additional fearsomeness with which a Christan culture has invested the figures of the psyche in demonizing them. He also makes a comment that will be a basis of Chapter 7: *all* images can be seen as animal images, as animal powers. It is interesting to recall that when Joseph Campbell came to write—with some help from Joan Halifax—the volume on hunter-gatherer mythologies, including the mythologies surrounding shamanism, in his *Historical Atlas of World Mythology*, he called it *The Way of the Animal Powers*.[43]

The paragraph closes with Hillman's repeated emphasis on how we must practice imaginal dream work with animals:

> The least we can do for them is to pay them that primordial respect of the cave man drawing in the dark, face to the wall, that respect of Adam, so closely considering them that he could find for each one its name. We need large caves and loving attention. Then they may come and tell us about themselves.[44]

The sense of Hillman's paragraph might be summed up by saying that images are "animals" and animals are helping beings, "familiars" who assist us on our underworld journey each night. As he elaborates in other writings like "The Animal Kingdom in the Human Dream" and "Going Bugs,"[45] these images, *all* inner images, are "power animals." The power is imagination, here seen with post-Jungian eyes as a provider of the soul's realities, not either a copier of outer objects or a frivolous mind game of make-believe.

That the latter definitions of imagining dominate in our culture suggests that, like the dream which is its nightly expression, the imagination is endangered in many and insidious and even well-meaning ways. Also like the dream, soul in the West will continue to be lost unless we learn to serve imagining, to protect its depths; modern man and woman, postmodern persons, have been searching for it since before Jung's day, but it continues to elude them, despite his example of descent to the objective psyche. It will take an imaginal shamanism to recover soul, and the dream work Hillman models for us so elusively, so exasperatingly, but so insightfully, starts us on the underworld journey that can help in such a shamanic recovery.

Continuing this journey in the day, finding in dayworld imaginings the powers so persuasively present in the night, will be our next topic. However, this work with waking dreams has almost nothing to do with "lucid" or "controlled" dreaming. Carlos Castaneda's most recent books—after his hoax became public knowledge—propose a kind of controlled dreaming as a "Toltec" mode of sorcery, and psychologists like Steven LaBerge promote lucid dreaming.[46] There may indeed be parallels between such conscious dreaming and the imaginal process of fiction writing, as Ronald Sukenick has suggested.

But with an excess of control, this process veers into the ego heroics that Hillman would disallow and that an imaginal shamanism would do well to avoid. Like the dream sharing and dream shaping attributed to the Senoi of Malaysia in another shamanthropological hoax,[47] controlled dreaming as an ideal is suspiciously akin to the cross-cultural fantasies surrounding Castaneda's neoshamanism.

Assuredly waking dreams will concern us, but not as a way to exercise our ego's power: that will only keep us distanced from soul's depths and fail as an imaginal shamanism. What we need in all our work with images is careful attention to *their* needs, respectful dialogue with their depths, which never end at rock bottom where we could get their meanings straight to serve *our* needs. Our waking dream work will need to be continuous with honoring the uncontrolled dreaming our ego undergoes each night.

« 7 »

IMAGINING WITH ANIMAL POWERS

*T*he final section of James Hillman's final chapter in *The Dream and the Underworld* is called "Attitude toward Dreams," and I recommend reading all of it, several times. Our attitude, he says at the start of this final section, needs to be multisensory in perceiving the underworld creatures: ". . . we begin to perceive more and more in particulars, less and less in overviews. We become more and more aware of an animal discrimination going on below our reflections and guiding them."[1]

This is only the first of the "more and more" reflections of "Attitude toward Dreams." But it is noteworthy that animals are again Hillman's helpers, not only as images but also as our model of how to feel, touch, hear, taste, and smell, as well as see, in the underworld through their modes of sensing. "Our" images are not ours, and on our shamanic journey as Westerners we must confront these animal powers at the farthest edge of our familiar campfire's light, in their forest. So we need something like their senses, their "language," to initiate a dialogue that can initiate us.

In Robert Bosnak's *Tracks in the Wilderness of Dreaming*, recently published as a follow-up to his *Little Course in Dreams*, imaginal psychology comes at the dream and its animals from a slightly different, but still similar, direction:

> If the dreamworlds and their dwellers are real and entirely unknown to us, they must belong to wilderness, to unknown lands with laws of their own and creatures untamed, fascinating, and frightening. In psychoanalysis we call these realms "unconscious"—which, of course, means "I don't know," or "I don't know what I'm talking about."

> A profound not-knowing is hard to bear. We wake up and try to get a grip
> on our dreams. We tame them with interpretations. We try to make them
> into pets, to render them relatively harmless, not like the unpredictable
> wild creatures they really are.[2]

He goes on to ask how it would be to enter dreams as mysteries, meaning by
that word both the general idea of something resistant—irreducibly resistant—to reasoned interpretation and, more specifically, the ancient Greek
mysteries. "Since olden days," he says, "initiatory experiences with the ultimate
unknown in a ritual setting had been called the mysteries," and he refers to
"the Eleusinian mysteries, the widespread initiation rituals in antiquity, during
which initiants were confronted with the mysteries of the Underworld."[3]

So Bosnak, too, has recourse to the mythic space of the underworld—
a Western shamanic otherworld, I have been suggesting—in order to work
imaginally with dreams. But his major metaphor for the space of dreaming is
the wilderness. This is both because his book is set in the Australian outback,
where he is comparing notes with an Aboriginal "dream doctor" from a culture we of the West have tried to obliterate, and because he sticks to the
depiction of dream images as "creatures untamed, fascinating, and frightening."[4] These creatures, of course, are under our attack.

Images are no less wild—no less endangered—in waking dreams.

GOING TO MEET OUR POWER ANIMAL

IT IS JULY of 1990 again, at the workshop entitled "The Way of the
Shaman: The Shamanic Journey, Power, and Healing." The leader, Michael
Harner, neoshamanism's most active shamanthropologist, former scholar,
defender of Carlos Castaneda, and now director of the Foundation for
Shamanic Studies, is beginning to drum in the hall full of one hundred
people, lying on their backs, heads on cushions, bandannas covering their
eyes. I cannot actually see this since I, too, am lying down and loosely
blindfolded, waiting to see where the journey will take me and who, or
what, I will meet.

We have already done a divination exercise with a stone, working in
pairs to gather images from the lines and colorings of the stone in answer to
some general question we had posed about our personal life. With this "rock-
seeing" now behind us—a laudable loosening-up exercise for the imagination, though perhaps too focused on ego-wants—we are next prepared for
our "lowerworld journey." We must settle upon a lowerworld opening that
we have seen in actual physical space, Harner instructs us, so we can more
easily make the transition from ordinary to nonordinary reality.

The possibilities we are given are familiar from his 1980 book, *The Way of the Shaman*: caves, hollow trees/knotholes, wells or springs, whirlpools, animal holes, behind a waterfall or in a lake or bay, or the *sipapu* or underworld emergence place in the floor of a Pueblo kiva or ceremonial chamber. Fairy tales are full of these openings and journeys through them, Harner observes, but shamans *do* these things as a routine activity.

I have selected St. Warna's Well for my lowerworld opening. This is a small "holy well," now untended, framed by a trilithon of granite, in an overgrown hillside of a remote island out in the Atlantic beyond Land's End, Cornwall. Several of my trips to southwestern Cornwall have included excursions to the Isles of Scilly, a group of one hundred small islands, five inhabited, that I had read about in novelist John Fowles' nonfiction book *Islands*. There are remote but evocative associations with the otherworld "Isles of the Blest" in Greek mythology, as the word "Scilly" may be related to the German word *salig*, meaning blessed.

The particular island with the well was St. Agnes, and St. Warna was the saint associated with shipwrecks—perhaps supplicated to *cause* them, since shipwreck plunder was once a major source of livelihood in the islands. This is further suggested by a television documentary on local treasure-diving which called St. Warna a "sorceress." Her well was a perfect lowerworld opening for me.

With Harner's steady drum beat as induction, I have entered the narrow opening of the well. Having already said that the terms "imagination and fantasy" are theories of what's happening, and that we should leave the baggage of theories behind, he has also answered a final question before beginning to guide our journey. An older woman in the group has asked him how you know the difference between "visualizations you're creating with your imagination" and the "shamanic reality of the SSC" (Shamanic State of Consciousness). His answer is that you cannot know until eventually you can "perform miracles"—get practical results.

He has added that people who have done guided imagery say it is qualitatively different from the SSC. Both the question and Harner's answer have called forth all my complex post-Jungian objections to *his* theoretical baggage. But I have again set such considerations aside in favor of carrying out the simple task he has set us for this first journey: to ask an animal to be waiting for us at the other end of the tunnel. I have tried not to anticipate, to clear my mind of favorite animal images, and to remain open to whatever appears.

I am going down steps into the water of St. Warna's Well, steps that take me under the water. There is the feeling of breathing under the water, and some sense of cave-like walls around me. I may reach a shore, in a cave at the end of the tunnel. This drifts into the image of two young girls, around ten years old, seen from the rear pushing a baby's stroller. They have shortish hair, one perhaps brown-haired, the other a blond. In the stroller I have the sense that there is an iguana-like lizard that is looking back over the back of the stroller, looking back toward me. There are several periods of drifting off from this scenario, but Harner's drumming allows me to refocus. I am in a vehicle now, maybe a bicycle, on a narrow lane. There is a wall on my left, a sheer cliff on my right. Now the lane, with the wall and cliff, turns left and I wonder if it will run out and maybe I will go over the precipice. But I see that the iguana, now on foot, is leading me around the corner to the left. I see a river far below, like the Grand Canyon, but there may also be a sloping mowed lawn below me. There are associations to the American Southwest. The drumming speeds up, calling me back.

NOT MUCH, BUT NOT NOTHING, I think as I sit up and remove my bandanna. The presence of a totally unanticipated animal, and one definitely not native to the British Isles, is the genuinely startling ingredient of my brief journey. I will later speculate that this iguana is a form of dragon, a creature which is at least native to British folklore, including the lore of Merlin which strikes me as so shamanic. But my "power animal," as Harner calls it, is definitely an iguana. Though it had first seemed only an "iguana-like lizard," which might allow some latitude in deciding *exactly* what it was, the word "dragon" did not "occur to me."

And just what occurred to me is what must be honored as an imaginal reality: a tropical reptile in a lowerworld beneath the Isles of Scilly. Where the two girls came from—besides this same lowerworld—I have no idea. I never saw their faces. They may have been twins, or at any rate sisters. The journey did not explain them any more than it explained why an iguana should be in a baby's stroller. The images were simply presented, present, suddenly there, and not to be interpreted symbolically any more than Hillman would do with dream images, preferring instead to have them inform our dayworld existence.

That the iguana was leading me along the precipice lane as it turned left seemed the sort of thing a power animal, as a guardian spirit, might do in

Harner's version of the New Shamanism—even though a fanged reptile might also fall under his prohibition against interacting with such menacing nonmammals, just as insects were forbidden. They seem to represent illness for him, so they have no place in his vision of shamanic healing. But does not healing require facing illness, seeing its face and fangs?

These oddly cautious proscriptions seemed out of line with Harner's comment after the journey that it is good to have fear in the lowerworld because it shows you take the other reality seriously. In any case I was impressed with my initial experience of his journeying technique. The drumming, or "sonic driving," was a very effective vehicle for brushing aside distractions and providing an open space in your attention where new images could appear. The guidance he gave us in the task he defined was gentle enough to allow for the surprises I had encountered, while still insuring that I probably would meet an animal in the lowerworld. He had called the task "a specific mission" in contrast to "a drug mission"—which is how he seemed to characterize any sort of directionless journey or unguided experience of inner imagery. But do not drugs, too, direct us?

Psychological questions keep surfacing for me, but now we are moving on to a second lowerworld journey.

ANOTHER JOURNEY: A JOURNEY FOR ANOTHER

OUR TASK THIS TIME is to specify beforehand that you will meet the animal that appeared in the first journey and, working with a partner, to bring it a broad personal question from this partner. Not only will this give us another experience of journeying, but it will begin to show us how to journey on behalf of someone besides ourself: a glimpse from the inside of the shaman's role as healer. Your animal, Harner says, may lead you to an answer to your partner's question by running away. Jump on its back or follow it, "reading the journey." Where you are taken to may be the answer.

My partner is Marya from Santa Fe. Her question is "Will Doug be a good partner for me?" The bandannas go back on and we lie down. The drumming begins:

> I am swimming with the iguana. Now we are sliding down a hill in a cave and into an open meadow by a bend in a stream with a tree. I ask him Marya's question and he moves his mouth. I somehow get "Yes," then "Dig Doug, dig down," and "a parting of the waves." Now the iguana is going across the stream; I ask "A parting of the ways?" and he shakes water off himself like a dog, which I take to mean no. Now we are running

across the meadow in long wavy grass. He says, "Come on, let's go." I say, "Where?" "Go(t) to find Doug," he answers. Now fleeting images of two men come to me: the side of a young man's head—short blondish hair and his cheekbone, athletic-looking—and a vague front view of the other man who has a dark mustache. I ask the iguana if these men are Doug and he winks or blinks his eye, which briefly looks rhinoceros-like.

The accelerated drumming concludes the journey and Marya and I proceed to share our findings.

Marya's wolf—into whom she was transformed at one point in her journey, seeing out of his eyes—has indicated my future with my partner would continue, though with periodic ups and downs, endings and beginnings. This had been imaged by movement through undulating small hills and an hourglass turning over and over. Father Time had appeared with a long white beard, and said that we would be in love until the end of our lives, though it was not clear whether it would be with each other. Marya as her wolf had then walked *through* Father Time and heard or saw a joyous ceremony or festival. Was it a wedding?

I can see how "my" iguana will take on more substance the more times I interact with him. And discussing his advice (he felt like a male iguana) for and with another person also lends a kind of consensual validation to his existence. That there was also a wolf in Marya's lowerworld, and a different topography, suggested a shared domain with a full array of creatures and features, just as the appearance of various boats in my successive dreams had done.

I am guarded about accepting this possibility; I had rather stick to the images that actually appear to me. But Marya has no doubts about this metaphysical issue: there is an otherworld, lower and upper, which exists apart from our contacts with it. This seems to go beyond Harner's term "Shamanic State of Consciousness," though not necessarily beyond Castaneda's "nonordinary reality," which Harner also favors in a somewhat contradictory combination of psychological and cosmological or metaphysical claims.

Marya later produces a pendulum and dowses me for answers to my question *and* channels information in the brogue of a Scottish lady. The results are a mildly positive prognosis for my future with my partner, who is about to move to New Mexico. I would not be able to join her there this next year, said Marya's Scotswoman, but maybe the year after. Did Marya's easy move from neoshamanist journeying to dowsing and channeling show the triviality of the former as a shallow New-Age mind game? Or did it suggest the latter media, like Harner's drumming-assisted exercise, can be a vehicle for genuine imagining beyond mere make-believe? I could not be sure, and could hardly put the matter to Marya, who had seemed both sincere and sincerely helpful.

THE NEXT MORNING we are again in a large circle for an opening song and a question-and-answer session. Harner begins the latter by saying "Let's get rid of these Western concepts of imagination, imagination and reality." That takes care of *my* questions! Similarly, no one else's question challenges his anti-psychological model in any way. The questions are all about the nuts and bolts of journeying: how to maneuver, what this or that animal may mean. No one asks him about his ties to Castaneda.

Appreciative of the experiences he is helping to induce, I am nonetheless impatient with his posture toward what he calls theoretical questions. At some point during the previous day he has said, for instance, that comparing the terminology of "spirits" to "the unconscious" does not help because the latter is an abstract concept in psychology: "I never met the unconscious," he had remarked. He went on to quip that "I'm not the Einstein of consciousness trying to correlate shamanism with psychology. I leave that to other people." He had not told us who these other people were. Yet he made the correlation with psychology sound so abstruse as to be utterly irrelevant to anyone interested in shamanism, especially anyone at his experiential workshop.

But it did not take an Einstein to explore such parallels, and with his Ph.D. and publications—and a little homework in post-Jungian thought (Hillman would share his view of "the unconscious" as an abstraction)—Harner was surely capable of doing so himself. Perhaps that job will be left to me, I muse.

In debriefing us from our second journey, Harner emphasizes how fast these methods work, explaining that our ancestors needed help or answers from shamans very quickly in what were often life-threatening situations: "They couldn't wait around." Perhaps not. But if fast relief were all he was offering it might satisfy American consumers while running counter, I worried, to the slower, lower processes of a soulful spirituality.

Introducing people to imaginal realities, on the other hand, seemed a genuine service to soul, a step toward shamanic imagining that needed only an appropriate psychological theory to let it see where it was truly going and free it for even greater spontaneity. Part of Harner's put-down of psychology may have been a disingenuous dodge, an evasion of the real issues about the New Shamanism that his workshop experiences raise. But much of it, I decided as I left for the drive back to Vermont, had to do with the legitimate fear of reductionism in the psychology he knew about, its falsification of journeying, for instance, as something that takes place "only in your head."

Coupled with this was his likely worry, at least partly a product of that same reductionistic psychology, that to admit that an experience was imagination, let alone fantasy, was to consign it to unreality. Having had his own encounters with imaginal realities in the South American jungle guided by indigenous healers, but lacking the theoretical knowledge of imaginal psychology, Harner was thrown back, I surmised, upon his rhetoric of "spirits" in the SSC—and upon his understandable suspicion of both the psychology he knew and imagining as usually understood.

I had been grateful to meet my power animal and (later) my celestial teacher—although the "my" implied more possessiveness than felt proper for an equal dialogue. It reminded me of a talk I had heard the previous year by the Native American scholar and writer Vine Deloria, Jr., in which he wise-cracked that Harner's power animals sometimes sounded like Mafia henchmen from *The Godfather*, sent to do some boss's bidding. More importantly, however, post-Jungian psychology had taught me that *all* inner images, experienced in sleeping or waking dreams as expressions of soul, of anima, are anima's powers, animal powers. Specific images of animals would thus appear in order to teach us with special autonomy and particularity (their rhinoceros eyes staring back at us from the otherworld) how *any* soul image works in us, works on us.

THE HEALING ART

As SUCH THEY COULD become, as Hillman called them, "healing fictions"—and, I am adding, appropriate medicine for a mindfully imaginal shamanism. This would be a New Shamanism similar to but importantly different from what Harner seemed to be attempting. It would be one which moved beyond the contributions of his neoshamanism by wielding a psychological theory that freed it *from* blind fantasies taken as indigenous fact—*à la* the Carlos Castaneda hoax to which he had tied himself. This was a theory that freed it *for* honoring the reality of the non-literal realm, like Carl Jung's objective psyche, where Western seekers could find a shamanic imagining of their own.

It is entirely possible that the New Shamanism of Castaneda and Harner, Halifax and Andrews—and scores of other writers and workshop leaders in or out of shamanthropology who follow in their footsteps—will never be deeply *healing* until it actively faces and thereby fully honors the imaginal process of fictive power upon which it fundamentally rests. I have admittedly heard reports of people being helped in various ways by the work of Harner and his trainees—Sandra Ingerman's "soul retrievals," for instance, or Susan Grimaldi's practice where I live in Vermont. And Joan Halifax has a reputation for charismatic clarity born out of her own self-healing and Buddhist meditation experience that sounds shamanically authentic. These are practitioners who have only my best wishes for their neoshamanist efforts.

My suspicion, nevertheless, is that where their neoshamanism heals it does so by means of the very imagination (e.g., in "journeying") it neglects to recognize as central to *any* Western effort at shamanizing. Just as the shamanovels of Castaneda and Lynn Andrews achieve their fascinations through unacknowledged fiction writing. Passive fantasies of indigenous healing—and even Harner's "core shamanism" and Halifax's "Teachings of the Shields" workshops fall prey—may answer to real spiritual yearnings, but they seem a problematic solution, shakily won, and subject to ready demystification when debunkers like Richard de Mille do their work.

Better than these passive, unconscious fantasies is conscious engagement in what Jung called "active imagination," an interactive dialogue with imaginal realities that brings the sort of healing a Western shamanism can honestly claim.

In a late letter he has some advice about this process that is often quoted to show very concretely how it works:

> The point is that you start with any image, for instance, just with that yellow mass in your dream. Contemplate it and carefully observe how the picture begins to unfold or to change. Don't try to make it into something, just do nothing but observe what its spontaneous changes are. Any mental picture you contemplate in this way will sooner or later change through a spontaneous association that causes a slight alteration of the picture. . . . Note all these changes and eventually step into the picture yourself, and if it is a speaking figure at all then say what you have to say to that figure and listen to what he or she has to say.[5]

Robert Bosnak calls this meditative process "returning to dream reality," and it both allows for further dream work and, by using a dream image as a starting point, gives to an active imagination experience the dream's feeling of reality. Bosnak explains this by saying that "in doing active imagination it is important first to alter our state of awareness into an image consciousness. We can accomplish this through the very detailed recall of a dream image."[6] Bosnak's *A Little Course in Dreams,* as we have noted, emphasizes dream recall in just such a fashion. For this reason it is as close to a practical guide to "doing" the dream-related method of active imagination as we really need in order to interact with animal powers. (The boat in my dream is one such animal power: I can go back and watch it prowl, menace, and slink with its boaty movements. Perhaps it will speak. My lowerworld iguana, somewhat more made-to-order, may not do as well, unless he also shows up in the underworld of my dreaming.)

Notwithstanding the seeming simplicity of practicing active imagination, however, understanding the full ramifications of this method—and how it compares to the journeying of neoshamanism—requires exploring further. In Hillman's book entitled *Healing Fiction*, he refers to Jung's active imagination method as "the healing art."[7] Before we can examine what Hillman means by that designation in his own realization of Jung's legacy, we need to back up and review, starting with Jung himself, what the Jungian tradition has had to say about how active imagination can be healing—and how it can fail to be healing if it is misconstrued.

A MAJOR WAY it can be misconstrued, according to Jung's earliest formulations and his later followers, is by confusing it either with Freud's "free association" technique or with a passive relationship to the flow of fantasy images. These two confusions probably amount to the same thing—or are largely overlapping—while a third possible misconstrual, mistaking active imagination for a guided imagery exercise, may be a special case of passive imagination. It will concern us below as we return to Harner's neoshamanism for some comparative assessments.

If we look at Jung's first statements on active imagination we find that for him this process is not "free" but "focused," not a passive "going-with-the-flow" but a delicately willful interaction. An acceptable analogy could be the actions of the parachutist who finds it healthiest to descend not in in a total free-fall, a passive plummeting, but rather, with chute opened, in a more two-sided interchange with the independent elements of air, wind, and gravity. In this analogy pulling the ripcord might be likened to the initial active engagement with the central image to be addressed and heeded in this downward dialogue. (My earlier analogy with being a glider pilot might make the same point.)

As early as his *Psychological Types* book in 1921—but already eight years after his split with Freud and thus a product of the descent he had made following it—Jung distinguished between "active and passive fantasy."[8] He added that while passive fantasy is antithetical to consciousness (and this is the negative sense in which I have generally been using the term "fantasy"), "active fantasy is one of the highest forms of psychic activity. For here the conscious and unconscious personality of the subject flow together into a common product in which both are united."[9] Of course, we know that Jung was speaking out of his own experience of dialogue with the daimons of the objective psyche, the biographical source of active imagination as a modern Western psychological discovery, a rediscovery of an ancient skill.

It is also noteworthy that his notion of a "common product" of the conscious and unconscious mind echoes his discussion of the "transcendent function" five years earlier in a key essay of that title.[10] In this 1916 essay he also began to sketch out the method of active imagination as a "practice," including the use of expressive arts media to both induce and record the equal conversation between the ego and the inner images of the soul.

In passages such as these Jung essentially referred to active imagination without employing the term, which he began to do eventually in the mid-1930s in several published and unpublished writings and lectures. Although he had earlier used labels like "creative fantasy" or, in one instance, "active phantasying," by the autumn of 1935 in what are called his Tavistock Lectures, he had settled upon "active imagination," even implying that the word imagination by itself connotes an active, purposeful creativity.[11]

Perhaps because of this Jung emphasizes in various places that first the images must be given free play, allowed their own activity, and must be accepted as if absolutely real. Only then should the conscious ego participate in "having it out" with the unconscious on equal terms.

This must be why he wrote of the need to relax "the cramp in the conscious mind" so that one can "let things happen"[12] in the unconscious as the initial stage of the process—and why, finally, *inter*active imagining may be a better name for his method.

Indeed, the *ego*'s activity (its "mastery" of this art) is more akin to the "creative letting-be" of Taoist meditation or the "action through nonaction" practiced by the Christian mystic Meister Eckhart, as Jung himself commented in his preface to the Chinese alchemical text *The Secret of the Golden Flower*.[13] Elsewhere he described a patient who, "through her active participation . . . merges herself in the unconscious processes, and she gains possession of them by allowing them to possess her."[14]

As mentioned earlier, the model of the shaman as macho technician of ecstasy may be more a matter of Mircea Eliade's Western (and masculine) fantasies than an inevitable feature of indigenous shamanism. Even aside from traditions, such as the Korean, in which shamans are usually women, a mastery which is delicate rather than dominating may characterize more versions of shamanism than the opposite style.

HOW DO FICTIONS HEAL?

IF WE LOOK now at Hillman's overall views on active imagination we find that, as in most areas, he offers a new twist on the Jungian consensus while remaining faithful to Jung's own radical legacy of personal dealings with the daimons of the imaginal underworld. First, what is that Jungian consensus?

With only minor differences in nuance, Jung and Jungian writers like Marie-Louise von Franz and Barbara Hannah, Ira Progoff, Rix Weaver, and Adolph Ammann—or, more recently, Robert Johnson, Pieter Middelkoop, and Verena Kast, as well as assorted tapes and articles by Jungian therapists—all agree on at least one point.[15] Although the conscious interaction with the figures of the unconscious psyche must be a respectful conversation between equals, with the images allowed to happen spontaneously in an unmanipulated manner, the merely passive observation of freely flowing inner associations is inadequate. It is inadequate, in particular, to the goal of healing in traditional Jungian therapy—the individuation of the self or achievement of the analysand's unique balance of intrapsychic oppositions—which requires rather the cooperation of ego consciousness with unconscious processes expressed through the imagination.

For Hillman active imagination is "the healing art" no less than it has been for Jung and these other successors. But what he means by healing modifies their views somewhat, in a fashion that subtly reconnects us to the theme of fictive power we have explored in charting the founding of the New Shamanism.

From Hillman's perspective, with his three-part distinction between spirit/mind, soul, and body/nature in place, the psychological disease that active imagination heals is literalism, the literalism which tends to characterize both spiritual goals (peak experiences) and material grounds (the bedrock of physiology, fauna, and flora). These he contrasts, we recall, to the *metaxy* or middle realm between and connecting them: psyche's domain, where ambiguous imaginings undermine any fixity or singleness of meaning. In other words, active imagination as a healing art deliteralizes all meanings by returning them to this middle region of "as if." For such an art, passive imagination would be losing oneself in the fantasy or fiction without seeing through it *as* fantasy or fiction, without consciously engaging it as nonliteral, imaginal, as-if.

While the usual Jungian aim of individuated wholeness seems to be submerged under Hillman's elusive antiliteralism, there is an important connection between Hillman's healing agenda here and a conviction of Jung's that fantasy's bad reputation stems "from the circumstance that it cannot be taken literally."[16] Elsewhere Jung elaborates on the related difficulties of the fantasy–reality relationship in psychological experience, and we see that these are the same difficulties that Carlos faced in the don Juan tales and that neoshamanism has yet to face by owning up to its Castanedan origins in fantasy. Moreover, these are the very difficulties that prompt Hillman to focus on active imagination as healing through de-literalization. How did Jung articulate them?

He begins with a familiar emphasis. "The fantasy," he says, "to be completely experienced, demands not just perception and passivity, but active participation." Then he goes on to point out an obstacle not generally dealt with in the Jungian tradition until we come to Hillman's radically imaginal re-visioning: namely that, as Jung puts it, "it is almost insuperably difficult to forget, even for a moment, that all this is only a fantasy, a figment of the imagination that must strike one as altogether arbitrary and artificial. How can one assert that anything of this kind is 'real' and take it seriously?"[17]

Jung's implication here is clearly that we *should* try to forget that this is only a fantasy or a "figment," merely make-believe—or perhaps that we should forget the "only," the "merely"—and indeed take the fantasy seriously as a reality. But Jung also cautions that we "must not concretize our fantasies,"[18] must not take them literally. Carlos, we recall, really *flew*, but not as a bird flies—and even this happened inside a cross-cultural fairy tale. Much of the problem of granting fantasies their own kind of reality, imaginal reality, is that, as Jung notes, we Westerners are caught in "the scientific credo of our time," which has a "superstitious phobia about fantasy,"[19] denying reality to fantasy because scientific belief sees only the literal as real.

THIS IS A BRILLIANT INSIGHT by a man schooled in science, another one of those word-bridges we traveled in our middle chapter. He then concludes the insight with a crucial statement: "But the real," he insists, "is what works. And the fantasies of the unconscious work, there can be no doubt about that."[20] The question for us then becomes how can *we* work with them, work with these fantasies as nonliteral realities in order to heal? Jung decides in this regard that "while we are in the grip of the actual experience we cannot take them literally enough," though "when it comes to understanding them" we must overcome "the tendency to concretization"[21] or literalization.

Again, despite the apparent simplicity of the active imagination method, this is not easy advice to follow in drawing on active imagination as a resource for an imaginal shamanism.

But it is an indispensable maneuver for Westerners who seek a shamanic spirituality that recovers soul: to experience the fantasy images—waking dream images—as more than the mere figments which our deeply engrained scientific credo would call them. To take them, rather, as real, literally so in the experience itself (and perhaps this would describe an initial, more passive stage of active imagination) but nonliterally so in the inevitable interpretive moment that follows immediately thereafter (which then might be more akin to a fully active imagining).

Jung goes on to say that neither the literal reality of the conscious world nor the nonliteral reality of the unconscious world is *absolutely* real[22]—quite a drastic statement from someone who has been seen by his critics as an "essentializing" metaphysician! Hillman's way of handling this issue of the *relative* reality of the literal world in its equality with the nonliteral realm is to call for a general deliteralization. We could say that where Jung continually spoke of "psychic facts" out of a kind of political regard for our scientific investment in factuality, Hillman speaks of "healing fictions," *seeing through* that scientific investment as itself an imaginal fantasy unacknowledged as such. (This would be in line with Hillman's early book title, "the myth of analysis.")

So his healing strategy for today is to become conscious that nothing, not even a literal fact, as Jung said, is *absolutely* real, and to begin to work very much more respectfully with the reality of the nonliteral, the fictive, the imaginal. We have already seen how Hillman makes good on this in his work with dream images, and he is no less revolutionary in relation to the realities of waking dreams in the active imagination process.

"Don Juan shows us we live in fictions," said Ronald Sukenick the literary liar, "and we live best when we learn to master the art." This gentle mastery is equivalent to Hillman's version of the healing art of active imagination: to actively encounter the fictive power informing every reality. "A 'healed consciousness,'" Hillman writes in *Healing Fiction*, "lives fictionally."[23] This is mainly because such a consciousness lives in full cooperation with the unconscious. And the unconscious, he observes, "produces dramas, poetic fictions; it is a theater."[24] Furthermore, he proceeds, extending a metaphor favored by Jung,

> healing begins when we move out of the audience and onto the stage of the psyche, become characters in a fiction . . . and as the drama intensifies, the catharsis occurs; we are purged from attachments to literal destinies, find

freedom in playing parts, partial, dismembered, Dionysian, never being whole but participating in the whole that is a play, remembered by it as actor of it.[25]

As always, Hillman is aware of his words, and we should be, too: being "dismembered" is a dire shamanic eventuality to which being "remembered" may be a healing response. Toward the end of the book there is a similar point made with a different metaphor, providing perhaps the most explicit linkage between Jungian active imagination and Hillman's post-Jungian healing fictions. He states of this meditative work with images that "the method of inquiry is like writing fiction," though with an understandable difference. The difference lies in "the active intervention of the interlocuter him- or herself. These dialogues," he repeats, "demand that one take a role in one's own story, all the while pretending to play the role of the main character, the first person singular, 'I,' as close to social realism as possible. . . ."[26]

Then he offers a remarkable example of what he means by this last idea—at least remarkable given our interests: ". . . much as Carlos Castaneda, for instance, maintained his guise of social realism by playing the anthropological interviewer in his imaginary dialogues with 'Don Juan.'"[27]

COMING FULL SPIRAL—NEOSHAMANISM REIMAGINED

AND SO WE HAVE come full circle, or perhaps full spiral, back to the fiction of Carlos and don Juan, now called social realism—which is how the fairy tale disguised itself for its readers, unconscious of the hoax. It is connected by Hillman to the Jungian method of active imagination, in which participants know that its realism is a disguise (its fictive, imaginal realities not being socially or consensually factual, but still real).

If the imagining of Castaneda the fiction writer was an active, conscious involvement, however hidden behind his masquerade of factual reportage, this was not the experience of his readers or of those drawn to the New Shamanism. Prompted by belief in the masquerade, this movement has for the most part kept its participants in unconscious fantasy, passive imagination. Accordingly, can it as yet be a fully healing fiction for these seekers, a conscious journey to the reality of fictions known to be fictions? If not, could it become such an experience?

The literalizing ego needs shamanic dismemberment. It is not clear that neoshamanism to this point, given its unexamined origins in the Castaneda hoax, can provide such a healing initiation, even when modified by the important contribution of Harner.

In his 1980 handbook, *The Way of the Shaman*, Harner encouraged a deliberate disregard for Castaneda's duplicity: "The books of Carlos Castaneda," he wrote in his introduction, "regardless of the questions that have been raised regarding their degree of fictionalization, have performed the valuable service of introducing many Westerners to the adventure and excitement of shamanism and to some of the legitimate principles involved."[28] Since Harner was content to leave it at that, forgoing the learning available by contemplating the questions surrounding his friend's fictionalizing, let us see if he arrives at such learning—how the fictive power of the imagination can convey Western seekers to a healing akin to shamanism—through his own formulations.

It is discouraging to discover that neither the word "imagination" nor the name "Jung" appears in the index to *The Way of the Shaman*, let alone the word "fiction." Recounting a stage of his own instruction at the hands of a Jivaro healer in Ecuador, Harner recalls feeling that he and his teacher "were children playing a game of make-believe" as contrasted with "being in genuine contact with reality."[29] The issue raised by such a statement, of course, is whether his book consigns all imagination to the category of mere make-believe. A post-Jungian psychology of imagination would help him guard against this reductionism. But his book refuses psychological explanations—despite his strong reliance on the terminology of "mind" and "consciousness."

We have earlier noted Harner's own fear of the reductionism of orthodox scientific psychology when it interprets the states of mind characterizing shamanism, and this is a laudable resistance. But it seems his antireductionism only goes so far, and he would need something like the unscientific psychology of Hillman and colleagues to take it farther: to where, in affirming the fictive power of imagining, he can approximate the healing art provided by active imagination for Western seekers of shamanic spirituality. Involved in his own form of healing work, Harner has a nervous relationship to medical claims, and this may keep him in a deferential posture toward the scientific credo of our time.

He does sometimes come close, in *The Way of the Shaman* and in interviews and essays thereafter, to the insights a post-Jungian psychology would offer him. For example, following Eliade's imaginative construction of shamanism, the book describes the ecstatic trance of the shaman as follows: "His experiences are like dreams, but waking ones that feel real and in which he can control his actions and direct his adventures."[30] This sounds close to the active imagination process discovered by Jung and developed by Hillman. And the reference to waking dreams calls to mind Mary Watkins' book of that title.

There she surveys the history and theory of imaginal work in psychotherapy while contributing her own sensitive perceptions to post-Jungian efforts.[31]

But Harner does not cite Watkins' *Waking Dreams*, and this is unfortunately as close as his book comes to embracing a process of interactive imagining. Indeed, his comment may indicate a zeal for the controlling mastery in Eliade's definition of the shaman or the Senoi fantasy of controlled dreaming, instead of an appreciation of equal dialogue. Ironically, given the guiding instructions for journeying set forth in his book, Harner's own control may make for a more passive experience in the journeyer, bound by instructions.

In a 1987 interview with Gary Doore, there is a more promising remark, this time about Jung's work. Jung, says Harner, "showed [psychologists] a door that most did not choose to enter because things inside seemed vague and unfamiliar in terms of the methodology to which they were accustomed."[32] He implies a correlation between Jung's explorations, perhaps including his work on the active imagination method, and his own practical work in attempting to replicate shamanic experiences. Still, on the level of theory neither had Harner himself, in 1987, entered the door Jung had opened some seventy years earlier, so he remained blind to options Jung's theory presents to his neoshamanist practice.

A year later in an essay there is another encouraging passage:

> . . . evidence of progress in this return to our shamanic roots can be seen in the fact that now shamanic journeys are being labelled "guided imagery" or "visualization" and are even being accepted in some official medical circles. Nevertheless, it should be noted that the real shamanic journey goes well beyond what is called "guided imagery."[33]

What he says here may well be true of indigenous shamans on their ecstatic flights. If it were also true of the drumming-induced neoshamanist journeys he and his trained counselors were leading by 1988, then his method had moved beyond a mainly passive experience of imagining constrained by the workshop leader's guidance. Alas, my experience at his own workshop in 1990 did not show this to be the case.

I ASKED HARNER during a break at his workshop whether the people who he had said found his journeying qualitatively different from guided imagery had published their findings anywhere. He smiled and said he did not know of any publications on the matter. A year later, however, the *Newsletter* of his own Foundation for Shamanic Studies published just such a finding—or just such a claim.

The author is Leilani Lewis, a Ph.D. clinical psychologist and Harner-trained "shamanic counselor" who advances a list of comparisons between his journey method and guided imagery. Harner's shamanic journey, she says in her most debatable claims, is "free form" versus the step-by-step guidance of another person in the guided imagery experience; there is a sense of "go to, travel to" in the shamanic journey versus "imagine going to" with guided imagery; empowerment is in and through the journey rather than the "dependence on [the] ordinary reality guide" of the guided imagery participant; Harner presents an actual lowerworld and upperworld to which one journeys versus the suggested imagery of a "special place in nature"; and there are encounters with "spirits separate from [the] self" on the shamanic journey versus meetings with "parts of [one's own] inner self" in the guided imagery work. A final remarkable comparison is terse: the shamanic journey is "real" while participation in guided imagery is "imaginary."[34]

Two among several objections that can be raised are that Lewis's list ignores the instructions given prior to Harner's journeys, instructions which include a quite directive collection of assigned encounters and approved interactions. Likewise, the idea that guided imagery exercises instruct participants to *imagine* going somewhere, somewhere "imaginary," whereas the neoshamanist journey involves *actual* travel to a "real" lowerworld or upperworld, loses sight of what the post-Jungian perspective clearly perceives: locations like these latter "worlds" are just as much imaginal fictions, however real.

While the implication of the guided imagery experience may be the *unreality* of what is encountered, it is possible to avoid this implication and at the same time acknowledge the central role of images, whether produced by directive guidance or occurring more spontaneously. Lewis says she believes that "the primary difference between the two methods is how they are each conceptualized."[35] It is hard to know how she means this. But I believe that both Harner's neoshamanist journeys and typical instances of the guided imagery method are better conceptualized by comparison with the active imagination approach of the Jungian tradition, including Hillman's concept of healing fictions.

Seen from this angle, Harner's journeys as I have read about and experienced them constitute a subtle form of guided imagery, but guided imagery nevertheless. As such they limit unduly one's active relationship to the irreducibly imaginal components of the experience. "Animal powers" are encountered—spontaneous images of power animals, celestial teachers, and otherworld topography—but these are threatened with domestication by Harner's rather rigid framework, perhaps put in place to insure that consumers like me have a safe, fast, and simple version of shamanism.

Just as domesticated animals serve us in many ways, guided imagery, blatantly controlling in "creative visualization" or less constantly directive in neoshamanist journeying, has its uses, from stress reduction and weight loss to enhanced sports performance and fighting cancer. These are certainly worthwhile goals of the ego.

Wild imagining with spontaneous powers of the psyche serves deeper and non-ego-dominated goals, however. This may be why, like undomesticated species, the forces of soul in waking as well as sleeping dreams are endangered. And why forms of active imagination that rely on interactive dialogue instead of directive guidance are more soulful and, honoring the animal powers, closer to a shamanism Westerners can claim as theirs: a spirituality that can help recover the lost soul of ourselves and our world.

SUFFERING THE RECOVERY OF SOUL

*F*ictions heal when we face and engage their power as imaginal realities which deliteralize as they deepen the incurable beauty of our lives. We cannot really say how Carlos and don Juan's social-realist fictions will come out. Castaneda keeps creating more of them, all the while maintaining he is merely reporting factually on the strangeness of the social reality he experienced in the Sonora Desert.

But if, employing the post-Jungian resources we have gathered, we can actively reimagine his fairy-tale adventures and the exercises of the New Shamanism which those adventures led to—seeing through the fiction of their literal reality to the nonliteral reality of their fiction—we will then have re-visioned a neoshamanism that can truly contribute to the soulful spirituality of Western seekers.

This re-visioned neoshamanism could then combine with an overall reorientation toward our inner imaginings through the initiatory journey of dream work and a practice of active imagination. The shift toward this new orientation, the care of the soul that Thomas Moore has called for, would at the same time be the basis from which the re-imagining of neoshamanism could proceed. And the shamanic fantasies of the latter could still provide evocative imagery to work with, a fairy-tale connection to indigenous shamanisms (and to the lost shamanic heritage of the West), a connection now understood as such.

We will not therefore live happily ever after, to be sure. But we might have thereby built an imaginal shamanism that will let us live healingly ever after—as long as we realize that healing only comes out of suffering and that "ever after" is also a fiction, a way of pretending we will not die.

A soulful psychology knows this is one of the many fantasies we weave, lifelong, around the inevitability of our death. The soul-making process is always mindful of this inevitability, working with it to undermine the literalism of the ego's belief in ever after, its own continuing control. Death deliteralizes, serving soul, as do the injuries, illnesses, accidents, and other traumas that mortal flesh is heir to. Soulful living involves schooling our ego-mania for winning with the depressive reality of loss: we are, finally, losers, for we will lose our lives.

To ponder this sort of thing, we say, is a "downer." Yes, it deepens us, a "gift of depression" Thomas Moore calls it, like the beauty of the blues or the late quartets of Beethoven. Falling apart, we also regain our multiplicity, no longer ruled by the stifling singleness of meaning that ego's literalism requires: "Heightened consciousness now refers to moments of intense uncertainty, moments of ambivalence," says Moore's teacher James Hillman, and the symptoms we suffer teach us with their wounding, opening us like the shedding of tears to feel the full depth of our lives.[1] Thus dismemberment itself can provoke the deep remembering that can heal. "Pathologizing," or falling apart, to use Hillman's terminology, is not so much the loss of soul, suggests post-Jungian psychology, but its recovery. As true seekers after shamanism we must also be sufferers.

From a broadly developmental perspective, pathologizing in adulthood may be the way that soul offers itself to be recovered after having been lost in childhood. Ironically lost, says Mary Watkins, because of a too-narrow developmentalism.

SUFFERING THE SOUL LOSSES OF CHILDHOOD

WATKINS' BOOK *Waking Dreams*, still the best overview of work with inner images after twenty years, has itself an interesting and highly relevant history, as she explains in a new preface to the 1984 edition by Spring Publications (Spring is the name of Hillman's press as well as the journal he edited). The first impetus for the explorations that led to writing the book was a violent, very disturbing dream and then an auditory image, a divine voice with affirmative advice seemingly at odds with the dream, heard upon awakening. In order to understand and reconcile these powerful irruptions of the imaginal she pursued, as a college student and thereafter, both experiential and academic avenues.

The latter search was mainly a solitary one, as the psychology department of the institution she was attending cared little for research into either sleeping dreams or waking dreams. On her own she especially investigated the cultural history of these phenomena and of the modern psychotherapies that had emerged to work with them. Already underway with the studies that produced her book, Watkins then encountered a key text. It was the account in Jung's autobiography of his "confrontation with the unconscious," the descent to the objective psyche where, as we have seen, soul was rediscovered in the modern West:

> Reading this I was tremendously reassured. Jung had not stopped at giving a theory, nor was his discussion couched in rituals and cultures which were strange to me, as were many of the other readings I was surrounded by. He spoke of his own feelings about the influx of imaginal experiences which occurred spontaneously after his break with Freud, experiences for which he did not have a framework at the time, except his knowledge of their insistency and his intuitive sense of their being allowed to unfold.

> This making room honestly, phenomenologically for such experience in a contemporary depth psychological way started my interest in Jung.[2]

Thus Watkins' work in *Waking Dreams* would be a further realization of Jung's legacy, the legacy that leads to the possibility of an imaginal shamanism. In particular she was intent upon drawing out the implications of his active imagination method, placing it in a developmental as well as an historical context.

She had almost completed her book in the mid-1970s—the heyday of Castaneda's popularity, just before Richard de Mille had blown the whistle on his imposture but not before Ronald Sukenick had resonated to his literary lying—when she encountered post-Jungian psychology. It began with her reading of Hillman's *Suicide and the Soul*, an early work which dramatically differentiated between the medical need to prevent suicide and the psychological appropriateness of honoring the soul's need to imagine death as another form of existence.[3]

Suicide and the Soul was, in fact, one of Hillman's first forays into the idea he would develop as pathologizing in *Re-Visioning Psychology*. As he says in the latter volume, referring to the former, "my first essay in this method was an attempt to deliteralize suicide by grasping the pathologizing fantasy there going on as a metaphorical search for death by a soul caught in a naturalistic literalism called life."[4]

For Watkins, still moved by the bloody assault of her original dream, it was important to find in Hillman's book that

> there was no effort to cure through sweetening, lightening, transforming, substituting, or controlling the imagery. The path was to follow out these

images imaginally and metaphorically; to ask what they want; to follow
their effort to initiate one into the imaginal world, which is so often experienced as a death of the familiar, the predictable.[5]

It is important for us, too, to find this radical move toward imaginal initiation in Hillman's work and in post-Jungian psychology more generally.
Without it the potential for a contemporary Western spirituality parallel to
traditional shamanism's religious valorization of suffering would not exist.

In Watkins' case, Hillman's insights also confirmed her own experience
that pathologized incursions such as suicide fantasies are "how we moderns
force [the imaginal] to gain our attention, due to our allegiance not to angels
but to the profane, secular, and material world we cling to."[6] By the time her
book had been out for eight years and was accepted for the 1984 reprinted
edition by Spring, she felt she had come home.

WAKING DREAMS CONTRIBUTES significantly to an imaginal psychology and
to an imaginal shamanism, evoking as well as informing, frequently taking
us as readers on an underworld journey of remembering our own soul loss.
This begins with her first sentence, which immediately introduces her developmental perspective, but in an imaginal rather than abstract fashion:
"What has happened to those imaginary playmates of ours who ate more
from the family dinner table than we did?"[7]

Just as the modern West had to put away such playmates—and all other
inhabitants of the imaginal underworld—to build its edifice of reason in a culture come of age, so must the individual put away childish things like imagining so as to develop cognitively and morally. This bespeaks a lamentably partial
notion of development, one upon which Watkins casts strong suspicion in
Waking Dreams and thoroughly critiques in an important second book, Invisible Guests.[8] There she takes on the major theorists of developmentalism with a
critical question: What have their models of how to grow up done to the development of imagination? Most of us, with our well-intentioned parents
instructed by these models, have been told, at some point in childhood, to stop
daydreaming, to abandon our dolls and toy trucks, to be a "big girl" or "big
boy," to leave imaginary playmates and imagination itself behind.

When I think back to my own childhood, I can recall one of my earliest
experiences of imagining, of being both immersed and yet dimly aware it was
"not real," "just pretend." Indeed, I knew it was a movie that was directing my
enchantment—though at that time, to be sure, I had none of my later misgivings about the Disney version of imagination. All I knew, as an almost
physical sensation, was that magic had happened: an elephant could fly.

Dumbo did powerful things to my budding imagination with his magic feather of imaginal power. I felt his weight when the stork carrying him to be born rested on a cloud, and the Dumbo bundle began to sink through; his fear and then his amazing lightness as he was coaxed with the feather by three blackbirds to flap his ears and fly; even his mother's sadness and longing when they were separated. Dumbo was my first power animal, perhaps my first animal power, and hearing Bonnie Raitt's recent rendition of "Baby Mine," the lullaby from the film, can almost take me back across some fifty years of "growing up." Almost, but not quite.

That child is long gone, much of his imagination repressed, returning in adult neuroses—pathologizing that is more often poorly processed than seen in its soulful necessity. Besides, I no longer approve of the Disney animations that once elicited my little boy daydreams.

These are animations, alas, that betray the anima, that betray the imagination of the child they enchant with their shallow success. They arrest the development of imagining in America: imagination, thanks to Disney, is *only* child's play, and in order to imagine any adult must become childish. In Disney's world, there are no animal powers appropriate for adults to encounter, only cartoons without genitals in sanitized heroic fantasies hatched by a right-wing technologist with an eye for a fast buck. His franchising of the imagination may have done as much as Descartes (or developmentalism) to cause the soul loss of the modern West, and the imagining he controls is the opposite of shamanic imagining.

Watkins counters all such sponsorship of an undeveloped imagination with her critique in *Invisible Guests*, but even before that in the intuitions and eloquence of *Waking Dreams*:

> When the last doll is tucked securely in the garbage pail, my friend, the imagination has not been overcome. We have, it is true, taken away a few more of its toys. But the imagination is a far deeper affair. It is not just a child to whom we toss toys as appeasement, to get it off our mind or nerves. It travels with us to the spaces behind closed doors to contemplate our fate and our faith. Our loneliness and our successes and failures. It sits with us at the breakfast table as we straighten our hair and head for work, and read the cries of the newspaper chroniclers. . . . It urges us to worry about our height and our fingernails and our ever-present symptoms. . . .

Here Watkins becomes especially persuasive as she indicates how the soul loss of childhood's imaginings leads to the pathologizing of adulthood. And how ill-equipped we are by modern culture to understand and honor its insistent expressions:

When the imaginal has been pruned from the trees and exorcised from the animals, having chased the night creatures under the rocks by the light of our reasonableness—when everything is still, clean and free of the beasts of the imaginary—within the hour we feel their movement from within. One forgets a well-known name, says something unintended, cries "without reason," becomes angry at one thing and not another, loves one man and not another and does not know why. One person becomes afraid to climb stairs, another has an eye twitch. One's actions and fleeting thoughts cannot be attributed to the person one believes oneself to be. . . . There is another force influencing our thoughts, emotions, movements, and actions. One can no longer say it is a god or a spirit and yet one has those ancient feelings of possession and movement by a force that does not answer to logic or common space and time.[9]

Few if any Western perspectives can take account of this state of affairs, the mild or wild self-alienation that led the first psychotherapists to be called "alienists." Something Other is in us, and there is no living heritage of native Western shamanism that has survived to guide us through the dissociation, the often fearsome ecstasy, that the activities of this Other entail. Mary Watkins does not propose a post-Jungian neoshamanist response to our loss of soul, but she helps to make one possible.

There are two passing references to Castaneda in *Waking Dreams*, but no engagement with the full ramifications of his writing. Her aim in her two books is to bring us into a waking dialogue with our dreams and other imaginings, not to coax, as Castaneda did with his sham, an identification of our consciousness with the fantasy object—thereby, in a sense, losing the former and literalizing the latter into fact. The distance she and her sources counsel in both books keeps us from this literalism while still attesting to the powerful reality of what we are imagining.

REFUSING JUNG'S RADICAL LEGACY WITH FUN AND GAMES

DESPITE ITS VIRTUES, the same cannot be said of another book that tries to remedy the soul-loss of suppressed imagining in child development. *Put Your Mother on the Ceiling* subtitles itself "Children's Imagination Games," and it is a well-intentioned attempt to help teachers and parents keep the imaginations of young children alive. Unfortunately, it also illustrates the subtle ways in which the development of imaginal dialogues can be denied with the best of motives. In addition, this book spirals us back again, most improbably but most pertinently, to Castaneda's neoshamanism.

It begins with the author's new preface to the 1976 Penguin edition of a text first published in 1967:

Imagination exists to be used, but many neglect it. About halfway through World War One, Carl Gustav Jung wrote: "Imagination . . . has a poor reputation among psychologists, and [up to now] psychoanalytic theories have treated it accordingly." Jung valued imagination as an agent of spiritual growth, which it announced through dreams and daydreams. He urged people to discover themselves by heeding the products of imagination.[10]

The year of the preface, launched with this citation of Jung, is the same year the author's first expose volume, *Castaneda's Journey*, appeared: the author's name is Richard de Mille.

At best, unfortunately, de Mille's is a sloppy reading of Jung, at worst a gross distortion. We know that in Jung's psychology, imagination was much more, much other, than a tool we can wield. Image is equivalent to psyche itself. And soul-making (it is doubtful that Jung ever spoke of "spiritual growth") demands a deep conversation with inner images, not the "use" of an "agent."

While de Mille is aware that Jung's work, as he says, "inspired . . . some contemporary psychotherapists [who] have described a middle ground between spontaneous and imposed fantasy,"[11] he never mentions the active imagination method. He seems unaware of its interactive rather than instrumental approach to imagining, alluding only to the "directed daydream" technique of Desoille, which differs importantly from Jung's method, as Watkins' *Waking Dreams* makes clear.

Not surprisingly, de Mille goes on to neglect the spontaneous aspects of image work entirely, suggesting that the only options are the therapist guiding the imagery through suggesting the fantasy elements to be imagined or the patient doing so, adding that "the reader will find similar elements in this book, as well as opportunities for the imaginer to take control of his own fantasy."[12] Nowhere in this misunderstanding of Jung's legacy are the animal powers of the imaginal world allowed to go undomesticated, their wildness honored—an indispensable attitude for any shamanic imagining Westerners might develop.

DE MILLE'S GAMES ARE no doubt as fun for children as going to see *Dumbo* was for me once upon a time, but the fun comes at a high price for the development of imaginal dialogues. Throughout he wants to keep imagination or fantasy distinguished as sharply as possible from anything real, just as he does in debunking Castaneda. Indeed, his imagination games are finally more to provide the child with "reality training" than to support his or her imagining.

However, not only is this training meant to safeguard the *child* from fearsome fantasies (he chides child psychologists who think *Alice in Wonderland* is too violent but promises he will show children that the scary bear under the bed is unreal). It is also advanced, we can infer, because de Mille wants the adults they will grow into to deny the reality of *their* imaginal experience as well. Indeed, there is finally little difference between his limited attitude in approaching the Castaneda imposture and his narrow preoccupation in *Put Your Mother on the Ceiling* with "teaching children to recognize what is fact and what is fiction."[13]

Like the upbeat promoters of personal growth through "creative visualization," de Mille serves the development of the heroic ego—who wants so badly to sort things out and is happy to use any agent to do so—more than he supports imagining. He therefore contributes more to the loss of soul than to its recovery with his right-minded goals and good intentions, even while serving us well, heroically well, with the doggedness of the attack on Castaneda. De Mille's earnest but severely partial effort points up in a valuable way how revolutionary the post-Jungian resources we have been marshalling are by comparison—and how revolutionary they *need* to be to help us build an imaginal shamanism.

The comparison his work makes possible is nowhere more striking than in a further error characterizing *Put Your Mother on the Ceiling*. We have found that he failed to understand that Jung did *not* "use" the imagination and *did* see it as a reality. In his emphasis on fun and games, de Mille also fails to see the healing power of pathologized images. His 1976 preface does touch on Freud's view that "happy people . . . never made up fantasies; only unsatisfied people did that"[14]—but quickly dismisses it. This is the nearest he gets to acknowledging the connection between suffering and imagination.

Would the careful nurturing of the child's developing imagination (Waldorf schooling, parents who read aloud) lead to a grown-up with no lost soul to recover, only pleasant fantasies? While this is a question beyond my competence to answer with any exactitude, I can note that even if the traumas of childhood were nonexistent, the unhappy prospects of aging and death would still loom. Similarly, accident, abandonment, loss, and illness are bound to nip the bud of even the most upbeat unabused upbringing, constantly hospitable to the child's invisible guests. In my own late childhood a long illness—pre-television—actually helped to *restart* my imagining, at least for a time, after earlier efforts to educate me out of it had threatened to succeed.

Thus the course of childhood imagining may indeed run smoothest when there are setbacks to our "growth," downfalls in the upwardness of that growth. Childhood illness no less than adult illness brings us down, as Alfred Zeigler, a Jungian analyst and a physician specializing in psychosomatic medicine, points out:

> While Health moves and draws us upward—flies, after a manner of speaking—Disease moves us heavily downward with its complaints, fatigue, paralysis, pain, and confinement (to bed, if nothing else!). . . . We are mired down, pulled under, drowned. Progression is "downhill," down, into bed. One slip, one fall, and it may be some time before we get "out" or "over" it. [15]

This time spent in the underworld of illness can be healing, as it was for me, to an imagination that has been subordinated to the upward flight of healthy development.

In some cultures, according to Eliade, significant illness or injury early in life, like the presence of deformity, can mark a person for shamanship. To a lesser degree, childhood illnesses that are non-life-threatening but of some duration may initiate any of us into realizations that are shamanic: imaginal healing of this sort helps to define an imaginal shamanism.

PATHOLOGIZING AS A SHAMANIC PATH

OF THESE PERPLEXITIES de Mille says nothing: as long as children are happily reality-trained, avoiding both hallucinations and hallucinogens, he is satisfied. Not so Hillman—more likely on Freud's side than that of de Mille—who provides, for purposes of an imaginal shamanism, the most considered perspective on the relation of suffering to the recovery of soul.

For Hillman the child, within the adult fantasy called "childhood," plays a complex part in the pathologies of adulthood. Deeply distrustful of developmentalism, Hillman sees the child arriving with a positive primordial relationship to the world, not a host of ills. Even more strongly than Mary Watkins he sees theories of child development as themselves a major ill, miseducating the child out of his or her native wonder, as when "school tries to put the child's psyche within the mind of practical reason: clocktime, factual truth, and a Xerox notion of images, i.e., accurate representation."[16]

This betrayal of childhood imagining, asserts Hillman, is carried out with the best of good will, following developmentalist ideas of the child in our psychology and schooling, providing adult guidance to the child that suppresses soul, the intense childhood involvement with the terrors and joys of the imaginal:

> No wonder that actual children become so anaesthetized that they are content with the pseudostimuli of television, so that by adolescence they have

to shoot up to feel. They sit in classes without motivation, walk the streets in sullen rage, and seek desperately for sensuous transcendence in sounds, speeds and sex for an altered state of mind as an alternative script to the soulless and joyless dealing, handling, coping, managing life as a program of practical reason. Unconsciously, they recollect something else, something more, which they would find again, sometimes by suicide.[17]

Thus the adult experience of psychological *pathology* that Hillman says Freud assigned to the child as source[18] might be found to have roots in "civilization," our cultural repression of the imaginal realities of the child's world in favor of an idea of ego development. To recover these realities, then—to recover soul as we are seeking to do in imaginal shamanism—requires a return to the child's relationship to them, a return which the developed ego and an ego-centered culture resist. Hillman calls this "a collapse into the infantile realm of the child. Our strong ego-centered consciousness fears nothing more than just such a collapse."[19]

This fear is one of the faces of pathologizing, a process that troubles the ego while offering a shamanic imagining the opportunity to recover soul. Only imagination can cure imagination, said Ronald Sukenick, and only pathologizing fantasies can psychologically heal pathology. Hillman affirmed Sukenick's insight in a 1993 address to the American Art Therapy Association.

THERE HE OBSERVED, first, that in regard to memories, or even false memories, of childhood trauma, what we are dealing with is primarily a "disordered imagination." For such patients, he said,

> . . . the imagination is not large enough to encompass the past history and its traumas. The past always remains a trauma rather than initiation, a violation rather than a learning about power, evil, and the inhumanity of inhuman forces that take part in human life. These . . . powers are what makes facing the canvas and the clay and the body [in art therapy] so terrifying. Let's not forget that. It's not just play! Meeting the image is frightening. Ask any artist.[20]

Meeting the image can be terrifying. Art can be terrifying. That is part of its central role in the practice of pathologizing, for fear is indispensable to that shamanic path.

This also means that the terror the artist faces is part of art's healing beauty: powers have been faced, animal powers of the wild underworld, that demand an initiation. An art therapy such as that taught by Howard McConeghey or Shaun McNiff requires a radical respect for the art-making process that insures we will be confronted by the image, faced with an initiation that can reorder our ego's relationship to imagining. And McNiff does draw the parallel between this encounter and shamanic experience very pointedly in his soulful work *Art as Medicine*.[21]

For his part, Hillman went on to tell the art therapists that

> the main trauma of early abuse is the damage it does to imagination. Imagination gets trapped in literalized fantasies of biography. And the emotions remain stuck in a narrow childhood box of bitterness. The way out of the box which has trapped imagination is by means of imagination. . . . When restricted imagination manifests as excessive emotion, that's imagination's way to protest.

Here Hillman made an important move, reminding us of the close connection between image and emotion. This then allowed him to propose an imaginal response to feelings run rampant. Neither medical sedation nor therapeutic release, cathartic expression, is fully adequate: "We need valid images, serious rituals, and heartfelt sacrifices"—of precisely the sort a post-Jungian art therapy can provide:

> I'm suggesting that the restoration of the imagination is the correct response to disordered emotions. Especially that imagination I've pleaded for for years, one which welcomes the gift of the gods. And art therapy is doing this! With its dance and music and masks and paint, clay, and colors art therapy is actually entering the spirit world of ritual and sacrifice. Don't take it literally, though, and start doing shamanism.

No, never take it literally. We cannot, as Westerners—and need not, for an *imaginal* art therapy contributes to an *imaginal* shamanism that can be more powerful than neoshamanist workshops which literalize our colonialist fantasies of direct indigenous access. Through its confrontation with the frequently terrifying image, an art therapy which *makes art* "is actually entering the spirit world of ritual and sacrifice." This dialogue in depth with the imagination by aesthetic means—always a crucial ingredient of Jung's revolutionary legacy—is a very big step on the path of what Hillman calls pathologizing.

THE PRACTICE OF PATHOLOGIZING

THE PATH OF PATHOLOGIZING is a slippery one both conceptually and experientially, but Hillman explains how we as Western seekers and sufferers might walk it. It is in his masterwork *Re-Visioning Psychology* that he shows how the pathologizing process is central to soul-making. We already know it is central to shamanism. For Eliade's insight that it was shamanic practices that first gave a religious value to suffering holds true however much his emphasis on the shaman's celestial flight was an imaginative construction based on his own preoccupations. Without dismemberment, or falling apart, in other words, there can be no shamanism of any sort.

So the section of *Re-Visioning Psychology* that deals with suffering points us toward a conclusive parallel between post-Jungian psychology and traditional shamanism that needs to inform any imaginal version in the future of the West. *The soul in ourselves and our world cannot be recovered if sickness unto death is not seen and felt as one of its imaginal realities.*

Hillman's book sets forth his fundamental shift of perspective away from ego psychology to soul-making in four long chapters. All illuminate the complex ways and means of soul, which he seeks to characterize in a brief introductory section:

> . . . the word refers to that unknown component which makes meaning possible, turns events into experiences, is communicated in love, and has a religious concern. These four qualifications I had already put forth some years ago; I had begun to use the term freely, usually interchange-ably with psyche (from Greek) and anima (from Latin). Now I am adding three necessary modifications. First, "soul" refers to the *deepening* of events into experiences; second, the significance soul makes possible, whether in love or in religious concern, derives from its special *relation with death.* And third, by "soul" I mean the imaginative possibility in our natures, the experiencing through reflective speculation, dream, image, and *fantasy*—that mode which recognizes all realities as primarily sym-bolic or metaphorical.[22]

It should be noted that this passage draws on Hillman's work with ancient Greek and Renaissance traditions rather than mainstream Christianity (there is little or no indication here or elsewhere in post-Jungian psychology, for instance, that "the immortality of the soul" is a concern) and that his refer-ence to fantasy specifies a *conscious* relationship to the process of imagining that produces fantasies. This is something lacking to date, as we have seen, in the New Shamanism. Moreover, a further comment by Hillman that his book is "an attempt to discover and vivify soul through my writing and your reading"[23] reminds us of how often the process of imagining begins with books, and nowhere moreso than in neoshamanism with its literary lying and its debt to shamanthropology.

I urge you to read this particular book of his in responding to the neoshamanism movement, just as I recommended *The Dream and the Underworld* (and I would add *Healing Fiction*). Hillman's writing is seldom entirely easy to follow: discovering and vivifying soul through his books is a large agenda for readers as well as writer, and requires our closest attention. The rewards of patient reading and reflection can be great, however, and certainly anyone stirred by Thomas Moore's more accessible books should consider a serious study of Hillman's work. For those who seek a soulfully Western version of shamanism that work is indispensable, perhaps especially the work on pathologizing he presents in Chapter 2 of *Re-Visioning Psychology*.

As ever, Hillman starts with a dual distinction established between soul and spirit or mind, on the one hand, and soul and body or nature, on the other. Thus his discussion of pathologizing is not about either spiritual ideas of sin or medical ideas of physiological sickness, except as these relate to the primary concern with the suffering soul, the disordered and disordering imagination. This also means that neither spiritual salvation nor perfect bodily health is the goal of a concern for pathologizing. Even the activities of the shaman, misunderstood along Eliadean lines as exclusively heroic journeying to the heights of heaven, are ruled out by Hillman as too groundlessly spiritual.[24]

We are envisioning Western shamanism otherwise, however, as a soulful spirituality counter to ego-control. Thus pathologizing as a necessity of the soul is entirely pertinent to our purposes. And its necessity, its determining reality for our psychological life, is what Hillman seeks to demonstrate:

> Each soul at some time or another demonstrates illusions and depressions, overvalued ideas, manic flights and rages, anxieties, compulsions, and perversions. . . . For we are each peculiar; we have symptoms; we fail, and cannot see why we go wrong or even where, despite high hopes and good intentions. We are unable to set matters right, to understand what is taking place or be understood by those who would try. Our minds, feelings, wills, and behaviors deviate from normal ways. . . . Destruction seeps out of us autonomously and we cannot redeem the broken trusts, hopes, loves. . . . These are the actualities—the concrete mess of psychological existence as it is phenomenologically, subjectively, and individually—in which I want to set these chapters. Through them, I hope to find some psychological necessity in the pathologizing activity of the soul.[25]

This lengthy passage makes plain how very serious Hillman is about something shamanism has known in its own ways. Illness is as normal as health, failure as frequent as success—a loss of soul is the ultimate diagnosis of a self or a culture out of balance with these perennial components of actual life in the world.

AND YET HILLMAN'S PURPOSE is finally a constructive one. Pathologizing is defined as "the psyche's autonomous ability to create illness, morbidity, disorder, abnormality, and suffering in any aspect of its behavior and to experience and imagine life through this deformed and afflicted perspective."[26] But the pathologizing psyche is not *wrong*, for all that, and to realize deeply that it is not wrong, but rather necessary, is healing. His aim is therefore to show its necessity, to show that the soul's pathologizing is not, in itself, wrong either physiologically or morally.

In order to do this he speaks of "rejoining soul and symptom,"[27] since it was symptoms, in the patients of Freud and Jung but also in themselves, that led to the cultural rediscovery of the soul in the modern West. Symptoms can also lead to the recovery of the soul for any one of us, if we honor our illnesses, the suffering that allows the imagination to be heard again. If we have patience with this process, become true "patients" who imagine the illness onward, we manifest the pathologizing fantasy without which healing therapy is impossible: "It is the patient who . . . makes possible practice of whatever sort of style. Without the archetypal fantasy of pathology there would be no shaman," says Hillman, "no medicine man, no psychopharmaceutica, no analyst."[28]

What are the main components of this fantasy, the suffering of which and from which is so essential to soul-making?

There is no schematic diagram to be had, though Hillman does point out that "pathologizing is present not only at moments of special crisis but in the everyday lives of all of us. It is present most profoundly in the individual's sense of death, which he carries wherever he goes."[29] The sense of death must, however, be made conscious, forced upon our awareness through layers of denial. So sometimes moments of crisis are needed to make us attend to such a dark matter, central to soul.

Hypochondria, of course, as Hillman affirms, may proclaim the soul's necessary affliction as well as actual crisis does. Psychologically it is not so much literal threat as fantasized death that asks us to be conscious of its necessity:

> Whenever a symptom appears, or an anxiety about our state of mind or physical welfare, it is immediately carried by fantasy into its worst potential, into the incurable possibility: the stiff neck becomes immediately the incipient meningitis; the little lump, cancer; and the nightmare a presentiment of madness, accident, or ruin.[30]

Indeed, hypochondria in Hillman's lexicon almost seems synonymous with soul's pathologizing, although its negative connotation tends to return wrongness to the latter's expression. Awakened through crisis or hypochondria, however, the consciousness we need—it is the same image consciousness or anima consciousness with which we are to approach dream work or active imagination—constitutes the shamanism Western seekers can authentically experience as they address their suffering and that of their world. "Shamanic imagining" I have called it, and in the context of Hillman's discussion of pathologizing it is important to draw the parallel: shamanic imagining will suffer the soul to approach in all its darkness, its animal powers attacking as well as serving our ego's expectation, the equilibrium of our normalcy upset by fears we can learn not to repress.

Irrepressibly, of course, we will want the method for achieving all this, some technique or clear-cut steps to such a consciousness. Just as surely Hillman will not supply such a simple blueprint. He does say what he can, though, without dishonoring the soul's native ambiguity. He suggests, for instance, that "reverting" all pathologizing fantasies to mythic persons or plots from ancient Greece or Rome with which they have resonance makes for a culturally suitable means of carrying them in our consciousness, mirroring them. This follows the pathologizing psyche's own reversion to a mythical style of consciousness, he notes, drawing on "the same distorted, fantastic language."[31] Like the underworld of Hades as a metaphoric receptacle for working with our dreams, a figure like Saturn with his mythic attributes is for Hillman a better designation for how we live a depression than are clinical abstractions that speak a very different language.

Another way we can attend to our pathologizing and bring soul to our symptoms is to feel our fear as fully as possible without finding it wrong. Hillman explains that "since pathologizing is frightening, we are obliged to follow fear, not with courage but as a path that leads deeper into awe for what is at work in the depths of the soul."[32] Always death is the referent of our pathologizing fantasies and fears. And this connection is their great value as they weave through our symptoms with the afflicted images soul often favors: "Symptoms are death's solemn ambassadors . . . and life mirrored in its symptoms sees there its death and remembers soul. Pathologizing returns us to soul, and to lose the symptom means to lose this road to death, this way of soul."[33]

Again the shamanic parallel to this psychology needs drawing: *Remembering soul responds healingly to the dismemberments of a life lived in thrall to the ego; the lost soul is recovered by a memory inseparable from imagining.*

These methodological factors in the making of soul through the conscious fantasy of pathology—occasional crises and everyday complaints, mythic reversion and its exaggerations, courage and fear, healthy concern and hypochondria, deathly symptoms and their denial—all came together for me one sunny day in South Wales, on a path to meet Merlin.

WAS THIS TRIP NECESSARY?

I AM ON BOGGY GROUND in a green valley, having just passed a stone chapel at the end of a shaded lane from the road. Despite it being January, the weather is mild, maybe in the fifties, and the one day of sun during my trip comes at a good time. I pick my way along the fence of an open pasture, heading for a large hill. To my left is a lovely sight: a little flood plain contains a pond with two white swans and a single ancient oak. Beyond these is the meandering River Tywi, running to the sea near Carmarthen, "Merlin's Town."

It is 1993, three years after my partner left me in Vermont to follow her soul to the Southwest, two years after I spent the spring in Boulder to be closer to her, the first of many visits, and a year from when I bought a house with her in Albuquerque—but still over a year before I can work it out with my college to move down and share our house and start what I hope will be a new life. The overnight flight has brought me from snowy New England to wet Wales for a conference on "Performance, Ritual, and Shamanism" at the Centre for Performance Research in Cardiff. A professional acquaintance of some years, Ronald Grimes, who has written about experimental theater as "parashamanism" in one of his books on ritual studies,[34] knows of my work on imaginal shamanism and has recommended me to the conference organizers.

The sessions will start this evening. But the day is free and I have rented a car to find Merlin here outside the village of Llandeilo. It is the same day I arrived, sleepless, at a London airport for the brief visit. Due to the disruption in my usual routine, I have neglected to take certain medications. But the day is fine, the scenery serene, and the quest is proving pleasant.

Merlin has many graves in the British Isles and Brittany. As Myrddin Wyllt, however, Wild Merlin, shamanic Merlin, his home is Wales. In Ean Begg and Deike Rich's guidebook *On the Trail of Merlin*, there are many Welsh sites associated with his legend, and Llandeilo is one of them.[35] Actually, it is in Dynevor Park, just outside the village, that he lies sleeping, entombed by the fairy enchantments of Viviane/Niniane/Nimue. Edmund Spenser, writing *The Faerie Queene* in the 1690s when the lore of *faerie* and the otherworld that he drew on still preserved Celtic echoes of shamanism (and just as Europe was first hearing about the actual shamans encountered by travelers to Siberia), pointed to the place I had chosen for a modest quest. Merlin is buried, in Spenser's poem, at

> That dreadful place.
> It is an hideous hollow cave (they say)

Under a rock that lyes a little space
From the swift Burry tumbling apace,
Amongst the woody hills of Dynevawr.

Spenser got the river wrong, Begg and Rich quickly interject,[36] but Dynevor was clearly indicated as a final resting-place for a Merlin who, submitting to his fate, may nevertheless be restless.

THE PATH THROUGH the woods to the chapel had been easy to follow. Now I was not so sure, and had only the fence railing to guide me to the foot of the wooded hill. Above I could see steps made out of railroad ties dimly evident in their dark green surroundings. At the top of this long climb, another book has assured me, will be a ninth-century castle ruin overlooking the Tywi Valley several hundred feet below. In these environs is a cave or stone or hawthorn clump or tower of mist, never found, beneath or within which Merlin, spellbound, sleeps. Will he stir, hearing my footsteps, and call out?

I am breathing heavily now as I approach the wooden steps, and my chest is beginning to hurt. Beyond the top of the steps I will meet a curving gravel road that climbs up almost to the castle. I remember now that I have not taken my heart pills, either last night on the plane or this morning when we landed at Heathrow. They are back in Cardiff with my luggage. On a regimen of medication, diet, and exercise I have had no angina for years, and have successfully avoided the bypass operation for which I was told I am a candidate. But now, as the chest pains increase, I begin to wonder: Should I turn back?

I decide to keep climbing, telling myself that the pains will go away when I get to the top and can rest. Still, I fear that this is a foolish daredevil maneuver that may even cost me my life. I, too, may have my final resting-place on this Welsh hill.

I also imagine that Merlin may be signalling me, perhaps warning me, through these feelings in my heart. Will I die here, finally, and be with him "ever after"? There is no one at the castle ruin, so I can pant and massage my chest in private. The ruin contains an impressive round tower—a stone structure, not a tower of mist, but could Merlin be inside, watching me? As I rest I ponder this possibility, but the chest pains persist and part of my mind is fending off panic. I am in intense uncertainty, my consciousness having been heightened in a way I would not have wished, my agreement with Hillman's psychology notwithstanding.

"Angina" and "anxiety" (also "anguish") are from the same root meaning to be choked, congested, constricted. What, aside from my arteries, is choking me, constricting my emotional life? Is Merlin causing this, or just the fact that I forgot to take my medication? And was my forgetfulness itself only a matter of jet lag? Did Merlin send the pain to say that I should stop being so heroic on my unmedicated climb, that the price of surmounting obstacles is too steep? Where did realistic medical assessment, "healthy concern," end and hypochondria begin? Could they ever be separated? Caught between genuine crisis and self-deluding melodrama, was my heart breaking? Was it courageous to be heartbroken on this hill, alone above the vale, reverting my pathologizing to a half-human figure of British lore if not to a Greek or Roman god? Or was this merely a case of stupidly indulging myself during a physical threat in need of medical prudence, risking the well-being of my partner and my children?

I suppose I should summon my iguana against the dragon that seems to be squeezing my chest in this landscape whose emblem, since Merlin's day, has been a red dragon. Or perhaps Dumbo can fly me off this hilltop, back to the fantasied safety of childhood. But I can only think of two things: *This is silly, it cannot possibly be that I will die here*; and: *Maybe I will.* I have my camera, and, following the first thought, I continue to take pictures. The second thought, though, puts Merlin in the picture as my fellow corpse— maybe as my murderer, for reasons unknown.

Even as I descend the hill and retrace my steps to the car my chest does not stop hurting; that it has stopped getting worse is not particularly encouraging. Only during the drive back to Cardiff on the congested motorway, as I realize I am drenched with sweat on this January day, do the pains subside, then disappear.

Back in my room I take my pills. It all seems like a dream, as if I am still in the plane sleeping, carried through the night on a magical flight, high above the ocean that separates me from the places where the shamanism of my heritage once healed lost souls like me. Was this trip necessary? Did the pathologizing provoked by the climb, the hill defeating my health, take me to depths where suffering acquires its imaginal necessity, its sacred shamanic value? Or was it all wrong, an episode of ego-heroics to surmount my body, an attack on my heart, despite Merlin's warning?

HEART TROUBLES

SOON AFTER RETURNING from Wales, I drive to New Mexico, having taken a leave for the spring semester to be with my partner in the house we had bought the previous year. At the end of the summer, August 1993, I drive back to Vermont to teach for another year, then work out an arrangement to reduce my teaching and move permanently to Albuquerque, flying back for brief residencies and corresponding with students in between. Less than a year after this relocation in the summer of 1994 my partner, descending with terrifying suddenness into a species of insanity, announces our ten-year relationship is over. There is no explanation, no grievance against me, no other person, no remorse—and no willingness to try to work things out with a couples counselor. Later, as we separate, there will be behavior on her part that others call violently psychotic, and vicious legal assaults I could not have imagined in my naïveté. "Breaking up," for me, is a falling apart, another kind of heart attack.

For most of 1995, I am in the stage of trauma that Greg Mogenson writes about in *God Is a Trauma*, a book I find and keep by my bed: "After the miscarriage, the break-up, or the tragic car accident, we may find ourselves utterly unable to imagine our lives forward. The soul, spellbound by events which have overwhelmed it, cannot lay hold of its other images."[37]

This trauma, however, brings me closer to my son, who has lost his partner in—precisely—a tragic car accident three years earlier in Vermont while I was out buying the house in New Mexico. Preoccupied with the uncertainties of purchasing a home I might only ever be able to visit, I do not return for the memorial service. My rationalizations soon prove ineffective, and I feel a rift between us that only closes with my own grieving. A fiction writer like his partner Brigid Clark, Christopher has completed a grief memoir, *In the Unlikely Event of a Water Landing*, that will appear in 1996. It is an experience of art therapy to write and to read. I wish there were an easier way we could have come together—I certainly wish our losses had never happened—but that is, in fact, life. Christopher and his sister Rebecca, with whom I am on the phone daily for damage control, have flown down to Albuquerque, unbidden, to support me as I fend off the truly incredible emotional devastation of my ex's mad attack. Once the immediate trauma lifts—and it lasts for most of a horrible year—pathologizing and the difficult healing it brings can slowly begin.

My breaking heart on Merlin's hill may have been a physical premonition of an emotional future, a warning from a very old man about what I will have to pass through to become an old man myself.

And now, having retreated to Vermont to write my own book, I am beginning to pass through this painful transition, working toward a more heartfelt realization of the initiatory function of my personal trauma, the loss of innocence that individuation entails as outrage yields to sad acceptance. Despite continuing legal onslaughts from afar that flash me back to the trauma, and my tendency to use the writing project itself as a heroic surmounting of my troubles, there is some psychic movement. There are, for instance, those British boat dreams to work on.

Beyond concepts *about* imaginal healing, there is imaginal healing itself, available to any of us through the inevitable pathologizing life brings—opportunities for a shamanic imagining that cannot be shamanic if it is fast, safe, simple, or fun.

Hillman once told an interviewer that "basically, if you give the soul a chance through defeat, a lot of things happen: Imagination happens; feeling happens; heartbreak, depression, fateful moves, lost loves—what I call soul."[38] These are some of the basics we each need to learn as we suffer the recovery of soul, the mending of the heart. We apparently need to learn them over and over, as soul-making is endless and our hard-won deepening proceeds by difficult fits and starts.

As WITH MY CHILDHOOD illness and my adult angina, the body can be an ally to shamanic imagining if we do not take its suffering only literally. Writing about cardiac dysrhythmia, or irregular heartbeat, Alfred Ziegler says that

> [it] can be understood as varying forms of being "beside oneself." Generally occurring as paroxysms, they are emotional seizures which find their expression primarily in the body because other outlets are denied them. The body gives expression to what otherwise would be passion, a fluttery anxiety, a racing rage, a sense of transcendence, or simply the occasional chaos of emotionality that is part of human experience. It is as if we fall apart or come to a fall when emotions "descend" into body and make themselves into disease syndromes of indeterminate origin. . . .[39]

I am myself a sufferer from this syndrome, as occasional dysrhythmia has visited me even as angina has generally been held in abeyance, and I am sure that otherwise-unexpressed "emotional seizures" play their part—as they surely do when, every decade it seems, acute anxiety overtakes me for a devastating day or two.

Ziegler's insight complements that of Elaine Scarry: fearful imaginings are "somatized" in painful physical symptoms just as such symptoms *prompt* imagining, according to Scarry's thoughtful study, *The Body in Pain*.[40] In either direction, so to speak, the body negotiates an ecstatic experience, an experience that can become shamanic if some consciousness is brought to it as in an active imagination process.

A third writer further illuminates the role of the body in imaginal healing, this time based upon her own very intimate acquaintance with illness.

The Alchemy of Illness is Kat Duff's sensitive exploration of the difficult journey of soul-making she experienced through suffering for several years from chronic fatigue syndrome. She tells us that "defying the rules of ordinary reality, illness shares in the hidden logic of dreams, fairy tales, and the spirit realms mystics and shamans describe," adding that

> I have begun to suspect that in the otherworld reality of illness, anything and everything can kill and heal, whether it is digitalis in heart medicine, a lover's touch, or God's grace. There is no apparent rhyme or reason to the geography of illness, only the ultimate authority and agency of physical pain.[41]

THE DARK HEART OF HEALING

DUFF DOES NOT stress that pain provokes imagining or ecstatic flights of aversion from the body, as Scarry does, although she confesses to having fantasies of torture instruments when afflicted. She does, however, underscore how alien the land of sickness is to those "in" good health, and vice versa. Being sick is thus itself an *ec-stasis*: we stand outside of, descend beneath, the "normal" selves we thought ourselves to be and our culture expects us to be. Duff discusses this otherness of illness itself:

> Because the experience of illness is so difficult to accept, communicate, and integrate, it sinks into the mute flesh of our bodies as we recover. In fact, the word "recover" literally means "to cover up again." We lose that piece of our lives, that corner of truth, in order to reclaim the world we share with others. The experience may be forgotten altogether, or obscured by the workings of memory into the shadows of insignificance, with euphemistic understatements like "It was just a bad dream" or "I had a little trouble with my heart." It appears that the terrain of the sick, like the underworld in Greek mythology, is surrounded by the waters of forgetfulness.[42]

Her mention of the Greek underworld recalls Hillman's use of its mythic image to orient his work with dreams, the initiatory strangeness of which we similarly consign to the lost memories of the familiar dayworld. It is therefore confirming that Duff should go on to make the same connection with no reference to *The Dream and the Underworld*. She reflects that

> the longer I am sick, the more I realize that illness is to health what dreams are to waking life—the reminder of what is forgotten, the bigger picture working toward resolution. If I were to name that intelligence, that deep knowing which operates through the agency of our dreams and flesh, I would call it soul. . . .[43]

Pathologizing is an indispensable path to imaginal shamanism and the soul recovery it suffers, a central instance of the radical resources post-

Jungian psychology provides to seekers of this mode of healing spirituality—which cannot be without its dark heart.

Illness, on the other hand, cannot be a route to the underworld of shamanic healing if these resources and their difficult demands are not realized: fully understood—intellectually or otherwise—and then incorporated into one's life. The advice of Thomas Moore can help. He writes about "the body's poetics of illness" in *Care of the Soul,* a book that begins, in the very first sentence, by saying that "the great malady of the twentieth century, implicated in all of our troubles and affecting us individually and socially, is 'loss of soul.'"[44] What he says in his endorsement of Duff's *Alchemy of Illness*—that it is "an excellent corrective to our society's usual soulless way of dealing with illness"—could be said for this section on the body in his own book. Reading it, I felt it offered a corrective not just to society in general but to me personally in my relatively soulless way of dealing with my heart trouble. Of course, my heroic handling of this disease is partly a product of powerful social forces from which none of us is immune; I, too, am a party to the soul loss of Western culture.

AMONG ITS OTHER STRATEGIES, Moore's corrective asks us to "imagine a medical approach more in tune with art, one that is interested in the symbolic and poetic suggestiveness of a disease or a malfunctioning organ."[45] As an example of how this aesthetic approach might work, he recounts a conversation, personally compelling to me, with a nutritionist who warned him to reduce his cholesterol intake to guard against heart disease.

He says to her "I don't doubt that cholesterol is a fact . . . but I wonder if we take it too factually." The nutritionist's husband then suggests an analogy between congested arteries and congested highways—neither of which North Americans have much patience with—that elicits Moore's favorable response:

> I appreciated his comment because it took us out of the literal realm of chemistry and treated the symptom as a symbol, a lens through which to see the problem in an altogether different context. . . . seeing the metaphorical comparison is the beginning of giving the body poetic weight.[46]

That said, Moore points to his mentor Hillman, who had lectured on the heart when they were both in Dallas. He had criticized the current narrow view of it as a pump or vessel:

> Hillman's point was that we are attacking the heart when we treat as a mere physical organ what poetry and song for centuries have treated as the seat of affection. It isn't easy for us, so imbued with modern categories of

thought, to remember our own biases in this matter. Of course the heart is a pump. That's a fact. Our problem is that we can't see through the thought structures that give value to fact and at the same time treat poetic reflection as nonessential. In a sense, that point of view is itself a failure of heart. We think with our heads and no longer with our hearts.[47]

It is crucial that those of us who are pursuing the possibility of a Western shamanism "take to heart" these observations of Moore and Hillman. And again they apply not only on the personal level—though they emphatically apply there for me—but also culturally.

We clearly must heal our cultural loss of the *anima mundi*, the soul of the world, as part of any imaginal healing of ourselves that shamanic imagining can bring. We live in a culture with heart trouble: our heroic and anaesthetized attitudes toward ourselves, one another, and the world are destroying the soul-connection that sustains our life. A soulful neoshamanism is not about heroic flights in behalf of ego's mastery, the acquisition of personal power. The healing process of the shamanism we seek recovers the relationship to soul that ego development has suppressed in our childhood— as Watkins makes plain—and is submerging under ugliness and pollution in the outer world. Pathologizing takes place in that world as well as the inner. Its imaginings there must be brought to consciousness for the sake of the community just as what we know of the shaman includes his or her restoration of balance socially and ecologically.

On the individual level our imaginal version of the New Shamanism works with the pathologizing that initiates the ego, that asks of the heart another kind of courage. Our lack of this courage starts in our head, necessitating the sort of rethinking as well as reimagining this book has asked of its readers. But "the heart has reasons that reason knows not of," said the philosopher Pascal. To know those reasons we need to find what Hillman calls the thought of the heart, a heartfelt aesthetic imagining akin to Kat Duff's "deep knowing." The legacy of Carl Jung allows us to do so. But unless we realize that legacy in a radical way we cannot have a shamanism of our own, only unconscious fantasies that devalue the indigenous Other even as they delude our seeking.

COMPREHENDING MERLIN'S CRY

*T*he day after my heartfelt encounter with Merlin, at the conference in Cardiff, I participated in a body-movement workshop with a man named Nunez from Mexico who leads such workshops for actors. Having survived my climb in Llandeilo, I was suitably medicated, but curious about how I would respond to some strenuous exercise. There was an hour and a half of it at least, a nonstop circling around the studio space which I endured with Nunez constantly imploring us, in wonderful Mexican-accented English, to "Make the effort! Make the effort!" It was all, alas, too heroic, though I was glad the angina did not return.

I think Nunez said that his exercises had the blessing of Carlos Castaneda, using a term—"tensegrity"—that I was later led to believe is borrowed from Buckminster Fuller and made use of by the brilliant literary liar of Los Angeles.

Or at any rate it is used in his name by his female disciples of the mid-1990s, who market a video of their own body-movement "passes" under that title. Castaneda has changed publishers for his 1993 book, his ninth, about the ego control of dream states; he has not, however, changed his story that it is not a story.[1] His new disciples, female and male, also produce a *Nagualist Newsletter* that shows how, after twenty-five years, they still do not seem to have learned the lesson of his hoax, and continue to float passively in literalized fantasies of Mesoamerican sorcery. Varieties of that sorcery may indeed exist—totally aside from Castaneda's fairy tales. And totally aside from "practical applications" of them, which a recent book by Victor Sanchez puts forth even when he acknowledges that don Juan may be the creation of "don Carlos"![2]

Meanwhile, there *is*, I believe, a "path with heart" that leads out of the experience of reading Castaneda. But it does not go around the circle I shuffled in Cardiff with the amiably insistent Senor Nunez.

Following that path, I am afraid, was instead a dance of avoidance, refusing for the time being the imaginal route my congested arteries had opened up at Merlin's behest. I hope that since then I have begun to travel the latter route, partly because meditating on the role of Merlin in my angina episode—knowing it could not be a factual role—may have initiated the conscious pathologizing required for imaginal healing. Merlin, having retired from the world, was being welcomed psychologically into the confused ambivalence of my actual life. A step may have been taken, beyond my ego-heroics in Wales, to join symptom to soul.

My personal experience, of course, is just one small example of what comprehending Merlin's cry entails. The imaginal shamanism here lies in giving reality to a fantasy—*feeling* Merlin's real presence in my pathologized imagining—without taking it literally, and thereby recovering a bit of lost soul.

This is not necessarily an easy shift in attitude, even as a purely intellectual maneuver. To say of the Wizard of Oz (or the Wizard of Los Angeles), "Pay *more* attention to that man behind the curtain," seeing through the wizardry, but *without* losing the felt reality of the story, is no mean feat. Anthropologists approaching shamanic rituals and related phenomena have had their own kind of difficulty in achieving this imaginal perspective. One who has achieved it was another participant in the conference on "Performance, Ritual, and Shamanism" in Wales that January.

FROM SPIRITS TO IMAGINALS

EDITH TURNER, a respected anthropologist, sweetly but strongly challenged me all through the conference about what she feared was the psychological reduction—in effect, the psychological dismissal—of the real spirits she had encountered doing field work in Africa and Alaska. She worried that my post-Jungian approach denied their reality by seeing it as only mental, much as her anthropological colleagues had typically distanced themselves from the force of such phenomena for being scientifically inadmissible data. My response, as ever, was that the rhetoric of "spirits" risked a literalism that denied the imaginal.

We left Cardiff feeling we had more to learn from one another. At least I felt that way, if only because the interface between performance and ritual which she and her late husband Victor Turner had investigated with great distinction was a place where an imaginal shamanism could well be embodied, as Ronald Grimes had also suggested with his idea of parashamanism. Theater as therapy and drama therapy as shamanic imagining were connections hinted as well by the use of theater arts analogies in Jungian explanations of the active imagination process. But equally important ideas, recalling our conversations in Cardiff, remained to be learned by me from Turner's perspective, and perhaps by her from mine.

Sometime after the conference, I encountered her 1992 article whose title alone signalled the importance of her topic for the issues between us: "The Reality of Spirits."[3] This article lends anthropological weight to imaginal shamanism even as the Jungian resources we have marshalled lend psychological weight, by implication and outcome, to her anthropology. It is necessary to review her essay closely to see just how this is so. It will richly repay us in concluding our search for the soul of shamanism.

Explaining that she and her husband had been trained not to "go native," she starts her article by recalling a period of field work with the Ndembu of Zambia in the 1950s: "Their ideas were strange and a little disturbing, but somehow we were on the safe side of the white divide and were free merely to study the beliefs."[4] Still, there were powerful experiences in Africa that this attitude did not entirely account for, and then a performance workshop at New York University in which, experimenting with a trance ritual from Brazil, a student was actually induced into trance, with seemingly paranormal aftereffects to follow.

Next came Turner's own striking experience, back in Zambia in 1985, of sighting a "spirit form," as she calls it, "a large gray blob of something like plasma," emerge from a sick woman's back at the height of a healing ritual.

> Then I knew the Africans were right. There *is* spirit stuff. There *is* spirit affliction: it isn't a matter of metaphor and symbol, or even psychology. And I began to see how anthropologists have perpetuated an endless series of put-downs about the many spirit events in which they participated—"participated" in a kindly pretense. They might have obtained valuable material, but they have been operating with the wrong paradigm, that of the positivists' denial.[5]

Here was our disagreement again: her understandable suspicion of psychology but also, I saw, her ignorance of Jung's radical legacy.

We know that indigenous healers sometimes use sleight-of-hand as part of their performances—not just to deceive but to produce real psychosomatic change. Turner certainly must know about this element of "extractions" in healing ceremonies better than I do. But she also knows she saw something. The question is how to take account of the "something" in our Western categories.

My inclination, evident throughout this book, is to lean over backwards to avoid literalism while fully honoring, in effect, the "rightness" of the Africans' reality. The real shamanic trick for us as Western seekers is to find a way to do the latter without committing the former, stretching the Western paradigm away from its positivist extreme without presuming that we—again as Westerners—can simply abandon it. The language of "spirits" fails, I feel, at this delicate task (while also potentially confusing Hillman's careful distinction, upon which our search depends, between "spirit" and "soul").

For Westerners like Turner and me spirits are "somethings" that have been claimed to be literally existing entities, entities whose existence we happen to have been taught to disbelieve as "supernatural." To believe in them—or to use this term to name some real experience, which amounts to the same thing—is to literalize, to "concretize," as Jung put it in condemning it. Ironically, this literalism is no more respectful of indigenous realities than is the "positivists' denial" Turner laments.

TURNER'S CONCLUSION from her African experience, aside from this continuing terminological issue, is to favor "going native," encouraging "radical participation" in the anomalous events anthropologists sometimes observe. In 1987 she experienced an event I do not remember her mentioning in Cardiff six years later, despite the references in my presentation there: a Michael Harner workshop.

She describes an "upperworld journey" assisted by drumming in which she was, as I was, guided to meet a celestial teacher. Instead, she sees a disturbing image of dark red internal organs on a large TV screen. Harner, she emphasizes, did not interpret this image, or those of the other participants, in psychological terms.

As we saw in Chapter 7, however, this ostensibly unobjectionable move does not tell the whole story of Harner's relationship to psychological perspectives, and certainly not to post-Jungian ones. Obviously Turner's terminology of spirits, and the problems with it, also echoes that issue in Harner's neoshamanism as we have critiqued it earlier. These questions are not in the foreground of her concern in the essay, however, nor does she discuss the reasons for her apparent deference to the Harner approach—or, for that matter, her reasons for participating in his workshop in the first place. Perhaps his standing as an anthropologist and her interest in performance as ritual had something to do with it.

Her point, in any case, is that the bloody image from the upperworld recurred four months later in Alaska in the actuality of a dead seal, its stomach split open, its internal organs displayed.

This perceived precognition alerted Turner to other more-or-less unaccountable phenomena of the Eskimo world in which she immersed herself. She says that her host, Ernest Frankson, "often accused me of not believing in these manifestations, but I protested that I did. How could I help it? Ernie usually had a bad time from whites, who labeled his experiences 'magical beliefs.'"[6] I may or may not have argued in Cardiff that the rhetoric of "belief," in my view, could be as problematically positivist as that of "spirits."

Her intention, again, was not to question terminology, at least not right away, but to develop a methodology which could allow anthropologists to study a "mentality" like the Eskimos' "from inside,"[7] to foster an anthropology, in other words, that deliberately goes native. We might call it a shamanthropology of a sort, though she does not, and she has not, to my knowledge, abandoned academia for the workshop circuit. Instead her article here returns to a criticism it had touched on earlier: she castigates anthropologists for using concepts of metaphor or symbol to deny the reality of indigenous experience and thereby maintain an "intellectual imperialism."[8]

With my strong investment in the imagination, terms like "metaphor" and "symbol" were very positive. Still, I could feel the validity of her critique and found myself challenged once more. I could see how describing occurrences as metaphorical might serve, as she details, an ethos of dissection on the part of Western anthropologists which disrespected the truth of their hosts' lives. I support her intentions here if we do not disrespect imagination in the bargain, since it is our embattled but available Western means of contacting the sorts of realities she honors in other cultures' spirituality.

And so Turner, in an article which contributes from the outside, so to speak, to our sense of what an imaginal shamanism needs to be, comes to the question "What are spirits?" She searches through other terms—"power," "energy," "*ki* or *chi*"—for help in answering this question, but returns to "the old-fashioned term, 'spirit manifestation,'" as "much closer" to doing justice to "these manifestations [which] constitute the deliberate visitation of discernable forms that have the conscious intent to communicate, to claim importance in our lives."[9]

Having intensively explored the radical view of image in post-Jungian psychology we are entitled to see her words, in our friendly war of words, as exactly applicable to the imaginal realities, the animal powers, our version of

Western shamanism interacts with. As her article approaches its conclusion, her position and mine, for all their differences, appear to converge—and such a convergence would be all the more valuable due to the different backgrounds and understandings we bring to it.

First, however, she sums up her critical diagnosis of her field's distance from the realities it encounters:

> Again and again, anthropologists witness spirit rituals, and again and again, some indigenous exegete tries to explain that the spirits are present and, furthermore, that rituals are the central events of their society. The anthropologist proceeds to interpret them differently. There seems to be a kind of force field between the anthropologist and her or his subject matter, making it impossible for her or him to come close to it, a kind of religious frigidity. We anthropologists need training to see what the Natives see.[10]

Turner ends up seeking her "training" in a familiar place.

OUR SHAMANIC AWARENESS

"THIS MIGHT BEST BE DONE," Turner goes on, "by following the method of a luminous, shaman-type lady, Mary Watkins, who in her book, *Waking Dreams* (1976), leads us through practically all the ways of thinking of the Native religions with unerring skill."[11] Turner's recourse to Mary Watkins' work is not anthropological confirmation of the validity of our post-Jungian resources (it does not require such validation), let alone a capitulation to my point of view in the discussions between us. But it does represent a rich convergence, with another sort of shamanthropology—Turner's methodology of radical participation—pointing to the possibility of an imaginal shamanism.

And the word "imaginal" itself, taken from Henry Corbin and James Hillman to specify the realities a Western form of shamanism can legitimately contact for the healing recovery of soul, acquires a new twist in Turner's use of *Waking Dreams*:

> Are there spirits "out there"? In her book, Mary Watkins does not refer to "spirits" but to "dream figures," "images," or "imaginals." But she might as well have been describing spirits. She sees her "imaginals" as conscious beings with self-determination, with autonomy.[12]

Exactly: everything Turner seeks to accomplish by establishing, as her title puts it, "the reality of spirits" is accomplished by the post-Jungian terminology of images, imagination, and imaginal realities—without the massive shortcomings of literalization that neoshamanism has suffered and that the rhetoric of spirits risks.

If Turner's use of "imaginals" as a plural noun is her own coinage (I find it nowhere in Watkins, or in Hillman or Corbin), we can nevertheless accept it as a helpful contribution. Although it has been important to explore the post-Jungian sense of the inner image as a nonliteral reality, the term "image," we have also seen, is often taken to mean an outer image as copy or even a false front. So Turner's term "imaginals"—or "an imaginal"— might be preferable for our purposes were it not a bit obscure. What she does with it at the close of her essay is assuredly pertinent.

Having quoted excerpts from Watkins' chapter entitled "Movements From and Toward the Imaginal" (i.e., the imaginal realm) in order to underscore equivalences to her own emphasis on spirits as real, Turner draws her insightful conclusion:

> Watkins recognized the autonomy of something that she defines as deriving from inside a person—"an imaginal." An almost identical recognition runs through many cultures, but it is of spirits "out there." The initiative is theirs, not ours. Who is right, the dream analyst or the traditional seer? A symbologist might recognize Watkins's statements as concerned with shamanic awareness. Should we begin quite seriously to experience and recognize this entity—this "X," whether "spirit" or "imaginal"?[13]

I do not believe that Watkins, any more than imaginal psychology in general, following Jung's legacy, limits the source of the imaginal to "inside a person"—its interiority is not only personal, or even human, and such a limiting would imply the very reductionism from which post-Jungian thought like that of Watkins is significantly exempt. Likewise I am not sure what Turner means by a "symbologist"—perhaps it refers to the school of "symbolic anthropology" with which she and her late husband are identified. I am not even certain the terminology of "spirits" is as indigenous as she implies, since it is, after all, an English term, from the Latin, that we may well have imposed on other cultures.

But the answer to her question, for us as well as for her, is certainly yes: we *should* begin to "experience and recognize this entity," the soul image producing the imaginal realities of our lives and world—realities accessible to shamanic imagining.

This yes is not just a yes in behalf of anthropology and anthropologists studying other cultures, however, as it seems to be for her. She enlists ethnographers Dan Rose and Michael Jackson in her cause, and could as well have included Douglass Price-Williams, whose article on "The Waking Dream in Ethnographic Perspective," drawing on Jung, Hillman, and Watkins, came out the same year as hers.[14] Likewise Richard Noll, a psychologist with anthropological interests, has valuably speculated, without seeing shamans as schizophrenics, that they may have "image-prone" personalities.[15]

But *our* yes is in behalf of a psychology applicable to our own culture, to a "shamanic awareness" we as Westerners can experience and recognize as we allow ourselves to become consciously image-prone. In other words, Turner has suggested, perhaps unintentionally, that anthropological resources exist that fit with our post-Jungian psychological ones to support the possibility of a practice that is fully Western, thoroughly conscious, and totally respectful of the realities presented to *our* shamanic awareness. Indeed, she has been pressed by the very needs of her anthropology to employ post-Jungian psychology, as her fellow anthropologist Harner might yet be.

I have said that seeing through the story without losing the reality of the story—becoming sorcerers, in Ronald Sukenick's terms, who know that we live in fictions and know how to master the art—is no easy task. Deliteralizing without dismissing, we could also call it: deliteralizing the Western fantasies of neoshamanism without at all dismissing the imaginal realities it represents. For instance, remembering how, earlier in this book, we have handled the founding shamanovels of Mircea Eliade and Castaneda or the sustaining shamanthropology of neoshamanist workshops like Harner's.

Shamanic awareness is only available to Westerners in an imaginal shamanism that achieves this difficult feat; its achievement is, indeed, tantamount to that awareness, which we have otherwise called shamanic imagining.

Anyone can do this, I hasten to say, without having to become a full-fledged shaman, whatever that can mean in the West. It is probably safest to say that it is impossible for you and me, although others may mentor our imagination, and we theirs, in shamanic ways at certain times. I have suggested that Jung might be considered a Western shaman, but if so it would be because he opened up shamanic healing possibilities to an entire culture: ours. And his successors in imaginal psychology, realizing this legacy, shamanic in its radicality, have made it possible for each of us to live his or her life soulfully. *This soulful spirituality, in artful touch with dreams and imaginings, including especially those which connect us to our wounding, can be a shamanic spirituality of imaginal healing.*

AND WE CAN ACHIEVE this Western shamanism without ever pirating misunderstood pieces of indigenous shamanisms—including especially, for those of us in North America, Native American spiritual resources—to feed our passive fantasies. Vine Deloria, Jr., the Lakota writer I referred to in assessing my experience of the Harner workshop, is particularly eloquent and particularly scathing about the dangers of non-Native appropriation of Native cultural riches, including the insidious presence of that appropriation within our best intentions.

In a foreword to a 1980 anthology on images of Native Americans in the movies, Deloria probes several prevalent ones, starting with the "old chief" stereotype.[16] He shows how we fall into this fantasy in taking Castaneda's don Juan as a teacher conveying Yaqui indigenous wisdom: "Carlos Castaneda parlayed the old man image into a series of best sellers that have much more relationship with an LSD travel tour than with Indians. Whatever Don Juan is, he is far from a recognizable Indian except to confused and psychically injured whites who have a need to project their spiritual energies onto an old Indian for resolution."[17]

The insidious process continues when this supposedly benign image is made the standard which actual Native Americans are expected to live up to in a Euro-American society. "It has nothing to do with Indians, of course, but it is not supposed to represent the contemporary Indian since he is a pale imitation of the real Indians of the American imagination. . . . In almost every instance," Deloria comments, "we are forced to deal with American fantasies about the Indians of white imagination rather than the reality of the present."[18] A final point in Deloria's indictment drives home how deep the problem of "appropriation" goes as we are drawn to partake of indigenous shamanisms:

> The whites are sincere but they are only sincere about what they are interested in, not about Indians about whom they know very little. They get exceedingly angry if you try to tell them the truth and will only reject you and keep searching until they find the Indian of their fantasies. . . .
>
> The obvious solution to the whole thing would be for the whites to achieve some kind of psychological and/or religious maturity. But the whole psychological posture of American society is toward perpetual youth. Everyone believes that he or she must be eternally young. No one wants to believe that he or she is getting or will ever get old. Somehow only Indians get old because the coffee table books are filled with pictures of old Indians but hardly a book exists that has pictures of old whites.[19]

Clearly an appropriate response to this devastating analysis would be to deliteralize the fantasies, seeing through their falseness as fact while honoring the power of imagining within them that produces any fantasy. As inaccurate—and as real—as dreams, they are less likely to be acted upon, politically implemented, or institutionalized once their imaginal status is brought to conscious awareness. As a step toward the "psychological and/or religious maturity" that Deloria recommends, our book in search of a consciously imagined Western shamanism will close with a picture of an old white. It will be a verbal picture, to be sure, but it will have the immense value of being an obvious fantasy, a Western dream figure whose aging has much to teach us about shamanic healing. There is a further remark with which Vine Deloria concludes his foreword, however, that merits our attention.

NATIVE ALTERNATIVES

DELORIA'S FINAL POINT concerns an issue we have approached tentatively from other directions: the impossibility for most Westerners to have a full and authentic relationship with any non-Western shamanism, however defined, and the consequent need to develop one of their own should that mode of spirituality prove compelling. In the case of Euro-Americans the situation is also geographical and historical. The roots of the Western heritage where any sort of shamanic inheritance—e.g., ancient lore and imagery as present psychological material—might be sought are not to be found in North America, despite centuries of colonization. Even after generations on this soil, North America can never entirely be the native land of Euro-Americans, Deloria feels:

> Underneath all the conflicting images of the Indian one fundamental truth emerges—the white man *knows* that he is an alien and he *knows* that North America is Indian—and he will never let go of the Indian image because he thinks that by some clever manipulation he can achieve an authenticity that cannot ever be his.[20]

This is a strong statement by a respected spokesman for Native American rights and religion—though no stronger than statements by other Native American scholars, including some who specifically address the excesses of neoshamanism in the appropriation of Indian culture. But I have also encountered the opinion of some Native Americans, with whatever authority from their communities, that Euro-Americans—and no doubt immigrants of other ancestries—have been in North America long enough that they need to find a way to become truly natives among Native Americans.

How do these alternatives play into the creation of an authentic New Shamanism in the West?

My sense is that Deloria's perspective is at least worthy of consideration, and probably should inform any Western quest for a shamanic spirituality. My ancestors, I have said, came from Normandy by way of England

and from Scotland, and at least in the case of the Norman Noels, this seems to have happened over two centuries ago, before the Revolutionary War. Am I not a native?

In one sense, of course, given the dictionary definition of "native," I am: I was born here. But on another level I think the answer has to be "not completely"—here I agree with Deloria. There is unfinished spiritual business for those of us who came to North America as colonizers, as oppressors, even if those words do not reflect the intentions of our particular ancestors. The historical record is contorted, to be sure, for most of us are of mixed ancestry and many of us came from homelands that were not European, and may have come unwillingly. But in relation to Native Americans like Deloria, all of us immigrants are implicated to some extent in their colonialization and oppression, with the complex issues of our alienness or alienation a constant, if often unconscious, part of our existence on this continent.

The unfinished business we need to do involves reconnecting with roots and resources of the Western heritage so that we can, as he says, "achieve some kind of psychological and/or religious maturity." Clearly this ought to happen in terms of our cultural history as well as our individual seeking. Imaginal shamanism can contribute to this reconnection, this recovery of our alien soul, partly by turning our spiritual sights—and our grasping hands—away from indigenous cultural riches and toward our own rich heritage with the psychology it has developed, perhaps in compensation for much that it has squandered and suppressed. Having begun this effort, we of the modern West who live here might look toward becoming Native Americans one day, or "alter-natives" who at last have a shamanic spirituality we can offer in a true gift exchange with the original inhabitants whose treasure we have only wanted to take until now.

One way to address the need of imaginal shamanism to reconnect with its Western heritage is to combine the post-Jungian psychological resources we have detailed with an already-existing tradition which has roots primarily in the British Isles and northern Europe. Neopaganism is a modern revival of what has been called Wicca or witchcraft, but without any of the negative connotations of "Satanism" or "devil-worship" that Christianity has attached to the latter term. It is, rather, a nature-based spirituality which claims connections to ancient traditions of "the Craft," including folk healing and a prominent role for women, that stretch back thousands of years to "Old Europe."

This would be the cultural context within which Merlin arose as a Celtic shaman of sorts with a special relationship to animals like the stag, the wolf, and the raptor called a merlin, and to the forests and sacred springs of Scotland, Ireland, Wales, Cornwall, and Brittany. Most of the Merlin we know, of course, is a figure of legend, and even his shadowy historical ties are filtered through cultural memories that are never separate from fantasy.

Similarly, the neopaganism of today, as an intended revival, has established less a literal line of succession from the witchcraft of Merlin's earliest era than a fantasied one. To its credit, neopaganism's recent spokespersons seem to acknowledge that its factual origins are in the 1930s at the earliest, and that the imagination of fiction writers like Dion Fortune (also an early psychoanalyst) played a prominent role in its creation. That is, neopaganism is an "invented tradition," and unlike the neoshamanism we have had up to now it appears able to work consciously, in impressively communal rituals, from an admitted imaginal base.

With these strengths, can neopaganism provide imaginal shamanism with roots—imaginal roots—in the Western heritage as a response to the sort of advice Deloria gives to Euro-American spiritual seekers? Perhaps: although neopaganism's appeal to those implicated in the Western heritage but without European ancestry may be limited, it is surely worth exploring. The same limitation could be said to apply to Merlin as a Western shamanic role model, but I see his evocative reach as wider than his geographical origins might indicate, even without simply decontextualizing him.

This latter point leads to another concern in assessing neopaganism's pertinence to imaginal shamanism: its degree of psychological attunement to (as contrasted with uncritical absorption in) the imaginal, including how it would work with sleeping and waking dreams, whether it would draw on the arts more than the sciences to do so in order to avoid the lure of literalism. Further, I would be intent upon seeing if its ritual practices are able to refuse excessive ego control while honoring the pathologizing process whose necessity helps to make soul.

THIS IS A LARGE post-Jungian agenda to visit upon a movement with its own priorities. But there is some evidence that neopaganism already makes use of Jung's psychology in certain respects, not to mention expressing an interest in shamanism which seems more predictable—even if applying the term "shamanism" to European memories and revivals is itself an act of imagining.

If we cast our net a bit wider and include the so-called Western mystery tradition of esoteric magical practice (perhaps itself also an invented tradition) along with the modern witchcraft of neopaganism—and the two movements already markedly overlap—we are likely to find more points of contact with imaginal shamanism and its psychological approach.

The practice of "pathworking," for example, is at least as close to Jung's active imagination method as are Harner's guided imagery journeys. A popular neopaganist book entitled *Pathworking*, however, does not mention Jung or Jungians while citing Harner's *Way of the Shaman* and several of Castaneda's shamanovels.[21] On the other hand, T. M. Luhrmann's *Persuasions of the Witch's Craft*, the major social-scientific study of the two movements, cites neither Castaneda nor Harner but refers to Jung at various points and frequently discusses the role of imagination.[22]

Beyond this brief glance at two texts that are readily available to me, there is a volume on *Shamanism and Witchraft* in the "Witchcraft Today" series edited by Chas Clifton which further contributes to a dialogue that I should like to see continued.[23] This is a collection for which I wrote a chapter, but it is Clifton's own perceptive essays in the book that are worth consulting in the present context, since they build on his knowledge, exceeding mine, of the history of modern Wicca.

In "What Happened to Western Shamanism?" he synthesizes the work of historians like Carlo Ginzburg to explore how original traditions akin to shamanism emerged, continued, and died out in Europe from Greece to Ireland. Another chapter he contributed, "Shamanism and Neoshamanism," contains the kind of observations that can help guide future study of how and whether imaginal shamanism might be supported by neopaganism:

> For followers of Wicca, who drew power from and yet could feel uncomfortable with the sometimes negative connotations of the word witch, shamanism offered the lure of redefinition. The claim "witchcraft is European shamanism" was frequently made in the 1970s and on into the present. . . . this claim reinforced Wicca's alleged link with pre-Christian Europe, a tribal landscape with its own mysterious "wise ones" of whom the legendary Merlin was but the first among many.[24]

The modern Craft movement may be "European shamanism"—or better, neoshamanism—but how consciously imaginal it is as a contemporary attempt to comprehend Merlin's cry is still not totally clear to me. Clifton, however, does raise some helpful questions for an inquiry into this issue along the path toward a possible alliance.

Two final considerations in this brief and tentative comparison seem to hold out promise: neopaganism may offer to a post-Jungian shamanism the community involvement that the Craft's rituals entail; it might also contribute its focus on nature. Both are elements significantly paralleling central ingredients that have been reported in indigenous shamanisms.

While Hillman in particular has emphasized the imperative for imaginal psychology to move beyond individualism to *gemeinschaftsgefuhl*, Alfred Adler's idea of communal fellow-feeling, and to honor the soul outside of personality in the polis or sociopolitical sphere,[25] there is no explicit structure of community that has arisen from post-Jungian thought or therapy where imaginal shamanism could find a social home. Neopaganism and its rich ceremonial life might be more hospitable in this regard. Furthermore, its investment in being an earth-oriented spirituality suggests a possible postmodern animism as the appropriate revived cosmology to accompany our soulful neoshamanism.

That is, animism (as Western anthropology labeled it) is the likely religious context within which traditional shamanisms, as sets of spiritual practices, were (and are) set. An imaginal version in the modern West would do well to seek out its own connections to a similar cosmological context. While there are indications that post-Jungian psychology makes possible its own kind of renewed animism, much remains to be done to develop an "archetypal (or imaginal) ecology."[26] And neopaganism has already moved toward such an environmental philosophy, expressed especially through rituals which imaginal shamanism would lack.

COMPREHENDING MERLIN'S CRY

IN ANOTHER RELEVANT COLLECTION, *Psychology and the Spiritual Traditions*, the editor, R.J. Stewart, author of several popular works on Merlin, comments on my contribution to the collection, an earlier version of this book's introductory chapter:

> C. G. Jung, as Dan Noel suggests and offers evidence for, sought the inner Merlin in the forest of the collective unconscious, where he is buried deep but permeates extensively. Jung must also, of course, have sought Merlin in his own soul. This type of psychological realisation has bridged between the ancient traditions of Merlin and modern reassessment of such traditions.[27]

To these themes, which Stewart accurately summarizes, we shall return in closing: Merlin's final withdrawal and its psychohistorical consequences as we contemplate the possibility of an imaginal shamanism. First, however, we need to note Stewart's next point about Merlin, for it continues the idea that such a neoshamanism needs a new animism, or an imaginal ecology, as its cosmological context:

> We might take the overall image of Daniel Noel's essay a little further, for just as Merlin buried himself in the inner world of the Western psyche, laying strange trails and clues for our pursuit, so do the old traditions teach that he linked and merged himself with the physical land (something significantly different to a psychological interpretation). Our new awareness of our wholeness and inseparable link to the environment, now that [we] have brought it to the brink of destruction, is part of that Merlin-awareness that comes alive for us today, when we need it the most.[28]

I entirely agree with Stewart's extension of my reimagining of Merlin—or almost entirely agree. Merlin's symbolic merging with the landscape as he withdraws is a decidedly powerful ecological feature of the example he sets for us, as Jean Markale also makes very clear in his *Merlin: Priest of Nature*, especially in its closing section on "The Great Withdrawal."[29] Additionally, Merlin's having retired into the landscapes of the British Isles and Brittany sends a signal about Euro-Americans' unfinished spiritual business that Vine Deloria might applaud.

But none of this is necessarily opposed to a psychological interpretation, at least not to a post-Jungian one, given the latter school's interest in soul as the interiority of the world's outer things, the *anima mundi*, as well as of human personalities. Post-Jungians like Michael Perlman and Peter Bishop have written sustained discussions of these possibilities.[30] Likewise, James Hillman has enlisted in the recent "ecopsychology" efforts of Theodore Roszak, whose thought has developed in this direction since he defined the '60s counter-culture, resulting in a book called *The Voice of the Earth* and a co-edited anthology on ecopsychology to which Hillman has contributed a foreword.[31]

Indeed, the sort of "wholeness" that post-Jungian psychology endorses would emphasize, as we have seen, the soul dimension of imagination connecting body and nature to spirit and mind, a *metaxy* or middle realm providing precisely that "inseparable link to the environment" of which Stewart speaks. And, again, this is an implication of Jung's own thought. He referred to the earth-conditionedness (*erdbedingtheit*) of the soul, and even his interest in Merlin had an ecological dimension.[32] My hope would be to write further myself on what might be entailed by an imaginal shamanism that was simultaneously an imaginal ecopsychology.

We have already considered the anecdote in Jung's autobiography where he recounts his intention to carve "Le Cri de Merlin" on his special stone at Bollingen. "It might be said," he declares, "that the secret of Merlin was carried on by alchemy, primarily in the figure of Mercurius. Then Merlin was taken up again in my psychology of the unconscious and—remains uncomprehended to this day!"[33] But who was this Mercurius, who harbors, Jung claims, the secret of Merlin?

Assuredly Mercurius—Mercury—is the Roman mythological counterpart of Hermes, and it is significant that a Hermes figure was carved on the other side of the Bollingen stone from where Jung intended to chisel the French translation of Merlin's cry (just as a Mercurius-Trickster figure was carved on a wall near the stone). We may know something about Hermes' traits from mythology, and Hillman made use of him, we recall, to instruct the Herculean ego in traveling to the underworld of dreaming. The Mercurius of alchemy, however, is less easily identifiable.

In a long essay on "The Spirit Mercurius," Jung goes through a bewildering array of symbolic associations Mercurius has had. He is, of course, quicksilver in chemical terms, a magically shapeshifting and tricky element to handle.[34] There is no mention of Merlin in the essay, but the whole thing is prompted by a fairy tale that has significant correlations to Merlin's legend—once more to its final chapter.

The fairy tale, from the Brothers Grimm, is "The Spirit in the Bottle," and it concerns a poor woodcutter's son who roams the woods until he comes to an immense old oak tree. There he hears a voice calling from the ground, "Let me out! Let me out!" The youth then digs down among the roots of the great oak and finds a well-sealed glass bottle, which he opens. A spirit rushes out, threatens him, and has to be tricked back into the bottle. Promising a reward for his second release, the spirit is let out again and the boy is indeed rewarded with the gift of healing.[35]

WITHOUT GOING INTO ALCHEMY, which would take us too far afield, what can we make of this tale, generative for Jung's entire essay, in relation to Merlin and his secret? Strangely, in their chapter of *The Grail Legend* on "Merlin and the Alchemical Mercurius," which has a wide-ranging discussion of Jung's essay, Emma Jung and Marie-Louise von Franz provide no treatment of the Grimms' tale or of the tree imagery it features.[36]

Left to our own devices, we can obviously find parallels with the aging Merlin's entombment, and the oak is a tree with powerful resonances to the pre-Christian Celtic spirituality of the druids into which Merlin fits very comfortably. On a personal level, I realize, pondering "The Spirit in the Bottle," that the oak tree I passed before reaching the hill up to Dynevor Castle during my Merlin quest might have been where he was crying to my heart—to keep me from the climb. I will have to return to commune more closely with the roots of that tree. And who were those swans nearby, so improbable in a pond that seemed more like a large rain puddle in the meadow near the river? Were they fairy women guarding his imprisonment? The two girls strolling "my" iguana?

The entanglement in tree roots also adds to our discussion of the need for an imaginal ecology. Here Michael Perlman's work in *The Power of Trees* is especially worth consulting.[37] If Merlin is Mercurius, he is manifestly part of the land upon his withdrawal, as R. J. Stewart asserts.

Is his call, however, like Mercurius's, a clear-cut plea to be let out of his bottle, where he has been "hermetically" sealed as in an alchemical retort or even a kind of Grail vessel? Merlin is not said to be enchanted by Niniane into a bottle—though the motif of the *esplumoir*, or moulting-cage, one of his sites of entombment, bears some similarity, as would the glass castle in the sea, yet another location. But his cry is not heard in quite this unambiguous way, and it is far from clear that a simple request to be let out would do justice to the sweep of the Merlin legend.

Heinrich Zimmer, in the 1939 essay that was Jung's only source of the legend for years, felt Merlin's enchantment by Niniane was voluntary, so under this interpretation there would be no motivation to cry for release.[38] Also, trees figure prominently as means of ascent in Eliade's imagination of Siberian and other shamanisms—a point Jung makes several times, citing Eliade, in his essay "The Philosophical Tree," published within a few years of "The Spirit Mercurius" and immediately following the latter in the English edition of the *Collected Works*.[39] It is important to remember in this regard that, on the contrary, Mercurius is in the roots of the oak, not its top. Nor is Merlin ever entombed on a tree-top, although the tower of mist might resonate somewhat to the Eliadean requirement of shamanic elevation. And earlier in the legend Merlin as Wild Man was known to move through the tops of trees, a point Markale emphasizes, also citing Eliade.[40]

However, this is not at all where shamans must inevitably journey, we know, and not where Merlin ends up.

The thing to see in this is that Merlin and his partial alchemical counterpart Mercurius-in-the-bottle are both in the depths—in the depths of the woods and in the depths of the tree, where our shamanism should likewise be to be soulful. But there are some final points to understand about Merlin's withdrawal as we conclude this search for the soul of shamanism—which has to do, as we indicated at the outset, with how he returns today.

MAGIC DEPTHS

ZIMMER'S JUNGIAN SENSITIVITY to Merlin's disappearance goes beyond the insight that it may well have been a deliberate one. He ends his essay by saying that "Merlin and Niniane seem, in the end, to have exchanged sexes. He is content to be vanquished and to rest peacefully, while she, with the knowledge he has given her, is free to come and go."[41]

Merlin returns, I have asserted in introducing our explorations, through our attentiveness to the cries of the unconscious, the murmurs of the imaginal or soul realm which we Westerners lost in modernizing the world. But we have rediscovered this realm thanks to Jung and those who are realizing his legacy, allowing us to comprehend Merlin's cry and greet his return as we pursue the realities of shamanic imagining.

And he returns, Zimmer suggests, not only in male manifestations. His 1939 insight about Merlin's voluntary withdrawal implies that the aging wizard became his own anima-figure, the "contrasexual" expression of soul within masculine personality development, according to classical Jungian theory. Even in saying this much, Zimmer would be importantly observing that Merlin's wisdom is accessible through all of the soul-women with whom he is associated throughout his legend and its variants: his wife Guendoloena, in one version, and his sister Gwenddydd, as well as Morgan le Fay, the Lady of the Lake, and Niniane/Viviane/Nimue.

Yet such anima images of women would remain within the domain of masculine psychology. Zimmer's reading, however, can just as well be extrapolated to say that in being "the incarnation of the magic depths of the forest itself"[42]—the Western unconscious into which Merlin subsides—Niniane, as an independent female personification, fully and freely incorporates Merlin's potentialities. This interpretation seems not so much an endorsement of a bland androgyny as a plea for all of us, men and women alike (and in interaction), to heed "Le Cri de Merlin," to practice a transformative attention to *all* expressions of soul.

These can come, we have found, through a shift in attitude—and thereby a healing shamanic relationship—to our dreams and imaginings, our woundings and our worlds of culture and nature. At several points it has been stressed that the shamanic realities these modes reveal, the animal powers, do not respond well to the hypercontrolling ego. We can now see, with Zimmer's help, that this model of ego could also be called hypermasculine, and "his" approach to the under/inner/otherworld is not what the imaginal interactions of a soulful shamanism endorses.

Even our role model Merlin—who might be renamed Merlininiane or Nimuerlin—refuses such machismo as he retires from the world of arms and wars. (Here Merlin may represent a relinquishment of patriarchy which is the most difficult and soulful heroism men can achieve.) It is a fact worth reimagining that Merlin was, in one version of his story, entombed beneath a stone, and the women's spirituality movement was inaugurated, during these decades of neoshamanism, by a book entitled *When God Was A Woman,* the author of which was a woman named—Merlin Stone.[43]

THERE REMAIN, THEN, just two closing thoughts about this withdrawal, a withdrawal which can evoke our emergence into a New Shamanism in the West.

In line with the need to find our own "native ground" psychospiritually as well as geographically before presuming to receive any gifts that indigenous wisdom might offer, we have seen that Merlin's disappearance calls out to us from the Western heritage of animist involvements in the landscape, in the ensouled things of the *anima mundi.* It further speaks to us of the need to abandon a patriarchal relationship to the animal powers of both the outer and inner worlds as part of a subtle but radical change in attitude toward the imaginal that would already be an act of shamanism for us.

There are reverberations as well in the cultural history of the West to our comprehending Merlin's cry from the magic depths. Retiring from the outer realm of Arthur's kingdom of conquest and succession, the history of governments and the worldly rule of power and wealth, even of chivalry, he takes his shamanism with him. He therefore presages the withdrawal of shamanism itself from the outer affairs of Western culture, the loss of its wisdom as an indigenous practice available to the modern Westerner.

Merlin's retirement signals the movement of shamanic healing in our history from the daily life and religious devotion of pagan peoples—and the Judeo-Christian influx where it incorporated pagan healing wisdom—*to another site, a new location: psychology.* What was conscious in the West became unconscious, there to await the arrival, with Freud and Jung, of the means to hear its call and comprehend its requirements. Merlin is at least a prophet in anticipating this large shift in the evolution of consciousness; his renunciation may even have been the magic that started the shift, centuries in completion down to our own day.

Perhaps the vaunted rise of science also had something to do with Merlin's great withdrawal. Perhaps he meant to leave the understanding of worldly things to the West's new way of knowing, supplanting older wisdoms as "superstition" and practicing a very different kind of sorcery.

And so shamanism became an endangered species in the West, even an extinct one—unless, in a Merlin's dance with science and all the other forces of modernity, it simply needed to shift its ground, moving into interiority as he did, into the soul of the landscape and the imaginings of the Western psyche, there to be available once again when we heed the potentialities of psychologies like Jung's.

Certainly psychology, and only psychology (but not every psychology), contains a place of reconnection to the Western shamanism that Merlin represents. It can be a bridge across from science to a new imagining and reimagining, as we have said. Realizing how psychology can provide this bridge is, as Jung implied, the way to comprehend Merlin's cry. There *are* magic depths where his message can be heard and understood, if seekers do not ask for clear-cut certainty. Jung's own heritage makes that transaction possible when realized in a soulful spirituality.

And realized as well, according to that psychology, in the arts of imagining: in art therapies that honor the art process and in that process itself, in any medium, including the writing of books of poems and stories. Merlin, Nikolai Tolstoy reminds us, had as one of his aspects the role of *llyfrawr*, a Welsh word for wizard that comes from the Latin *librarius*, a master of books. Tolstoy calls him "the patron of writing," adding that "as embodiment of a literature which encompasses the human experience, he is to humanity what the author is to a book."[44] As a prophet he is always also a poet, a bard—which cautions us to never take his prophecies literally. He is closer to Wordsworth, Tolstoy implies, or even to Wallace Stevens, than to Nostradamus.

Everything we have said about him and his guidance of our search for the imagining soul of a Western form of shamanism comes in a story, or a set of stories. If there ever was a Merlin of historical fact, he has withdrawn into story just as he withdrew into the forest unconscious. Like that forest his story, too, has magic depths. Travel to it is magical flight, and we must be as mindful of this sorcery as we are of the power of shamanovels.

At the same time, without at all abdicating from conscious interaction, we must as well submit to the story, surrendering in love to the enchantment we know to be at work on us. As Merlin did, and as I have tried to do in reimagining his legend and the neoshamanist fantasies he helps us to see through. He inspires us to trust the nonliteral, believing without belief, beyond belief, as Stevens once advised.

In so doing we come upon an authentic shamanism that moves beyond Western fantasies literalized as fact. This shamanism honors the power within those fantasies by attending to the imaginal realities, the imaginal healing, such power can make possible. This would be a shamanism—as I hope I have shown—that could help us to recover the soul we as Westerners suffer and seek.

NOTES

INTRODUCTION: MERLIN RETURNS

1. Carlos Castaneda, *The Teachings of Don Juan: A Yaqui Way of Knowledge* (Berkeley: University of California Press, 1968).
2. Frank Waters, *Book of the Hopi* (New York: Penguin Books, 1963/1977).
3. Michael Whan, "'Don Juan,' Trickster and Hermeneutic Understanding," *Spring* (1978): 17–27.
4. Nikolai Tolstoy, *The Quest for Merlin* (London: Hodder and Stoughton/Coronet Books, 1985).
5. Ibid., 142.
6. Mary Stewart, *The Crystal Cave* (New York: Fawcett/Ballantine, 1970/1971), *The Hollow Hills* (New York: Fawcett/Ballantine, 1973/1974), *The Last Enchantment* (New York: Fawcett/Ballantine, 1979/1980), *The Wicked Day* (New York: Fawcett/Ballantine, 1983/1984); Marion Zimmer Bradley, *The Mists of Avalon* (New York: Ballantine/Del Rey, 1982); Jane Yolen, *Merlin's Booke* (New York: Ace, 1986).
7. R.J. Stewart, *The Prophetic Vision of Merlin, The Mystic Life of Merlin* (London and New York: Routledge & Kegan Paul/Arkana, 1986), *The Merlin Tarot* (Wellingborough, Northants.: Aquarian, 1988), *The Way of Merlin* (London: Aquarian, 1991); *The Book of Merlin,* ed. R. J. Stewart (Poole, Dorset, and London: Blandford, 1987), *Merlin and Woman,* ed. R. J. Stewart (Poole, Dorset, and London: Blandford, 1988); Norma Lorre Goodrich, *Merlin* (New York and Toronto: Franklin Watts, 1987); Nikolai Tolstoy, *The Coming of the King* (New York: Bantam, 1989).
8. Ward Rutherford, *The Druids: Magicians of the West* (Wellingborough, Northants.: Aquarian, 1978/1983); Nevill Drury, *The Shaman and the Magician* (London and Boston: Routledge & Kegan Paul, 1982); John Matthews, *Taliesen: Shamanism and the Bardic Mysteries of Britain and Ireland* (London: Aquarian, 1991); Tom Cowan, *Fire in the Head: Shamanism and the Celtic Spirit* (San Francisco: HarperSanFrancisco, 1993); Brian Bates, *The Way of Wyrd* (San Francisco: Harper & Row, 1983).

9. Jean Markale, *Merlin: Priest of Nature*, trans. Belle N. Burke (Rochester, Vt.: Inner Traditions, 1981/1995); Deepak Chopra, *The Return of Merlin: A Novel* (New York: Harmony, 1995).

10. Emma Jung and Marie-Louise von Franz, *The Grail Legend*, 2d ed., trans. Andrea Dykes (Boston: Sigo, 1986).

11. Heinrich Zimmer, "Merlin," Zimmer, *The King and the Corpse: Tales of the Soul's Conquest of Evil*, ed. Joseph Campbell (New York: Meridian, 1960), 181–201.

12. Marie-Louise von Franz, *C. G. Jung: His Myth in Our Time*, trans. William H. Kennedy (New York: G. P. Putnam's Sons, 1975).

13. C. G. Jung, *Memories, Dreams, Reflections*, ed. A. Jaffe, trans. Richard and Clara Winston (New York: Vintage, 1961), 228.

14. John A. Grim, *The Shaman* (Norman, Okla.: University of Oklahoma Press, 1983), 15.

15. Mihaly Hoppal, "Shamanism: An Archaic and/or Recent Belief System," in *Shamanism*, ed. Shirley Nicholson (Wheaton, Ill.: Theosophical Publishing House, 1987), 76–100; Ioan M. Lewis, *Ecstatic Religion* (Harmondsworth, Middlesex: Penguin, 1971); Amanda Porterfield, "Shamanism: A Psychosocial Definition," *Journal of the American Academy of Religion* 55, no. 4 (1987): 721–39; Sergei M. Shirokogoroff, *Psychomental Complex of the Tungus* (London: Kegan Paul, Trench, Trubner, 1935).

16. Andreas Lommel, *Shamanism: The Beginnings of Art*, trans. Michael Bullock (New York: McGraw-Hill, 1967); Rogan Taylor, *The Death and Resurrection Show: From Shaman to Superstar* (London: Anthony Blond, 1985); Henri F. Ellenberger, *The Discovery of the Unconscious* (New York: Basic Books, 1970).

17. Gloria Flaherty, *Shamanism and the Eighteenth Century* (Princeton, N. J.: Princeton University Press, 1992), 208–15.

1. BOOKING A MAGICAL FLIGHT

1. Lynn Andrews, *Shakkai: Woman of the Sacred Garden* (New York: HarperCollins, 1992), *Medicine Woman* (New York: Harper & Row, 1981).

2. Jonathan Adolph and Richard Smoley, "Beverly Hills Shaman," *New Age Journal* 6, no. 2 (1989): 22, 24, 26, 96–97.

3. Mircea Eliade, *Shamanism: Archaic Techniques of Ecstasy*, trans. W. R. Trask, Bollingen Series LXXVI (Princeton, N. J.: Princeton University Press, 1951/1964).

4. Joan Halifax, *Shamanic Voices: A Survey of Visionary Narratives* (New York: Dutton, 1979); Michael Harner, *The Way of The Shaman: A Guide to Power and Healing* (New York: Bantam, 1980/1982).

5. Daniel C. Noel, "Makings of Meaning: Carlos Castaneda's 'Lived Hermeneutics' in the Cargo Culture," *Listening: Current Studies in Dialog* 7, no. 1 (1972): 83–90, "Fact, Fiction, and Post-Modern Faith: Carlos Castaneda and the Incredible Shrinking Credibility Gap," *Philosophy and Religion: 1973*

Proceedings, ed. David R. Griffin (Tallahassee, Fla.: American Academy of Religion, 1973), 110–30.

6. Jonathan Z. Smith, *To Take Place: Toward Theory in Ritual* (Chicago: University of Chicago Press, 1987).

7. Ibid., 5.

8. See, for example, Edmund Leach, "Sermons By a Man on a Ladder," *New York Review of Books* 20 Oct., 1966: 28–31 (Leach refers to Eliade disparagingly as Merlin on 28); Michael Taussig, "The Nervous System: Homesickness and Dada," *Stanford Humanities Review* 1, no. 1 (1989): 44–81; *Shamanism: Soviet Studies of Traditional Religion in Siberia and Central Asia,* ed. Marjorie Mandelstam Balzer, (Armonk, N. Y.: Sharpe, 1990); Ronald Hutton, *The Shamans of Siberia* (Glastonbury, Somerset: Isle of Avalon, 1993).

9. Mircea Eliade, *Two Tales of the Occult,* trans. Willard R. Trask (New York: Herder and Herder, 1970).

10. *Waiting for the Dawn: Mircea Eliade in Perspective,* ed. David Carrasco and Jane Marie Swanberg (Boulder, Colo., and London: Westview, 1985).

11. Ibid., 19.

12. Mircea Eliade, *The Forbidden Forest,* trans. Mac Linscott Ricketts and Mary P. Stevenson (Notre Dame, Ind., and London: University of Notre Dame Press, 1955/1971/1978).

13. Ibid., 74–75.

14. Mac Linscott Ricketts, "Mircea Eliade and the Writing of *The Forbidden Forest,*" in *Imagination and Meaning: The Scholarly and Literary Worlds of Mircea Eliade,* ed. Norman J. Girardot and Mac Linscott Ricketts, (New York: Seabury, 1982), 104–112.

15. Eliade, *Forbidden,* 105.

16. Ricketts, "Eliade," 110.

17. Eliade, *Forbidden,* 317–18.

18. Ibid., 338.

19. Ibid., 336.

20. Ibid., 531.

21. Eliade, *Shamanism,* 9.

22. Ibid., 581 (index under "decadence").

23. Ibid., 264 (emphasis added).

24. Ibid. (emphasis added).

25. Ibid., 265 (emphasis added).

26. Ibid. (emphasis added).

27. Ibid., 269 (emphasis added).

28. Ibid. (emphasis added).

29. Mircea Eliade, *No Souvenirs: Journal, 1957–1969,* trans. Fred H. Johnson, Jr. (New York: Harper & Row, 1973/1977), 79.

30. Ibid., 92.

31. Mircea Eliade, *Autobiography: Volume I. 1907–1937. Journey East, Journey West*, trans. Mac Linscott Ricketts (New York: Harper & Row, 1981), 6–7, 18–19.
32. Taussig, "Nervous System," 57.
33. Ibid., 59.
34. Ibid., 57; see also Taussig, *Shamanism, Colonialism, and the Wild Man: A Study in Terror and Healing* (Chicago: University of Chicago Press, 1987).

2. TELLING TALES OF FICTIVE POWER

1. Carlos Castaneda, *The Teachings of Don Juan: A Yaqui Way of Knowledge* (New York: Ballantine, 1968/1969), 25.
2. Ibid., 128.
3. Ibid., 130–31.
4. Ibid., 131.
5. Ibid., 132.
6. Ibid., 198.
7. Carlos Castaneda, *A Separate Reality: Further Conversations with Don Juan* (New York: Simon and Schuster, 1971).
8. Ibid., 130.
9. Carlos Castaneda, *Journey to Ixtlan: The Lessons of Don Juan* (New York: Simon and Schuster, 1972).
10. Ibid., 13.
11. Ibid., 301.
12. Ibid., 299–300.
13. Sandra Burton, "Don Juan and the Sorcerer's Apprentice," *Time* 5 Mar. 1973: 45.
14. Carlos Castaneda, *Tales of Power* (New York: Simon and Schuster, 1974).
15. Burton, "Don Juan," 45.
16. Sam Keen, "Sorcerer's Apprentice," in *Voices and Visions*, ed. Sam Keen (New York: Harper & Row, 1974), 111.
17. Joseph Slade, *Thomas Pynchon*, "Writers for the Seventies" Series (New York: Warner, 1974).
18. Michael Korda, *Power! How to Get It, How to Use It* (New York, 1975).
19. Theodore Roszak, *The Making of a Counter-Culture* (Garden City, N. Y.: Doubleday, 1969). See also Philip D. Beidler, *Scriptures for a Generation: What We Were Reading in the '60s* (Athens, GA, and London: University of Georgia Press, 1994).
20. Carlos Castaneda, "Don Juan: The Sorcerer," interview with Theodore Roszak, Jeffrey Norton Publishers Tape Library 25021, 1968.
21. Carlos Castaneda, *The Second Ring of Power* (New York: Simon and Schuster, 1977), *The Power of Silence* (New York: Simon and Schuster, 1987).
22. Castaneda, *Journey*, 126.
23. Castaneda, *Tales*, 118–46.
24. Joyce Carol Oates, letter to Daniel Noel, in *Seeing Castaneda: Reactions to the "Don Juan" Writings of Carlos Castaneda*, ed. Daniel Noel (New York: Putnam's, 1976), 69.

25. Reprinted in Noel, *Seeing*, 116.
26. Ibid., 124.
27. Richard de Mille, *Castaneda's Journey: The Power and the Allegory* (Santa Barbara, Calif.: Capra, 1976).
28. See, for example, Ward Churchill, *Fantasies of the Master Race*, ed. M. Annette Jaimes (Monroe, Maine: Common Courage, 1992), 43–64, 291 (index under "Castaneda"); Wendy Rose, "The Great Pretenders," *The State of Native America*, ed. M. Annette Jaimes, (Boston: South End, 1992), 403–21.
29. *The Don Juan Papers: Further Castaneda Controversies*, ed. Richard de Mille (Santa Barbara, Calif.: Ross-Erikson, 1980).
30. Burton, "Don Juan," 44.
31. Oates, "Don Juan's Last Laugh," in Noel, *Seeing*, 127.
32. Sukenick, "Upward and Juanward," in Noel, *Seeing*, 114.
33. Castaneda, *Journey*, 79.

3. Lying with Shamanovelists

1. Mario Vargas Llosa, *The Storyteller*, trans. Helen Lane (New York: Penguin,1989–1990).
2. Ronald Sukenick, *Out* (Chicago: Swallow, 1973).
3. Ronald Sukenick, "Upward and Juanward," *Seeing Castaneda: Reactions to the "Don Juan" Writings of Carlos Castaneda*, ed. Daniel Noel (New York: Putnam's, 1976), 110.
4. Sukenick, *Out*, 115.
5. Ibid., 117–18.
6. Ibid., 134–36.
7. Sukenick in Noel, *Seeing*, 112.
8. Ronald Sukenick, "The Birds," in Sukenick, *The Death of the Novel and Other Stories* (San Diego: Serendipity, 1969), 155.
9. Ronald Sukenick, *Wallace Stevens: Musing the Obscure* (New York University Press, 1967).
10. Wallace Stevens, *The Collected Poems* (New York: Knopf, 1954), 102.
11. Sukenick, *Out*, 140.
12. Ibid., 147.
13. Ibid., 155–56.
14. Ronald Sukenick, "The Death of the Novel," in Sukenick, *Death* 49.
15. Sukenick, *Out*, 282–83.
16. Raymond Federman, "In," *Partisan Review* 41, no. 1 (1974): 142.
17. Ronald Sukenick, *98.6* (New York: Fiction Collective, 1975), 97.
18. Ibid., 172.
19. Ronald Sukenick in *Surfiction*, ed. Raymond Federman (Chicago: Swallow, 1975) 41.
20. *Innovative Fiction*, ed. Jerome Klinkowitz and John Somer (New York: Dell, 1973), *xvi*.
21. Roberto Assagioli, *Psychosynthesis* (New York: Viking, 1965).
22. Sukenick, *98.6*, 122.

23. Ibid., 180.

24. Ibid., 170.

25. Ibid., 123.

26. Ronald Sukenick, interview with Joe David Bellamy, Bellamy, *The New Fiction* (Urbana, Ill.: University of Illinois Press, 1974), 72–73.

27. Carlos Castaneda, *Tales of Power* (New York: Simon and Schuster, 1974), 244.

28. Sukenick in Bellamy, *New Fiction,* 74.

29. Quoted in Ihab Hassan, *Paracriticisms* (Urbana, Ill.: University of Illinois Press, 1975), 141.

30. Ibid., 107.

31. Mircea Eliade, "Waiting for the Dawn," in *Waiting for the Dawn: Mircea Eliade in Perspective,* ed. David Carrasco and Jane Marie Swanberg (Boulder, Colo., and London: Westview, 1985), 12.

32. Ibid., 13–15.

33. Ibid., 15.

34. Michael Harner, *The Way of the Shaman: A Guide to Power and Healing* (New York: Bantam, 1980/1982).

35. Mircea Eliade, "Waiting for the Dawn," address, University of Colorado, Boulder, 26 Oct. 1982, typescript, 26.

36. Ibid., 27–28.

37. Ronald Sukenick, *In Form: Digressions on the Act of Fiction* (Carbondale and Edwardsville, Ill.: Southern Illinois University Press, 1985), 14–15.

38. Ibid., 32.

39. Ibid., 81.

40. Ibid., 117.

41. Ibid., 219; Ronald Sukenick, *Down and In: Life in the Underground* (New York: Collier, 1987), 255.

42. Ronald Sukenick, *Blown Away* (Los Angeles: Sun and Moon, 1986), 24.

43. Sukenick, *In Form,* 224.

44. Sukenick, *Blown,* 28–29.

45. Ibid., 169.

46. Ibid., 140.

47. Ronald Sukenick, *Doggy Bag* (Boulder, Colo., and Normal, Ill.: Black Ice, 1994).

48. Annie Dillard, *Living By Fiction* (New York: Harper & Row, 1982), 99.

49. Eliade, "Waiting," typescript, 30.

4. Studying with Shamanthropologists

1. Richard de Mille, taped interview with Dick Hooper, New Age Communications WR136, 1977.

2. Ibid.

3. Sandra Burton, "Don Juan and the Sorcerer's Apprentice," *Time* 5 Mar. 1973: 43. The possible influence of the "ethnomethodology" approach of Castaneda's UCLA professor Harold Garfinkel has never been spelled out. The role of "the new ethnogaphy," explored later in this chapter, more effectively explains the

Castaneda move from anthropology to fiction. See Garfinkel, *Studies in Ethnomethodology* (Englewood Cliffs, N. J.: Prentice–Hall, 1970).

4. Harvey Bialy, untitled poem, *The Phoenix* [Boston] 29 Mar. 1972: 26.

5. Jorge Luis Borges, "Anxieties: The Anthropologist," trans. Jorge Luis Borges and Norman Thomas Di Giovanni, *New Yorker*, 20 Feb. 1971: 41.

6. R. Laurence Moore, *Selling God: American Religion in the Marketplace of Culture* (New York: Oxford University Press, 1994), 256.

7. Marilyn Ferguson, *The Aquarian Conspiracy: Personal and Social Transformation in the 1980s* (Los Angeles: Tarcher, 1980), 439 (index under "Castaneda").

8. Stephen Larsen, *The Shaman's Doorway: Opening the Mythic Imagination to Contemporary Consciousness* (New York: Harper Colophon, 1976); see also Stephen Larsen, *The Mythic Imagination* (New York: Bantam, 1990).

9. Joan Halifax, *Shamanic Voices: A Survey of Visionary Narratives* (New York: Dutton, 1979).

10. Richard de Mille, *Castaneda's Journey: The Power and the Allegory* (Santa Barbara, Calif.: Capra, 1976), 101n., 102n., 112n.; *The Don Juan Papers: Further Castaneda Controversies*, ed. Richard de Mille (Santa Barbara, Calif.: Ross–Erikson, 1980), 515 (index under "Myerhoff"); see also Jay Courtney Fikes, *Carlos Castaneda, Academic Opportunism and the Psychedelic Sixties* (Victoria, British Columbia: Millenia, 1993).

11. *Technicians of the Sacred: A Range of Poetries from Asia, Africa, Oceania and America*, ed. Jerome Rothenberg (Garden City, N. Y.: Doubleday, 1968).

12. Halifax, *Shamanic*, 238.

13. De Mille, *Don Juan*, 22, 513 (index under "Harner").

14. Michael Harner, *The Way of the Shaman: A Guide to Power and Healing* (New York: Bantam, 1980/1982).

15. James Clifford, "Introduction: Partial Truths," in *Writing Culture: The Poetics and Politics of Ethnography*, ed. James Clifford and George E. Marcus (Berkeley: University of California Press, 1986), 2.

16. Ibid., 6.

17. Ibid., 3–4.

18. William G. Doty, "Writing the Blurred Genres of Postmodern Ethnography," *Annals of Scholarship: Studies of the Humanities and Social Sciences* 6, no. 3–4 (1990): 277.

19. Clifford Geertz, "Blurred Genres: The Refiguration of Social Thought," reprinted in Geertz, *Local Knowledge* (New York: Basic Books, 1983), 20. For another view of how Castaneda's writing relates to the blurring of genre boundaries in anthropology, see David Murray, *Forked Tongues: Speech, Writing and Representation in North American Indian Texts* (Bloomington and Indianapolis: Indiana University Press, 1991), 153–56.

20. Donald Barthelme, "The Teachings of Don B: A Yankee Way of Knowledge," *New York Times Magazine* 11 Feb. 1973: 14–15, 66–67.

21. Doty, "Writing," 271.

22. Mary Louise Pratt, "Fieldwork in Common Places," Clifford and Marcus, *Writing*, 32.

23. Florinda Donner, *Shabono: A Visit to a Remote and Magical World in the South American Rainforest* (New York: HarperSanFrancisco, 1982/1992).
24. Quoted in Pratt, "Fieldwork," 28.
25. Ibid., 30.
26. Ibid.
27. George E. Marcus and Michael M. J. Fischer, *Anthropology as Cultural Critique: An Experimental Moment in the Human Sciences* (Chicago: University of Chicago Press, 1986), 69.
28. Ibid., 40.
29. Wendy Rose, "The Great Pretenders: Further Reflections on White Shamanism," in *The State of Native America*, ed. M. Annette Jaimes (Boston: South End, 1992), 403–21; Ward Churchill, "Spiritual Hucksterism: The Rise of Plastic Medicine Men," Ward Churchill, *Fantasies of the Master Race*, ed. M. Annette Jaimes (Monroe, Maine: Common Courage, 1992), 215–28.
30. Carlos Castaneda, *The Art of Dreaming* (New York: HarperCollins, 1993).
31. Ken Eagle Feather, *Traveling with Power* (Norfolk, Va.: Hampton Roads, 1992); Victor Sanchez, *The Teachings of Don Carlos*, trans. Robert Nelson (Santa Fe, N. M.: Bear & Company).
32. Florinda Donner, *The Witch's Dream* (New York: Simon and Schuster, 1985), *Being-in-Dreaming* (New York: HarperSanFrancisco, 1991).
33. Taisha Abelar, *The Sorcerers' Crossing* (New York: Penguin, 1992).
34. Sandra Ingerman, *Soul Retrieval: Mending the Fragmented Self Through Shamanic Practice* (New York: HarperSanFrancisco, 1991), *Welcome Home: Following Your Soul's Journey Home* (New York: HarperSanFrancisco, 1994).
35. Ailo Gaup, *In Search of the Drum*, trans. Bente Kjos Sjordal (Fort Yates, N. D.: Muse, 1992).
36. Felicitas Goodman, *Where the Spirits Ride the Wind: Trance Journeys and Other Ecstatic Experiences* (Bloomington, Ind.: Indiana University Press, 1990).
37. Joan Halifax, *Shaman: The Wounded Healer* (New York: Crossroad, 1982).
38. Joseph Campbell, *The Way of the Animal Powers* (San Francisco: Harper & Row, 1983), 300.
39. Joan Halifax, *The Fruitful Darkness: Reconnecting with the Body of the Earth* (New York: HarperSanFrancisco, 1993).
40. Ibid., 213–14.
41. Halifax, booksigning at Living Batch Bookstore, Albuquerque, N. M., 7 July 1993.

METAXY, THE MIDDLE: ENTERING JUNG'S HOUSE

1. C. G. Jung, *Memories, Dreams, Reflections*, ed. Aniela Jaffe, trans. Richard and Clara Winston (New York: Vintage, 1961).
2. *C. G. Jung: Word and Image*, ed. Aniela Jaffe, 2d ed., Bollingen Series XCVII: 2 (Princeton, N. J.: Princeton University Press, 1979/1983); Jaffe, "Creative Phases in Jung's Life," *Spring* (1972): 174.

3. Stephen Segaller and Merrill Berger, *The Wisdom of the Dream: The World of C. G. Jung* (Boston: Shambhala, 1990), 16, 20.

4. Daniel C. Noel, "Veiled Kabir: C. G. Jung's Phallic Self-Image," *Spring* (1974): 124–42.

5. Colin Wilson, *Lord of the Underworld: Jung and the Twentieth Century* (Wellingborough, Northants.: Aquarian, 1984).

6. Jung, *Memories*, 181.

7. James Hillman, *Healing Fiction* (Dallas: Spring, 1983), 53.

8. Richard Evans, *Conversations with Carl Jung and Reactions from Ernest Jones* (Princeton, N. J.: Van Nostrand, 1964), 62.

9. Hillman, *Healing*, 53–54.

10. Segaller and Berger, *Wisdom*, 20.

11. Jung, *Memories*, 183.

12. Hillman, *Healing*, 55.

13. Ibid.

14. Ibid., 56.

15. Ibid.

16. Ibid.

17. Jung, *Memories*, 103-104.

18. Hillman, *Healing*, 56.

19. Ibid. 59.

20. Jung, *Memories*, 192.

5. Realizing the Radical Legacy of Jung

1. James Hillman, *The Myth of Analysis* (Evanston, Ill.: Northwestern University Press, 1972), 7.

2. James Hillman, *Healing Fiction* (Dallas: Spring, 1983), 69.

3. Ibid., 155–56.

4. Hillman, *Myth*, 7.

5. Ibid., 40.

6. Ibid., 113.

7. Ronald Sukenick, *98.6* (New York: Fiction Collective, 1975), 122.

8. Ibid., 180.

9. Ibid.

10. Hillman, *Myth*, 132.

11. Ibid., 132–33, n. 12.

12. James Hillman, *Re-Visioning Psychology* (New York: Harper & Row, 1975), xi.

13. Ibid., 221.

14. Ibid., 224.

15. Ibid., 164.

16. Michael Whan, "'Don Juan,' Trickster and Hermeneutic Understanding," *Spring* (1978): 17–27.

17. Ibid., 26.

18. James Hillman, "Peaks and Vales: The Soul/Spirit Distinction as Basis for the

Differences between Psychotherapy and Spiritual Discipline," in *Puer Papers*, ed. James Hillman et al. (Dallas: Spring, 1979), 54–74.

19. C. G. Jung, *Collected Works*, ed. Herbert Read, Michael Fordham, Gerhard Adler, and William McGuire, trans. R. F. C. Hull, Bollingen Series XX (Princeton, N. J.: Princeton University Press, 1967), vol. 13, para. 75.

20. One of the few exceptions to this neglect of soul is the work of the humanistic psychologist Jean Houston, whose advisory relationship to Hillary Clinton led to dull-witted distortions of her activities—including her sensitive use of guided imagery—by the popular press.

21. Thomas Moore, *Care of the Soul* (New York: HarperCollins, 1992), *Soul Mates* (New York: HarperCollins, 1994), *The Re-Enchantment of Everyday Life* (New York: HarperCollins, 1996).

22. Thomas Moore, *The Planets Within: The Astrological Psychology of Marsilio Ficino* (Hudson, N. Y.: Lindisfarne, 1982), *Rituals of the Imagination* (Dallas: Pegasus Foundation, 1983), *Dark Eros: The Imagination of Sadism* (Dallas: Spring, 1990).

23. James Hillman, *A Blue Fire: Selected Writings*, introd. and ed., Thomas Moore (New York: Harper & Row, 1989).

24. Ibid., 15.

25. Ibid., 16.

26. Ibid., 5.

27. Ibid., 10.

28. Hillman, *Re-Visioning*, x.

29. Hillman, *Blue*, 112.

30. Moore, *Care*, 203.

31. Ibid., 210–11.

32. James Hillman, *Emotion: A Comprehensive Phenomenology of Theories and their Meanings for Therapy* (Evanston, Ill.: Northwestern University Press, 1961/1992).

33. Andreas Lommel, *Shamanism: The Beginnings of Art* (New York: McGraw-Hill, 1967).

34. Marianna Torgovnick, *Gone Primitive: Savage Intellects, Modern Lives* (Chicago: University of Chicago Press, 1990).

35. Maureen Korp, *Sacred Art of the Earth: Ancient and Contemporary Earthworks* (New York: Continuum, 1997).

36. Michael Tucker, *Dreaming with Open Eyes: The Shamanic Spirit in Twentieth-Century Art and Culture* (London: Aquarian/HarperSanFrancisco, 1992).

37. Shaun McNiff, *Art as Medicine: Creating a Therapy of the Imagination* (Boston: Shambhala, 1992).

6. DREAMING THE UNDERWORLD JOURNEY

1. Liam Hudson, *Night Life: The Interpretation of Dreams* (New York: St. Martin's, 1985), 1.

2. Ibid., 4–5.

3. Ibid., 8.
4. Ibid., 25.
5. Ibid., 35-36.
6. Ibid., 167.
7. James Hillman, *The Dream and the Underworld* (New York: Harper & Row, 1979), 6.
8. Ibid., 13.
9. Ibid., 23.
10. Ibid., 46.
11. Ibid., 34.
12. Ibid., 41.
13. Mircea Eliade, *Shamanism: Archaic Techniques of Ecstasy*, trans. Willard R. Trask, Bollingen Series LXXVI (Princeton, N. J.: Princeton University Press, 1951/1964), 33-34.
14. Hillman, *Dream*, 55.
15. Ibid., 96.
16. Patricia Berry, "An Approach to the Dream," *Spring* (1974): 61.
17. Ibid., 62.
18. Ibid.
19. Hillman, *Dream*, 102–103.
20. Ibid., 108.
21. Ibid., 112.
22. Ibid.
23. Ibid., 113.
24. Ibid.
25. Ibid., 115.
26. Ibid., 117.
27. Ibid., 122–23.
28. Robert Bosnak, *A Little Course in Dreams* (Boston: Shambhala, 1988), 7.
29. Hillman, *Dream*, 155.
30. Ibid., 130.
31. Ibid.
32. Ibid., 118.
33. Ibid., 133.
34. Ibid., 139–40.
35. Berry, "Approach," 61.
36. Hillman, *Dream*, 142.
37. Ibid., 142–43.
38. Ibid., 143.
39. Ibid., 144.
40. Ibid., 148.
41. Ibid.
42. Ibid., 150.
43. Joseph Campbell, *The Way of the Animal Powers* (San Francisco: Harper & Row, 1983).

44. Hillman, *Dream*, 150.
45. James Hillman, "The Animal Kingdom in the Human Dream," *Eranos Jahrbuch* 51 (1982): 279-334, "Going Bugs," *Spring* (1988): 40-72; see also Eligio Stephen Gallegos, *Animals of the Four Windows: Integrating Thinking, Sensing, Feeling and Imagery* (Santa Fe, N. M.: Moon Bear, 1991); and Alan Bleakley, *Familiars* (Woodstock, Conn.: Spring, forthcoming). Bleakley's book in particular promises to be specifically relevant to an imaginal shamanism, as are his earlier works *Fruits of the Moon Tree* (Bath, U. K.: Gateway, 1984) and *Earth's Embrace: Archetypal Psychology's Challenge to the Growth Movement* (Bath, U. K.: Gateway, 1989).
46. Stephen LaBerge, *Lucid Dreaming* (New York: Ballantine, 1985).
47. G. William Domhoff, *The Mystique of Dreams: A Search for Utopia Through Senoi Dream Theory* (Berkeley: University of California Press, 1985).

7. IMAGINING WITH ANIMAL POWERS

1. James Hillman, *The Dream and the Underworld* (New York: Harper & Row, 1979), 192.
2. Robert Bosnak, *Tracks in the Wilderness of Dreaming* (New York: Delacorte, 1996), 13.
3. Ibid., 16.
4. Ibid., 13.
5. C. G. Jung, *Letters: 1: 1906–1950*, ed. Gerhard Adler and Aniela Jaffe, trans. R. F. C. Hull, Bollingen Series XCV:1 (Princeton: Princeton University Press, 1973), 460.
6. Robert Bosnak, *A Little Course in Dreams* (Boston: Shambhala, 1986), 44.
7. James Hillman, *Healing Fiction* (Dallas: Spring, 1983), 78.
8. C. G. Jung, *Collected Works*, ed. H. Read, M. Fordham, G. Adler, and W. McGuire, trans. R.F.C. Hull, Bollingen Series XX (Princeton, N. J.: Princeton University Press, 1971), vol. 6, para. 712.
9. Ibid., para. 714.
10. Ibid., vol. 8, para. 131-93.
11. Ibid., vol. 18, para. 396-97.
12. Ibid., vol. 13, para. 23.
13. Ibid., para. 20.
14. Ibid., vol. 7, para. 368.
15. Marie-Louise von Franz, *C. G. Jung: His Myth in Our Time*, trans. William H. Kennedy (New York: G. P. Putnam's Sons, 1972/1975); Barbara Hannah, *Encounters with the Soul: Active Imagination As Developed by C. G. Jung* (Boston: Sigo, 1981); Ira Progoff, *The Symbolic and the Real* (New York: McGraw–Hill, 1963) and *At a Journal Workshop* (New York: Dialogue House, 1975); Rix Weaver, *The Old Wise Woman: A Study of Active Imagination* (New York: G. P. Putnam's, 1973); A. N. Ammann, *Aktive Imagination: Darstellung einer Methode* (Olten und Freiburg im Breisgau, Germany: Walter–Verlag, 1978); Robert A. Johnson, *Inner Work: Using Dreams and Active Imagination for Personal Growth* (San Francisco: Harper

& Row, 1986); Pieter Middelkoop, *The Wise Old Man: Healing through Inner Images*, trans. Adrienne Dixon (Boston: Shambhala, 1989); Verena Kast, *Imagination as Space of Freedom: Dialogue between the Ego and the Unconscious*, trans. Anselm Hollo (New York: Fromm International, 1988/1993). I encountered Ira Progoff's "twilight imaging" version of active imagination when I was his student at Drew University Graduate School in New Jersey in the early 1960s. While not directly about the active imagination method, two philosophical works are also deeply pertinent to its understanding and implementation: Gaston Bachelard, *The Poetics of Reverie: Childhood, Language, and the Cosmos*, trans. Daniel Russell (Boston: Beacon, 1960/1971); and Edward S. Casey, *Imagining: A Phenomenological Study* (Bloomington, Ind., and London: Indiana University Press, 1976).

16. Jung, *Collected Works*, vol. 7, para. 491.
17. Ibid., para. 350-51.
18. Ibid., para. 352.
19. Ibid., para. 353.
20. Ibid.
21. Ibid.
22. Ibid., para. 354.
23. Hillman, *Healing* 80.
24. Ibid., 36.
25. Ibid., 38.
26. Ibid., 93.
27. Ibid.
28. Michael Harner, *The Way of the Shaman: A Guide to Power and Healing* (New York: Bantam, 1980/1982), *xxi*.
29. Ibid., 14.
30. Ibid., 27.
31. Mary Watkins, *Waking Dreams*, 3d ed. (Dallas: Spring, 1976/1984).
32. Michael Harner, "The Ancient Wisdom in Shamanic Cultures," interview with Gary Doore, in *Shamanism*, ed. G. Doore (Wheaton, Ill.: Quest, 1987), 15.
33. Michael Harner, "What Is A Shaman?" in *Shaman's Path: Healing, Personal Growth, & Empowerment*, ed. Gary Doore (Boston: Shambhala, 1988), 11.
34. Leilani Lewis, "Coming Out of the Closet As a Shamanic Practitioner," *Foundation for Shamanic Studies Newsletter* 4 no. 1 (1991): 5.
35. Ibid.

8. SUFFERING THE RECOVERY OF THE SOUL

1. James Hillman, *Re-Visioning Psychology* (New York: Harper & Row, 1975), 110.
2. Mary Watkins, *Waking Dreams*, 3d ed. (Dallas: Spring, 1976/1984), *vii*.
3. James Hillman, *Suicide and the Soul* (Dallas: Spring, 1964/1976).
4. Hillman, *Re-Visioning*, 100.
5. Watkins, *Waking, viii*.
6. Ibid., *ix*.

7. Ibid., 1.
8. Mary Watkins, *Invisible Guests: The Development of Imaginal Dialogues* (Boston: Sigo, 1986/1990).
9. Watkins, *Waking*, 6–7.
10. Richard de Mille, *Put Your Mother on the Ceiling: Children's Imagination Games* (New York: Penguin, 1967/1976), *ix*.
11. Ibid., *xiii*.
12. Ibid.
13. Ibid., 4.
14. Ibid., *x*.
15. Alfred Ziegler, *Archetypal Medicine*, trans. Gary V. Hartman (Dallas: Spring, 1983), 22–23.
16. James Hillman, *A Blue Fire: Selected Writings*, intro. and ed. Thomas Moore (New York: Harper & Row, 1989), 233.
17. Ibid., 234.
18. Ibid., 235.
19. Ibid., 237.
20. James Hillman, "You Can't Fix It—And Besides, It Ain't Broke," American Art Therapy Association Meeting, Atlanta, 18–22 Nov. 1993.
21. Shaun McNiff, *Art as Medicine: Creating a Therapy of the Imagination* (Boston: Shambhala, 1992).
22. Hillman, *Re-Visioning*, *x*.
23. Ibid.
24. Ibid., 79-80.
25. Ibid., 55-56.
26. Ibid., 57.
27. Ibid., 70.
28. Ibid., 80.
29. Ibid., 70.
30. Ibid., 81.
31. Ibid., 99.
32. Ibid., 74.
33. Ibid., 110.
34. Ronald Grimes, *Beginnings in Ritual Studies* (Washington, D. C.: University Press of America, 1982), 254–66.
35. Ean Begg and Deike Rich, *On the Trail of Merlin: A Guide to the Celtic Mystery Tradition* (London: Aquarian, 1991).
36. Ibid., 81.
37. Greg Mogenson, *God Is a Trauma: Vicarious Religion and Soul-Making* (Dallas: Spring, 1989), 8.
38. James Hillman, "On Soul and Spirit," interview with Barbara Dunn, *The Common Boundary* 6, no. 4 (1988): 7.
39. Ziegler, *Archetypal*, 89.

40. Elaine Scarry, *The Body in Pain: The Making and Unmaking of the World* (New York: Oxford University Press, 1985).
41. Kat Duff, *The Alchemy of Illness* (New York: Bell Tower, 1993), 13–14.
42. Ibid., 17.
43. Ibid., 33.
44. Thomas Moore, *Care of the Soul* (New York: HarperCollins, 1992), *xi*.
45. Ibid., 155.
46. Ibid., 157.
47. Ibid.

CONCLUSION: COMPREHENDING MERLIN'S CRY

1. Carlos Castaneda, *The Art of Dreaming* (New York: HarperCollins, 1993).
2. Victor Sanchez, *The Teachings of Don Carlos: Practical Applications of the Works of Carlos Castaneda*, trans. Robert Nelson (Santa Fe, N. M.: Bear & Company, 1995), *xiii–xiv*.
3. Edith Turner, "The Reality of Spirits," *ReVision* 15, no. 1 (1992): 28–32.
4. Ibid., 28.
5. Ibid.
6. Ibid., 29.
7. Ibid.
8. Ibid., 30. Shamanthropologist Felicitas Goodman mounts a similar attack on metaphor and symbol as appropriate categories for capturing shamanic realities in a 1989 paper. She does not, however, advance from that understandable critique of conventional psychology's reductionism to Turner's eventual post-Jungian insights. See Felicitas D. Goodman, "Beware the Symbols: The Shaman Rides a Horse," in *Proceedings of the Sixth International Conference on the Study of Shamanism and Alternate Modes of Healing, September 2–4, 1989*, ed. Ruth-Inge Heinze (Berkeley, CA: Independent Scholars of Asia, 1989), 221–25. Roger Walsh, a transpersonal psychologist, discusses this crucial issue inconclusively in a section on "The Nature of Spirits" of his 1990 survey volume *The Spirit of Shamanism* (Los Angeles: Tarcher, 1990), 130-37. Walsh deals very briefly and inadequately with Castaneda while uncritically lumping Western neoshamanism like Harner's together with indigenous shamanisms. As a psychologist, he is more aware of Jungian perspectives than is Goodman, but he does not take account of Jung's radical legacy regarding imaginal realities. Perhaps, remembering Hillman's distinction, a book on the *spirit* of shamanism, whatever its virtues, will not be focused on finding the *soul* of shamanism.
9. Turner, "Reality," 31.
10. Ibid.
11. Ibid.
12. Ibid.
13. Ibid.

14. Dan Rose, *Living the Ethnographic Life* (Newbury Park, Calif.: Sage, 1990); Michael Jackson, *Paths toward a Clearing: Radical Empiricism and Ethnographic Inquiry* (Bloomington: Indiana University Press, 1989); Douglass Price-Williams, "The Waking Dream in Ethnographic Perspective," in *Dreaming: Anthropological and Psychological Interpretations,* ed. Barbara Tedlock (Santa Fe, N. M.: School of American Research Press, 1992), 246–62. Certainly Turner's own book from 1992 is also a valuable anthropological resource: see Edith Turner, *Experiencing Ritual: A New Interpretation of African Healing* (Philadelphia: University of Pennsylvania Press, 1992). Another excellent contribution to our efforts from anthropology is Jane Monnig Atkinson's bibliographical essay, which includes a "Postscript" on "Neo-Shamanism and Anthropology": see Atkinson, "Shamanisms Today," *Annual Review of Anthropology* 21 (1992): 307–330.

15. Richard Noll, "Mental Imagery Cultivation as a Cultural Phenomenon: The Role of Visions in Shamanism," *Current Anthropology* 26 (1985): 443–61. Among other, more "scientific" clinical and experimental psychologists, "mental imagery" is approached very differently from post-Jungian imaginal psychology, about which (unlike Noll) these writers seem strangely unaware. See *The Journal of Mental Imagery* and *The Potential of Fantasy and Imagination,* ed. Anees A. Sheikh and John T. Shaffer (New York: Brandon House, 1979).

16. Vine Deloria, Jr., "Foreword/American Fantasy," in *The Pretend Indian: Images of Native Americans in the Movies,* ed. Gretchen M. Bataille and Charles L. P. Silet (Ames: Iowa State University Press, 1980), *ix-xvi.*

17. Ibid., *xi-xii.*

18. Ibid., *xiii-xiv.*

19. Ibid., *xv.*

20. Ibid., *xvi.*

21. Pete Jennings and Pete Sawyer, *Pathworking,* 2d ed. (Chieveley, Berks.: Capall Bann, 1993).

22. T. M. Luhrmann, *Persuasions of the Witch's Craft: Ritual Magic in Contemporary England* (Cambridge, Mass.: Harvard University Press, 1989).

23. *Shamanism and Witchcraft* ed. Chas S. Clifton, Witchcraft Today: Book Three (St. Paul, Minn.: Llewellyn, 1994). See also Clifton, "A Goddess Arrives: The Novels of Dion Fortune and the Development of Gardnerian Witchcraft," *Gnosis* 9 (1988): 20–28.

24. Clifton, *Shamanism,* 7. See also Carlo Ginzburg, *Ecstasies: Deciphering the Witches' Sabbath,* trans. Raymond Rosenthal (New York: Pantheon, 1989/1991); and Hans Peter Duerr, *Dreamtime: Concerning the Boundary between Wilderness and Civilization,* trans. Felicitas Goodman (London and New York: Basil Blackwell, 1978/1985).

25. See, for example, James Hillman, "Anima Mundi: The Return of the Soul to the World," *Spring* (1982): 71–93.

26. Shaun McNiff, *Earth Angels: Engaging the Sacred in Everyday Things* (Boston: Shambhala, 1995); and Thomas Moore, *The Re-Enchantment of Everyday Life*

(New York: HarperCollins, 1996). See also Daniel C. Noel, "Soul and Earth: Traveling with Jung Toward an Archetypal Ecology," Parts I and II, *Quadrant* 23, no. .2 (1990): 57-73; 24, no. 1 (1991): 83–91.

27. R. J. Stewart, ed., *Psychology and the Spiritual Traditions* (Shaftesbury, Dorset: Element, 1990), 1.

28. Ibid., 1–2.

29. Jean Markale, *Merlin: Priest of Nature*, trans. Belle N. Burke (Rochester, Vt: Inner Traditions, 1990), 140–79.

30. Michael Perlman, *The Power of Trees: The Reforesting of the Soul* (Dallas: Spring, 1994), and *Hiroshima Forever: The Ecology of Mourning* (Barrytown, N.Y.: Barrytown, 1995); Peter Bishop, *The Greening of Psychology: The Vegetable World in Myth, Dream, and Healing* (Dallas: Spring, 1990), and "Facing the World: Depth Psychology and Deep Ecology," *Harvest* 36 (1990): 62–71.

31. Theodore Roszak, *The Voice of the Earth: An Exploration of Ecopsychology* (New York: Simon and Schuster, 1992); and *Ecopsychology: Restoring the Earth Healing the Mind*, ed. Theodore Roszak, Mary E. Gomes, and Allen D. Kanner (San Francisco: Sierra Club, 1995).

32. See Noel, "Soul and Earth."

33. C. G. Jung, *Memories, Dreams, Reflections*, ed. Aniela Jaffe, trans. Richard and Clara Winston (New York: Vintage, 1961), 228.

34. C. G. Jung, *Collected Works*, ed. Herbert Read, Michael Fordham, Gerhard Adler, and William McGuire, trans. R.F.C. Hull, Bollingen Series XX (Princeton, N. J.: Princeton, 1967), vol. 13, para. 239–303.

35. Ibid., para. 239.

36. Emma Jung and Marie-Louise von Franz, *The Grail Legend*, 2d ed., trans. Andrea Dykes (Boston: Sigo, 1960/1986), 366–78.

37. Perlman, *Power*.

38. Heinrich Zimmer, "Merlin," in Zimmer, *The King and the Corpse: Tales of the Soul's Conquest of Evil*, ed. Joseph Campbell, Bollingen Series XI (Princeton, N. J.: Princeton University Press, 1948/1971), 181–201. (The Merlin essay was originally published in the Zurich journal *Corona* in 1939.)

39. Jung, *Collected Works*, vol. 13, para. 304–482.

40. Markale, *Merlin*, 118–20.

41. Zimmer, "Merlin," 201.

42. Ibid., 197.

43. Merlin Stone, *When God Was a Woman* (New York: Harcourt Brace Jovanovich, 1976).

44. Nikolai Tolstoy, *The Quest for Merlin* (London: Hodder and Stoughton Coronet Books, 1985), 248.

INDEX

Abelar, Taisha, 103
active imagination, 170–77, 179,
  183, 215, 237 n.15
  and healing, 171–76, 179, 181,
    189, 203
Adams, Michael Vannoy, 127
Adler, Alfred, 217
Adler, Gerhard, 108–9, 112
alchemy, 219–20
Alchemy of Illness, The (Duff), 200–202
Alice in Wonderland (Carroll), 187
Ammann, Adolph, 173
Andrews, Lynn, 26–28
  Native Americans' protest of, 26–27
  as shamanovelist, 26–29, 38, 40–
    41, 61, 65, 104, 170
  workshops of, 26–27
"Animal Kingdom in the Human
    Dream, The" (Hillman), 161
animal powers, 163–66, 169
  attempts to control, 185, 187
animals, 55, 185, 214
  in dreams and fantasies, 159–61,
    162–67
  See also Power animals
animism, 217, 222
"Anthropologist, The" (Borges), 87
anthropologists, 39, 42
  Castaneda's works accepted by, 82,
    83–84, 87–92
  as founders of New Shamanism, 42,
    88, 93–97, 102
  as objective observers, 205–11
  See also Shamanthropologists
anthropology
  and literature, 82–92 passim,
    93–94, 231 n.3

and self-help healing, 90–91
  and shamanthropology, 93–97, 102
Anthropology as Cultural Critique
    (Marcus and Fischer), 97
"Approach to the Dream, An" (Berry),
    146–47
Aquarian Conspiracy, The (Ferguson),
    88, 94
art, 190
  and shamanism, 135–36, 138
Art as Medicine (McNiff), 138, 190
Arthurian legend, 15, 18
Art of Dreaming, The (Castaneda), 102
art therapy, 132–38, 190–91, 223
ascent, imagery of
  in works of Eliade, 32–38, 42, 69,
    91–92, 101, 131, 220
  See also Magical flight
Ashe, Geoffrey, 17
Assagioli, Roberto, 72–73
attitude
  toward dreams, 162, 211
  and healing, 145–46, 151, 221
awareness, shamanic, 210–11

Barthelme, Donald, 95
Bates, Brian, 17
Baynes, Anne, 18–19
Baynes, H. G., 18
Begg, Ean, 196–97
Being-in-Dreaming (Donner), 102
Berry, Patricia, 126, 136, 146–47
Bialy, Harvey, 86–87
"Birds, The" (Sukenick), 68
Bishop, Peter, 126, 133, 218
Bleakley, Alan, 126, 133, 236 n.45
Blown Away (Sukenick), 79–81

Blue Fire, A (Hillman), 129
"Blurred Genres" (Geertz), 94
Bly, Robert, 91
Body in Pain, The (Scarry), 200
body movement workshops, 204
Boer, Charles, 127
Book of the Hopi (Waters), 14
Boorman, John, 16
Borges, Jorge Luis, 86, 87, 94
Bosnak, Robert, 126, 152, 162, 170
Bradley, Marion Zimmer, 16
Brand, Stewart, 92
Burton, Sandra, 48

Campbell, Joseph, 18, 90, 104, 160
Cannibal (Harner), 103
Care of the Soul (T. Moore), 128,
        130–31, 136–38, 202
Carpenter, Edmund, 89
Carrasco, David, 29, 75, 77
Casey, Edward, 126
Castaneda, Carlos, 23, 43–62, 211
    anthropologists' acceptance of,
        82, 83–84, 87–92
    counter-culture's acceptance of,
        51–54, 57–58, 69–70
    defenders of, 58, 82, 83–84, 87–
        92, 101, 121, 163, 176–77, 204
    Don Juan writings of, 27, 43–49,
        54–55, 89, 107, 121–23, 212;
        See also titles of works
    factuality of works questioned, 49,
        55–61, 64, 71, 83–91, 95–98,
        101–2, 121–23, 126, 161
    fictive power in works of, 54–62,
        87–89, 92, 95, 121, 181
    as a founder of New Shamanism,
        10, 14, 22, 25, 27–28, 43, 60,
        84, 88, 93–94, 98, 113, 122
    and hallucinogens, 44–47, 53–54,
        70, 88–89, 124, 212
    See also under Fiction; *titles of works*
*Castaneda's Journey: The Power and
        the Allegory* (de Mille), 57–58,
        83, 86, 187
celestial journeys, 32–37

and hallucinogens, 44–47, 70, 212
    nonhallucinogenic, 47–48
center, Eliade's concept of, 29, 34–36, 69
C. G. Jung: His Myth in Our Time
        (von Franz), 19
C. G. Jung: Word and Image (Jaffe), 108
child development, 186–90
Chopra, Deepak, 17
Clark, Brigid, 199
Clifford, James, 93–94, 96–97
Clifton, Chas, 216
Clinton, Hillary, 234 n.20
Cobb, Noel, 126
Collected Works (Jung), 109, 220
Coming of the King, The (Tolstoy), 17
Corbin, Henry, 123, 209
Cowan, Tom, 17
creative writing, 88, 223
    as controlled dreaming, 68, 70
    See also Fiction
Crystal Cave series (M. Stewart), 16

Dark Eros (T. Moore), 129, 134
"Death of the Novel, The" (Suken-
        ick), 69–70, 81
*Death of the Novel and Other Stories,
        The* (Sukenick), 75
Deloria, Vine, Jr., 169, 211–15, 218
De Mille, Richard
    Castaneda unmasked by, 57–59, 64,
        66, 76, 78–93 passim, 101, 121–
        22, 125, 170
    on child development, 185–89
demons and spirits, 34
depth psychology, 60–61, 127
Descartes, René, 185
Dillard, Annie, 81
Doggy Bag (Sukenick), 81
Don Genaro, 46
Don Juan Papers, The (de Mille), 58
"Don Juan's Last Laugh" (Oates), 56
Don Juan writings, 27, 43–49, 54–55,
        89, 107, 121–23,   212
    See also titles of works
"'Don Juan,' Trickster, and Hermeneutic
        Understanding" (Whan), 15, 125

Donner, Florinda, 96–97, 102–3
Doore, Gary, 178
Doors of Perception, The (Huxley), 92
Doty, William, 94, 95
Douglas, Mary, 93
Down and In (Sukenick), 79
drama therapy, 205
Dream and the Underworld, The (Hillman),
     142–43, 146, 151, 158,
     162, 192, 201
dreaming, 70, 73–74, 139–61, 211
    and art, 135
    mindfulness of, 68, 73–74
    reading and writing as, 68–70, 74
Dreaming with Open Eyes (Tucker), 136
dreams, 181, 211
    animals in, 159–61, 162–63
    and depression, 145
    interpretation of, 139–61
    reality of, 144, 175, 186
    research into, 182
    theory of, 140–62, 184
    threat to, 139, 142
    water images in, 158–59
drugs, 13, 44–48, 51–54, 212
    literature of, 88–92
    See also Hallucinogens
druids, 17, 219
Druids, The (Rutherford), 17
drumming, 98, 103, 104, 163–67, 178, 207
Drury, Nevill, 17
Duff, Kat, 200–203
Dumbo (motion picture), 184–85
Duvignaud, Jean, 93

Eckhart, Johannes (Meister Eckhart), 172
ecology, imaginal, 217–19
ecopsychology, 218
ecstatic flight: *See* Magical flight
Eliade, Mircea, 10, 23, 25–41, 75–76
    as authoritative writer, 42, 54, 76
    center, concept of, 29, 34–36, 69
    as fiction writer, 29–37, 65, 77,
     84, 211
    magical flight in works of, 32–38,
     42, 69, 91–92, 101, 131, 220

New Shamanism of, 10, 23, 25–26,
    28, 42, 43, 97, 99, 113, 172, 177
    scholarly imagining of, 54, 60,
     73, 77, 92
    secret room in works of, 30–32, 34,
     36, 37, 39–40, 49, 78
    See also titles of works by
Emotion: A Comprehensive Phenomenol-
    ogy of Theories and Their Mean-
    ings for Therapy (Hillman), 133
environmental philosophy, 217–18
ethnomethodology, 231 n.3
ethnography, 93–98, 113
    blurring of boundaries in, 57, 93–
     98, 102
    personal narratives in, 96–97
    writing as central to, 93–96
Excalibur (motion picture), 16
experiential shamanism, 28
    literature of, 89, 90–91

fantasies of flight, 28, 37–40, 60,
    69, 71, 74, 77
    and hallucinogens, 44–47, 70
    nonhallucinogenic, 47–48, 56, 59
    See also Magical flight; Trances
fantasy: *See* Dreams; Imagination
Ferguson, Marilyn, 88, 94
Ficino, Marsilio, 129, 131, 137
fiction, 129
    and anthropology, 82, 83–84, 87–
     92, 93–94, 231 n.3
    as basis of New Shamanism, 38–39,
     49, 55–62, 65, 73, 87–89, 93–97,
     99, 105, 113, 119–24, 173, 181
    Castaneda's works as, 49, 55–61,
     64, 93, 95–97, 121–23, 170, 176,
     204, 211, 216
    healing, 171–76, 179, 181
    and politics, 63–64, 66–67
    recognition of, 87–88, 93, 122
fictive power, 68, 87–89, 92, 129
    of imagination, 121, 133–34, 160,
     177, 181
    tales of, 68–74, 80, 95, 181, 223
"Fieldwork in Common Places" (Pratt), 96

Fire in the Head: Shamanism and the Celtic Spirit (Cowan), 17
Fischer, Michael M. J., 97
"Five Denials on Merlin's Grave" (Williamson), 16
Flaherty, Gloria, 22
Forbidden Forest, The (Eliade), 32–38, 65, 77, 84
    imagery of ascent in, 30–37, 42
Fortune, Dion, 215
Frankson, Ernest, 208
Franz, Marie-Louise von, 18–19, 109, 112, 173, 219
Freud, Sigmund, 108, 121
    dream theory of, 140–41, 144–45, 152
Fruitful Darkness, The (Halifax), 104
Fuller, Buckminster, 204

Gablik, Suzi, 90
Garfinkel, Harold, 231 n.3
Gaup, Ailo, 103
Geertz, Clifford, 93, 94–95, 97
Geoffrey of Monmouth, 16
Giegerich, Wolfgang, 126, 133
Ginsberg, Allen, 53
Ginzberg, Carlo, 216
God Is a Trauma (Mogenson), 199
"Going Bugs" (Hillman), 161
Goldschmidt, Walter, 89
Goodman, Felicitas, 103–4, 240 n.8
Goodrich, Norma Lorre, 17
Grail Legend, The (E. Jung and von Franz), 18–20, 219
Grail quest lore, 15, 18
Gravity's Rainbow (Pynchon), 48
Grimaldi, Susan, 169
Grimes, Ronald, 196, 205
Grof, Stanislav, 92, 99

Halifax, Joan, 90–91, 92, 160
    as a founder of New Shamanism, 28, 93, 97, 102
    workshops of, 14, 104, 170
hallucinogens, 44–48, 212
    counterculture's acceptance of, 51–54, 88–89, 124

    indigenous uses of, 90–91
    and magical flight, 44–47, 70
    and perception of reality, 13, 46–48, 124
    rejection of, 47–48, 212
Hanley, Joan, 136
Hannah, Barbara, 173
Harner, Michael, 48, 176–78, 211, 215
    Castaneda defended by, 91–92, 101, 163, 176–77
    credentials of, 98
    as a founder of New Shamanism, 76, 91–94, 97, 131
    New Shamanism of, 10, 25, 28, 99, 165, 171, 207
    workshops of, 14, 92, 94, 98–104, 163–70, 178–79, 207, 211
healing, 20–21, 60, 77, 90, 112, 153
    and art, 190
    and attitude, 145–46, 151
    and imagination, 171–76, 179, 181, 189, 200, 203, 205, 211, 223
    and power, 91, 100, 119, 181
    suffering and, 188–95, 200, 203, 205, 211, 221
    women's role in, 214
    See also Shamanism and healing
Healing Fiction (Hillman), 120–21, 171, 175, 192
Henning, Doug, 16
Hillman, James, 11, 120–37, 141, 182, 202–3, 219
    and Castaneda, 122–26
    on child development, 189–90
    dream theory of, 142–61, 162
    and ecopsychology, 218
    on healing, 171–76, 182, 189–95
    imaginal psychology of, 21, 111–16, 119, 123–25, 129–35, 137, 146–47, 209, 216
    on imagination, 173–77, 190–95, 200
    on Jung, 111–17, 121
    on pornography, 134
    on soul recovery, 189, 193
    on suffering, 189–95, 200
    on suicide, 183–84

Historical Atlas of World Mythology
    (Campbell), 104, 160
holism, 127–28, 130
Houston, Jean, 234 n.20
Hudson, Liam, 140–42
Huxley, Aldous, 92
hypochondria, 194–95

illness, 188–89, 194, 200–2
    See also Suffering
imaginal psychology, 10–11, 73, 100,
    135–37, 177, 211
    and dream theory, 162, 184
    and ecopsychology, 218
    of James Hillman, 21, 111–16, 119,
    123–25, 129–35, 137, 146–47,
    209, 216
    and the New Shamanism, 20–21,
    119–21, 127, 138, 184, 203
imaginal reality, 59–61, 102
    and healing, 174, 181, 192, 223
    Hillman's concept of, 123–24, 133
    honoring of, 165, 169, 181, 223
    Jung's concept of, 115–16, 174–76
    and shamanism, 105, 127, 129, 208–10
imaginal shamanism, 113, 134–35, 138,
    181, 191, 236 n.45
    and dreams, 140, 143, 146–47, 150–
    51, 161
    and neopaganism, 214–17
    psychological approach of, 215
    search for, 117, 119, 122, 205–10
    sources of, 11, 132, 174, 183–84
    and suffering, 188–95, 203, 211, 221
imagination, 75–78, 107, 191
    active, 170–77, 179, 183, 215,
    237 n.15
    development of, 184, 188–91
    Disney version of, 184–85
    repression of, 80, 184–86, 188–90
    shamanic, 107, 169, 181, 185, 187,
    190, 194–95, 200, 203, 205,
    210, 221
    as soul of New Shamanism, 37–38,
    40–41, 65, 73–76, 84, 99, 105,
    119–23, 138, 203, 206

and suffering, 188–95, 200, 203,
    211, 221
In Form (Sukenick), 79
Ingerman, Sandra, 103, 169
In Search of the Drum (Gaup), 103
Interpretation of Dreams (Freud), 140,
    144
*In the Unlikely Event of a Water
    Landing* (C. Noel), 199
Invisible Guests (Watkins), 184–85

Jackson, Michael, 210
Jaffe, Aniela, 108
Johnson, Robert, 173
Journey to Ixtlan: The Lessons of Don Juan
    (Castaneda), 47–48, 53, 54
    doctorate awarded for, 58, 89, 91
Jung, C. G., 54, 106–17, 131, 215–16
    on active imagination, 173–77, 215
    autobiography of, 19–20, 108, 111,
    115, 182, 218
    depth psychology of, 60–61, 127
    and Freud, break with, 108, 110–11
    imaginal psychology of followers
    of, 10–11, 73–74, 100, 111–16,
    119–21, 124, 129–35, 146, 177,
    203, 211
    medical training of, 106, 108, 114
    Merlin as subject of interest to,
    19–20, 218–19
    misreadings of, 187–88
    and the objective psyche, 110–17,
    120, 123, 128, 131–32, 134, 144,
    161, 169, 172, 182–83
    as Western shaman, 10–11, 20, 100,
    107, 132, 211
Jung, Emma, 18–20, 109, 219
Jung, Franz, 107–8
Jung, Lily, 107–9, 122

Kant, Immanuel, 55
Kast, Verena, 173
Keen, Sam, 49, 55, 57
Knight, Gareth, 17
Korda, Michael, 51, 54
Korp, Maureen, 136

Kugler, Paul, 126

LaBerge, Steven, 161
Lailoken, 16
Larsen, Stephen, 90
Leach, Edmund, 93
Leary, Timothy, 54
Leger, Fernand, 132
Levi-Strauss, Claude, 93
Lewis, Leilani, 178–79
literary lying: See Fiction
literature: See Creative writing; Fiction
Little Course in Dreams, A (Bosnak),
    152, 162, 170
Living by Fiction (Dillard), 81
Lockhart, Russell, 127
Lommel, Andreas, 135
Lopez-Pedraza, Rafael, 126
Lord of the Rings (Tolkien), 18
Luhrmann, T. M., 216

Mabinogion, The, 16
magical flight, 21, 27, 34, 36–40,
    44–46, 60, 69, 77, 178, 223
    in Eliade's works, 32–38, 42, 69,
        91–92, 101, 220
    and hallucinogens, 44–47, 70
    during illness, 200–202
    nonhallucinogenic achievement of,
        47–48, 56, 59, 92
    of reading, 66, 71, 74, 81
    of spirituality, 131
"Magical Flight" (Eliade), 36
Making of a Counter-Culture, The
    (Roszak), 52
Malinowsky, Bronislaw Kasper, 96
Marcus, George E., 93, 96, 97
Markale, Jean, 17, 218, 220
Matthews, Caitlin, 17
Matthews, John, 17
McConeghey, Howard, 126, 132–38
    passim, 190
McNiff, Shaun, 126, 136, 138, 190
Medicine Woman (Andrews), 26–27
Memories, Dreams, Reflections (Jung),
    19–20, 108, 111, 115, 182, 218

Mercurius, 19, 218–20
Merlin, 92
    cry of, 19–20, 65, 205, 216–23
    disappearance of, 19–20, 217–22
    Jung's interest in, 19–20, 218–19
    legend and lore of, 15, 18–20, 165,
        196–98, 214–23
    as Western shaman, 10, 15–16, 18–
        20, 214–15
Merlin (Goodrich), 17
"Merlin" (Zimmer), 18–19, 220
Merlin (magic show), 16
Merlin: Priest of Nature (Markale), 17,
    218
Merlin's Booke (Yolen), 16
Merlin Tarot, The (R. Stewart), 16
Middelkoop, Pieter, 173
Miller, David, 126, 128
Mists of Avalon, The (Bradley), 16
Modern Man in Search of a Soul (Jung),
    132
Mogenson, Greg, 199
Moore, R. Laurence, 88
Moore, Thomas, 11, 127–34, 136–38, 192
    on care of the soul, 181–82, 202–3
    Catholic training of, 128, 138
    imaginal psychology of, 119, 127–
        35, 137
Murdock, Fred, story of, 85–87
Myerhoff, Barbara, 90
Myrddin, 16
Mystic Life of Merlin, The (R. Stewart), 16
Myth of Analysis (Hillman), 120,
    122–23, 145

nagual, 55
Naranjo, Claudio, 90
Native Americans, 211–14
    appropriation of spirituality of, 211–14
    neoshamanist workshops picketed
        by, 26–27
    stereotypes of, 212
neopaganism, 214–16
neoshamanism: See New Shamanism
"Nervous System: Homesickness and
    Dada, The" (Taussig), 39–40

New Age movement
  Castaneda's works accepted by,
    88, 90–91
  and holism, 127–28
  and the New Shamanism, 27, 88,
    92, 94, 100, 103, 127
  as successor to counter-culture, 88
New Shamanism, 14, 18, 20–22, 106, 213
  and imaginal psychology, 20–21,
    111, 119–21, 127, 132, 138,
    169, 183–84, 191
  imagination as soul of, 37–38, 40–
    41, 54, 65, 73–76, 82, 84, 95,
    99, 111–13, 116, 119, 203
  literary basis of, 38–39, 49, 55–
    62, 65, 73, 87–89, 93–97, 99,
    105, 113, 119–24, 173, 181
  as psychospiritual movement, 10,
    42, 44–46, 88, 90–92, 100, 102
  selling of, 88–92, 93, 98, 102, 127
  sources of, 10, 23–27, 38, 42, 46,
    49, 51, 54, 58–59, 76, 83–84, 88
  workshops in, 14, 26–27, 92, 94,
    98–105, 138, 148, 163–70, 178–
    79, 191, 206, 207, 211
  See also under Castaneda, Carlos;
    Eliade, Mircea; Halifax, Joan;
    Harner, Michael
Night Life: The Interpretation of
    Dreams (Hudson), 140–41
"Night of St. John, The": See Forbidden
    Forest, The
98.6 (Sukenick), 70–73, 123
Noaptea de Sanziene: See Forbidden Forest,
    The
Noel, Christopher, 199
Noel, Daniel, 217
Noel, Rebecca, 199
Noll, Richard, 210

Oates, Joyce Carol, 56–57, 59, 61, 84
Once and Future King, The (White), 18
On the Trail of Merlin (Begg and
    Rich), 196
oral tradition, 10
  disappearance of, 82

ordeals, shamanic, 40, 181–82, 184
Out (Sukenick), 66, 68–70

paranormal experiences, accounts of, 26
parashamanism, 205
Paris, Ginette, 126
pathologizing: See Suffering
Pathworking (Jennings and Sawyer), 215–16
patriarchy, relinquishment of, 221–22
performance workshops, 206–7
Perlman, Michael, 126, 218–19
personal narratives, in ethnography, 96–97
Persuasions of the Witch's Craft (Luhrmann),
    216
"Philosophical Tree, The" (Jung), 220
Planets Within, The (T. Moore), 128
pornography, 134
post-Jungian psychology, 111, 115,
    125–28, 132–35, 147, 169, 177
  and ecology, 218
  and shamanism, 138, 182
power
  in Castaneda's work, 54–55
  and creativity, 55, 68
  fictive, 55–62, 64–65, 68–74, 80,
    87–89, 95, 121, 129, 133–34,
    169, 173, 176, 181
  and healing, 91, 100, 119, 188, 212
  imaginal, 121, 133, 161, 212
power animals, 195, 208, 221–22
  interacting with, 170–71, 190
  See also Animal powers
Power! How to Get It, How to Use It
    (Korda), 51
Power of Silence, The (Castaneda), 54
Power of Trees, The (Perlman), 219
power plants, 44, 52–53, 90–91
  See also Hallucinogens
Pratt, Mary Louise, 96–97
Price-Williams, Douglass, 210
Progoff, Ira, 173, 237 n.15
Prophetic Vision of Merlin, The (R. Stewart),
    16
psyche, 132
  imaginal power of, 120–21, 134
  image as, 119, 128, 187

psyche *(continued)*
    objective, 110–17, 120–23, 128, 131–
        32, 134, 144, 169, 172,182–83
Psychological Types (Jung), 171
psychology, 134, 222–23
    depth, 60–61, 127
    post-Jungian, 111, 115, 125–28,
        132–35, 138, 147, 160, 177, 182
    soul-based, 127–34, 141
    See also Imaginal psychology
Psychology and the Spiritual Traditions
        (R. J. Stewart, ed.), 217
Psychomental Complex of the Tungus
        (Shirokogoroff), 22
psychosynthesis, 72–73, 123
Put Your Mother on the Ceiling:
        Children's Imagination Games
        (de Mille), 186–89
Pynchon, Thomas, 48, 50

Quest for Merlin, The (Tolstoy), 15, 19–20

Raitt, Bonnie, 185
reading, 81, 122
    as central to the New Shamanism,
        49, 105, 119, 123–24
    as controlled dreaming, 68–70, 74
    creative, 68, 71, 88
    and magical flight, 66, 71, 74
    as means of empowerment, 78, 82
    as shamanic imagining, 38, 40–41,
        46, 59, 69, 73–75, 84, 119,
        121–24, 192
reality, 55, 59, 206–10
    nonordinary, 13, 46–48, 60, 101,
        163, 166–67, 175, 209
    psychic, 112, 115, 116
    shamanic, 45–47, 54, 205, 209–11,
        221
    See also Imaginal reality
"Reality of Spirits, The" (E. Turner), 206
Re-Enchantment of Everyday Life, The
        (T. Moore), 128
Return of Merlin, The (Chopra), 17
Re-Visioning Psychology (Hillman),
        124–25, 130, 183, 191–93

Rich, Deike, 196–97
Ricketts, Mac Linscott, 31
rituals, 215, 217
    shamanic, 77, 136, 205–9
Rituals of the Imagination (T. Moore), 129
Robbe-Grillet, Alain, 71
Rose, Dan, 210
Roszak, Theodore, 52, 53, 57, 115
    ecopsychology of, 218
Rothenberg, Jerome, 91
Rutherford, Ward, 17

sacred pole myth, 29, 35
Sanchez, Victor, 204
Sardello, Robert, 126
Scarry, Elaine, 200, 201
"Sea Surface Full of Clouds" (Stevens), 69
Second Ring of Power, The (Castaneda), 54
Secret of the Golden Flower, The
        (Chinese alchemical text),
        Jung's preface to, 172
secret rooms in shamanovels, 30–32, 34,
        36, 37, 39–40, 49, 78, 88, 131
Seeing Castaneda: Reactions to the
        "Don Juan" Writings of Carlos Cas-
        taneda (Noel), 57, 95
Selling God: American Religion in the
        Marketplace of Culture (R. L.
        Moore), 88
Sells, Benjamin, 127
Separate Reality, A: Further Conversations
        with Don Juan (Castaneda),
        46, 47, 66, 67, 86
Shabono: A Visit to a Remote and Magical
        World in the South American
        Rainforest (Donner), 96–97, 102
Shakespeare, William, 79–80
Shakkai (Andrews), 26, 38–39, 61
Shaman and the Magician, The (Drury), 17
Shaman: The Wounded Healer (Halifax),104
shamanic imagining, 181, 205
    development of, 187, 211, 221
    and healing, 200, 203
    psychology as road to, 107, 169
    and soul recovery, 60, 190, 194–95
    See also under Reading

Shamanic Voices: A Survey of Visionary Narratives (Halifax), 90–91, 104
shamanism, 9, 21–22, 35, 222
  experiential, 28, 89, 90–91
  modern Western version of, 14, 18, 21–22, 65, 73, 111, 127, 217, 222–23
  ordeals of, 40, 181–82, 184
  as a religion, 21–22, 27, 42, 90–92, 100, 136
  as a spiritual practice, 10, 44–45, 102, 217
  suppression of, 46, 59, 65, 222
  See also Imaginal shamanism; New Shamanism; Shamanism and healing
Shamanism: Archaic Techniques of Ecstasy (Eliade), 28, 34–37, 76, 84
Shamanism: The Beginnings of Art (Lommel), 135
shamanism and healing, 20–21, 166
  and power, 90–91, 100
  rituals and practices of, 77, 136, 205–9
  search for, 60, 119, 212, 222
Shamanism and Witchcraft (Clifton, ed.), 216
shamanovelists, 10, 25, 30–37, 40, 62–82, 83, 113, 116, 121, 211, 216, 223
shamans, 100–101, 172
  as healers, 20–21, 166
Shaman's Doorway, The (Larsen), 90
shamanthropologists, 10, 25, 28, 43, 92–94, 138, 211
  as supporters of Castaneda, 82, 83–84, 87–92, 101, 163
shamanthropology, 57, 93–98, 102
Shirokogoroff, Sergei M., 22
Simmel, Georg, 89
Slade, Joseph, 50
Smith, Jonathan Z., 29, 34–36
Sorcerers' Crossing, The (Abelar), 103
"Sorcery: A Description of the World" (Castaneda), 58
soul, 220
  loss of, 131–32, 182, 184–86, 188–89, 202–3, 221, 231 n.20

recovery of, 60, 161, 189–94, 209, 214, 220–23
  and spirit, 127–28, 130, 137, 193, 207
Soul Mates (T. Moore), 128, 130
Spenser, Edmund, 196
"Spirit in the Bottle, The" (Grimm), 219
"Spirit Mercurius, The" (Jung), 219–20
Spirit of Shamanism, The (Walsh), 240 n.8
spirits
  and demons, 34
  reality of, 206–10
  and soul, 127–28, 130, 137, 193, 207
spirituality
  and earthly life, 130, 137
  indigenous, 208–14
  shamanic, 44, 211–14
Stevens, Wallace, 68–69, 74, 78, 81, 223
Stewart, Mary, 16
Stewart, R. J., 16, 217–19
Stone, Merlin, 221
Storyteller, The (Vargas Llosa), 63–65
storytellers, 10, 82
Strathern, Marilyn, 95, 97
suffering, 40, 181–82, 199
  and ecstasy, 200–202
  and healing, 188–95, 200, 203, 205, 211, 221
  and imagination, 188–95, 200, 203
  and soul recovery, 189–93
  valorization of, 184
Suibhne, 16
Suicide and the Soul (Hillman), 183–84
Sukenick, Ronald, 10, 55–61 passim, 64–75, 78–82, 84, 86, 95, 175
  cloud imagery of, 68–69, 80
  and Eliade, 78–79
  on imagination, 190
  as shamanovelist, 113, 116

Tales of Power (Castaneda), 48–49, 51, 54–56, 58, 61, 104
Taliesin: Shamanism and the Bardic Mysteries in Britain and Ireland (J. Matthews), 17

Taussig, Michael, 39–40, 66–72 passim, 78, 82, 152
Tavistock Lectures (Jung), 172
"Teachings of Don B.: A Yankee Way of Knowledge" (Barthelme), 95
Teachings of Don Juan: A Yaqui Way of Knowledge (Castaneda), 13, 27, 45–46, 47, 52, 61, 84, 124
    marketing of, 88–89
Technicians of the Sacred (Rothenberg, ed.), 91
Tempest, The (Shakespeare), sorcery in, 79–80
tensegrity, 204
Time magazine cover story about Castaneda, 48, 50, 56, 57, 60, 84
Tolkien, J. R. R., 16, 18
Tolstoy, Nikolai, 15–17, 19–20, 223
To Take Place (Smith), 29
Tracks in the Wilderness of Dreaming (Bosnak), 162–63
trances, 22, 31, 39, 104, 151, 177
    and hallucinogens, 44–47, 70
    inducement of, 206
    nonhallucinogenic, 47–48
    See also Magical flight
"Transcendent Function, The" (Jung), 172
Tucker, Michael, 136
Turner, Edith, 205–10, 240 n.8
Turner, Victor, 93, 205, 20
Two Tales of the Occult (Eliade), 29
Tyler, Steven, 94, 97

"Upward and Juanward" (Sukenick), 122

Vargas Llosa, Mario, 63–65, 75, 84–85, 92, 133
visions, 43–48
    and hallucinogens, 44–47, 70, 90
Voice of the Earth, The (Roszak), 218
Voices and Visions (Keen), 49
"Vol magique, Le" (Eliade), 36

"Waiting for the Dawn" (Eliade lecture), 75–77, 82
Waiting for the Dawn: Mircea Eliade in Perspective (Carrasco and Swanberg, eds.), 29, 75
"Waking Dream in Ethnographic Perspective, The" (Price-Williams), 210
Waking Dreams (Watkins), 177, 182–87, 209
Walsh, Roger, 240 n.8
Wasson, R. Gordon, 91
Waters, Frank, 14
Watkins, Mary, 11, 126, 177, 182–86, 203, 209–10
    imaginal psychology of, 119, 184
Way of Merlin, The (R. Stewart), 16
Way of the Animal Powers, The (Campbell), 104, 160
Way of the Shaman, A Guide to Power and Healing, The (Harner), 76, 91–92, 94, 98, 102, 163, 176–77, 216
Way of Wyrd, The (Bates), 17
Weaver, Rix, 173
Whan, Michael, 15, 18, 19, 125–27, 133
When God Was a Woman (Stone), 221
Where the Spirits Ride the Wind (Goodman), 104
Whistling Elk, Agnes, 26, 39
White, T. H., 16, 18
Whole Earth Catalog (Brand, ed.), 92
Wicca, 214, 216
Williamson, Nicol, 16
Williamson, Robin, 16
Wilson, Colin, 110
witchcraft, 214–16
Witch's Dream, The (Donner), 102
Wolff, Toni, 109
women's spirituality movement, 221
writing: See Creative writing; Fiction
Writing Culture: The Poetics and Politics of Ethnography (Clifford and Marcus, eds.), 93, 96

Yaqui Indians, 43–44, 212
Yolen, Jane, 16

Ziegler, Alfred, 188, 200
Zimmer, Christiane, 18
Zimmer, Heinrich, 18–20, 220–21